Real-Resumes for Students

Anne McKinney, Editor

PREP PUBLISHING

FAYETTEVILLE, NC

PREP Publishing
1110½ Hay Street
Fayetteville, NC 28305
(910) 483-6611

Cover design by Chris Pearl

Library of Congress Cataloging-in-Publication Data

Real-resumes for students / Anne McKinney, editor.
      p. cm. -- (Real-resumes series)
    ISBN 1-885288-18-2
    1. Résumés (Employment) 2. College students--Employment.
3. College graduates--Employment. I. McKinney, Anne, 1948- II. Series.

    HF5383 .R3963 2000
    808'.06665–dc21

00-028560
CIP

Printed in the United States of America

By PREP Publishing

Business and Career Series:

RESUMES AND COVER LETTERS THAT HAVE WORKED

RESUMES AND COVER LETTERS THAT HAVE WORKED FOR MILITARY PROFESSIONALS

GOVERNMENT JOB APPLICATIONS AND FEDERAL RESUMES

COVER LETTERS THAT BLOW DOORS OPEN

LETTERS FOR SPECIAL SITUATIONS

RESUMES AND COVER LETTERS FOR MANAGERS

REAL-RESUMES FOR TEACHERS

REAL-RESUMES FOR STUDENTS

REAL-RESUMES FOR CAREER CHANGERS

REAL-RESUMES FOR SALES

REAL ESSAYS FOR COLLEGE & GRADUATE SCHOOL

Judeo-Christian Ethics Series:

SECOND TIME AROUND

BACK IN TIME

WHAT THE BIBLE SAYS ABOUT...Words that can lead to success and happiness

A GENTLE BREEZE FROM GOSSAMER WINGS

BIBLE STORIES FROM THE OLD TESTAMENT

Fiction:

KIJABE...An African Historical Saga

Table of Contents

A WORD FROM THE EDITOR:
ABOUT THE REAL-RESUMES SERIES

Welcome to the Real-Resumes Series. The Real-Resumes Series is a respected collection of books which have been developed based on the experiences of real job hunters and which target specialized fields or types of resumes. As the editor of the series, I have carefully selected resumes and cover letters (with names and other key data disguised, of course) which have been used successfully in real job hunts. That's what we mean by "Real-Resumes." What you see in this book are *real* resumes and cover letters which helped real students.

The Real-Resumes Series is based on the work of the country's oldest resume-preparation company known as PREP Resumes. If you would like a free information packet describing the company's resume preparation services, call 910-483-6611 or write to PREP at 1110½ Hay Street, Fayetteville, NC 28305. If you have a job hunting experience you would like to share with our staff at the Real-Resumes Series, please contact us at preppub@aol.com or visit our website at http://www.prep-pub.com.

The resumes and cover letters in this book are designed to be of most value to students. At last there is a book that addresses the unique problems students have when they create their resume. For example, how do you show off experience as a tutor, dormitory president, volunteer, or nonpaid research assistant? How do you show clinical rotations or internships? How do you use your part-time and summer work experience to your professional advantage?

If we could give you one word of advice about your career, here's what we would say: Manage your career and don't stumble from job to job in an incoherent pattern. Try to find work that interests you, and then identify prosperous industries which need work performed of the type you want to do. Learn early in your working life that a great resume and cover letter can blow doors open for you and help you maximize your salary.

This book is dedicated to students. The advice and samples in this book will help you launch your career.

Real-Resumes for Students

As the editor of this book, I would like to give you some tips on how to make the best use of the information you will find here. The purpose of this book is to help you land the best possible job after graduating from college, technical school, graduate school, or a professional training program. We also provide excellent advice on how to manage your career and show you resumes and cover letters that will be essential career tools.

Overview of the Book

Every resume and cover letter in this book actually worked. And the resumes and cover letters have common features: all are one-page, all are in the chronological format, and all resumes are accompanied by a companion cover letter. The book is divided into three parts. **Part One provides some advice about job hunting.** Step One begins with a discussion of why employers prefer the one-page, chronological resume. In Step Two you are introduced to the direct approach and to the proper format for a cover letter. In Step Three you learn the 14 main reasons why job hunters are not offered the jobs they want, and you learn the six key areas employers focus on when they interview you. Step Four gives nuts-and-bolts advice on how to handle the interview, send a follow-up letter after an interview, and negotiate your salary. At the end of Part One, you'll find advice about how to research and locate the companies and organizations to which you want to send your resume.

Part Two of the book goes into detail about cover letters, since cover letters are such an important part of a job hunt when someone is launching a new career. You will see an example of a resume of a newly credentialed teacher who is seeking her first job in teaching, and you will see how important a cover letter is in terms of introducing you. You will also see a resume accompanied by two different cover letters—one cover letter designed to explore opportunities in the public sector and the other cover letter designed to explore opportunities in the private sector. You learn more about cover letters when you look at several examples of cover letters for students seeking their first job in their field. When you have had no experience in the field you are trying to enter, your cover letter is of critical importance, and the sample cover letters in this section give you clear ideas about how cover letters should be phrased to be most effective.

Part Three is the meat of the book, and it shows real resumes and real cover letters for students. In this section you will find sample resumes of students trying to enter a variety of fields and possessing a variety of majors. Whether they are entering the job market with a major in accounting or the sciences, these students have much in common. For one thing, many students have job titles on their resume like "Groundskeeper," "Tutor," "Student Teacher," "Student Aide," "Resident Advisor," "Student Government President," "Intern," "Volunteer," "Waitress," "Lifeguard," and "Research Assistant."

But before you proceed further, think about why you picked up this book.
- Do you wonder if you even have enough job experience to put on a resume?
- Did you get your degree in one area but are thinking of pursuing work options in something unrelated?
- Are you aware of the importance of a great cover letter but unsure of how to write one?
- Do you need expert advice on how to plan and implement a job campaign that will open the maximum number of doors?
- Do you want to make sure you handle an interview to your maximum advantage?
- Do you want to learn the secrets and shortcuts of professional resume writers?

INTRODUCTION:
About Job
Hunting,
Interviewing,
and Locating
Potential
Employers

Using the Direct Approach

As you go into your upcoming job hunt, you need to be aware that most people end up having at least three distinctly different careers in their working lifetimes, and often those careers are different from each other. Yet people usually stumble through each job campaign, unsure of what they should be doing. Whenever you find yourself in a job hunt, the direct approach is the job hunting strategy most likely to yield a full-time permanent job. The direct approach is an active, take-the-initiative style of job hunting in which you choose your next employer rather than relying on responding to ads, using employment agencies, or depending on other methods of finding jobs. You will learn how to use the direct approach in this book, and you will see that an effective cover letter is a critical ingredient in using the direct approach.

Lack of Industry Experience Not a Major Barrier to Entering New Field

The "direct approach" is the style of job hunting most likely to yield the maximum number of job interviews.

"Lack of experience" is often the last reason people are not offered jobs, according to the companies who do the hiring. That should be good news to students, because that tells you that companies are screening recent graduates to try to identify strong personal qualities and certain types of interests that have been shown to be predictors of success in a particular industry. What that means to you later on in your career, too, is this: One day, for example, if you happen to be a manager changing industries, you will be glad to learn that even experienced professionals often are selling "potential" rather than experience in a job hunt. Companies often seek personal qualities that they know tend to be present in their most effective professionals, such as communication skills, initiative, persistence, organizational and time management skills, and creativity. Frequently companies are trying to discover "personality type," "talent," "ability," "aptitude," and "potential" rather than seeking actual hands-on experience, so your resume at any age and stage in your life should be designed to aggressively present your accomplishments. Attitude, enthusiasm, personality, and a track record of achievements in anything—in academic pursuits or in extracurricular activities including student government or sports—are the primary "indicators of success" which employers are seeking. If you have limited work experience, your volunteer interests may also be very revealing to employers; for example, if you spend much of your free time volunteering your assistance to Habitat for Humanity, you should make sure you include that fact on your resume. High-quality motivations in your personal life may be perceived as an indication of the fact that you could be a generous colleague who would work unselfishly in a team environment. Finally, don't worry if you are not exactly sure what you want to do in your next job. If you want to explore lots of options in many different fields, you can make sure your resume is written in an all-purpose fashion. You will see numerous examples in this book of resumes written in an all-purpose fashion so that students can approach various industries and types of companies.

Using references in a skillful fashion in your job hunt will inspire confidence in prospective employers and help you "close the sale" after interviews.

The Art of Using References in a Job Hunt

You probably already know that you need to provide references during a job hunt, but you may not be sure of how and when to use references for maximum advantage. You can use references very creatively during a job hunt to call attention to your strengths and make yourself "stand out." Your references will rarely get you a job, no matter how impressive the names, but the way you use references can boost the employer's confidence in you and lead to a job offer in the least time. You should ask from three to five people, including people who have taught you or supervised you, if you can use them as a reference during your job hunt. If you are working, you may not be able to ask your current boss since your job hunt may be confidential. A common question in resume preparation is: "Do I need to put my references on my resume?" No, you don't. And even if you create a page of references at the same time that you prepare your resume, you don't need to mail your references page with the resume and cover letter. The potential employer is not interested in your references until he meets and gets interested in you, so the earliest you need to have references ready is at the first interview. An excellent attention-getting technique is to take to the first interview not just a page of references (giving names, addresses, and telephone numbers) but an actual letter of reference written by someone who knows you well and who preferably has supervised or employed you. A professional way to close the first interview is to thank the interviewer, shake his or her hand, and then say you'd like to give him or her a copy of a letter of reference. Hopefully you already made a good impression during the interview, but you'll "close the sale" in a dynamic fashion if you leave a letter praising you and your accomplishments. For that reason, it's a good idea to ask instructors or previous employers if they will provide you with a written letter of recommendation which you can use in future job hunts. Most instructors or employers will oblige, and you will have a letter that has a useful "shelf life" of many years. Such a letter often gives the prospective employer enough confidence in his opinion of you that he may forego checking out other references and decide to offer you the job in the next few days. Whom should you ask to serve as references? References should be people who have known or supervised you in a professional, academic, or work situation. Most employers know that your pastor will almost certainly be your ally, so avoid asking your minister. You may not want to rely too heavily on your parents' friends, although a well-written letter from someone who has known you most of your life can provide a useful character reference to potential employers. References with big titles, like school superintendent or congressman, are fine, but remind busy people when you get to the interview stage that they may be contacted soon. Make sure the busy official recognizes your name and has instant positive recall of you! If you're asked to provide references on a formal company application, you can simply transcribe names from your references list. In summary, follow this rule in using references: If you've got them, flaunt them! If you've obtained well-written letters of reference, make sure you find a polite way to push those references under the nose of the interviewer so he or she can hear someone other than you describing your strengths. Your references probably won't ever get you a job, but glowing letters of reference can give you credibility and visibility that can make you stand out among candidates with similar credentials and potential!

In general, you will find that the approach taken by this book is to (1) help you master the proven best techniques of conducting a job hunt and (2) show you how to stand out in a job hunt through your resume, cover letter, interviewing skills, as well as the way in which you present your references and follow up on interviews.

The best way to "get in the mood" for writing your own resume and cover letter is to select samples from the Table of Contents that interest you and then read them. Don't necessarily look for someone with the same type of degree or major. You can learn a lot by looking over most of the resumes in this book. A great resume is a "photograph," usually on one page, of an individual, and you will meet some talented people between the covers of this book. If you wish to seek professional advice in preparing your resume, you may contact one of the professional writers at Professional Resume & Employment Publishing (PREP) for a brief free consultation by calling 1-910-483-6611.

With regard to references, it's best to provide the names and addresses of people who have supervised you or observed you in a work situation. However, students might also ask one or more of their teachers or instructors for a reference.

Part One: Some Advice About Your Job Hunt

What if you don't know what you want to do?

Your job hunt will be more comfortable if you can figure out what type of work you want to do. But you are not alone if you have no idea what you want to do next! You may have knowledge and skills in certain areas but want to get into another type of work. What *The Wall Street Journal* has discovered in its research on careers is that most of us end up having at least three distinctly different careers in our working lives; it seems that, even if we really like a particular kind of activity, twenty years of doing it is enough for most of us and we want to move on to something else!

That's why at PREP we strongly believe that you need to spend some time figuring out ***what interests you*** rather than taking an inventory of the skills you have. You may have skills that you simply don't want to use, but if you can build your career on the things that interest you, you will be more likely to be happy and satisfied in your job. Realize, too, that interests can change over time; the activities that interest you now may not be the ones that interested you when you declared your major. For example, some professionals may decide that they've had enough of managing people and want a job marketing a product or service, even though they have earned a reputation for being an excellent manager. We strongly believe that *interests* rather than skills should be the determining factor in deciding what types of jobs you want to apply for and what directions you explore in your job hunt. Obviously one cannot be a lawyer without a law degree or a secretary without secretarial skills; but a professional can embark on a next career as a financial consultant, property manager, plant manager, production supervisor, retail manager, or other occupation if he/she has a strong interest in that type of work and can provide a resume that clearly demonstrates past excellent performance in *any* field and *potential* to excel in another field. As you will see later in this book, "lack of exact experience" is the last reason why people are turned down for the jobs they apply for.

Figure out what interests you and you will hold the key to a successful job hunt and working career. (And be prepared for your interests to change over time!)

How can you have a resume prepared if you don't know what you want to do?

You may be wondering how you can have a resume prepared if you don't know what you want to do next. The approach to resume writing which PREP has used successfully for many years is to develop an "all-purpose" resume that translates your skills, experience, and accomplishments into language employers can understand. What most people need in a job hunt is a versatile resume that will allow them to apply for numerous types of jobs. For example, you may want to apply for a job in pharmaceutical sales but you may also want to have a resume that will be versatile enough for you to apply for jobs in the construction, financial services, or automotive industries.

"Lack of exact experience" is the last reason people are turned down for the jobs for which they apply.

Based on 20 years of serving job hunters, we at PREP have found that **an all-purpose resume** and **specific cover letters tailored to specific fields** is often your best approach to job hunting rather than trying to create different resumes for different occupational areas. Usually, you will not even need more than one "all-purpose" cover letter, although the cover letter rather than the resume is the place to communicate your interest in a narrow or specific field. An all-purpose resume and cover letter that translate your experience and accomplishments into plain English are the tools that will maximize the number of doors which open for you while permitting you to "fish" in the widest range of job areas.

Your resume will provide the script for your job interview.
When you get down to it, your resume has a simple job to do: Its purpose is to blow as many doors open as possible and to make as many people as possible want to meet you. So a well-written resume that really "sells" you is a key that will create opportunities for you in a job hunt.

This statistic explains why: The typical newspaper advertisement for a job opening receives more than 245 replies. And normally only 10 or 12 will be invited to an interview.

But here's another purpose of the resume: it provides the "script" the employer uses when he interviews you. If your resume has been written in such a way that your strengths and achievements are revealed, that's what you'll end up talking about at the job interview. Since the resume will govern what you get asked about at your interviews, you can't overestimate the importance of making sure your resume makes you look and sound as good as you are.

So what is a "good" resume?
Very literally, your resume should motivate the person reading it to dial the phone number you have put on the resume. (If you are relocating, that's one reason you should think about putting a local phone contact number on your resume, if possible, when your contact address is several states away; employers are much more likely to dial a local telephone number than a long-distance number when they're looking for potential employees.)

If you have a resume already, look at it objectively. Is it a limp, colorless "laundry list" of your job titles and duties? Or does it "paint a picture" of your skills, abilities, and accomplishments in a way that would make someone want to meet you? Can people understand what you're saying?

How long should your resume be?
One page, maybe two. Usually only people in the academic community have a resume (which they usually call a *curriculum vitae*) longer than one or two pages. Remember that your resume is almost always accompanied by a cover letter, and a potential employer does not want to read more than two or three pages about a total stranger in order to decide if he wants to meet that person! Besides, don't forget that the more you tell someone about yourself, the more opportunity you are providing for the employer to screen you out at the "first-cut" stage. A resume should be concise and exciting and designed to make the reader want to meet you in person!

Should resumes be functional or chronological?
Employers almost always prefer a chronological resume; in other words, an employer will find a resume easier to read if it is immediately apparent what your current or most recent job is, what you did before that, and so forth, in reverse chronological order. A resume that goes back in detail for the last ten years of employment will generally satisfy the employer's curiosity about your background, but only "older students" will have that much experience to put on a resume. Remember that your intention is not to tell everything you've done but to "hit the high points" and especially hit the employer with what you learned, contributed, or accomplished in each job you describe.

Your resume is the "script" for your job interviews. Make sure you put on your resume what you want to talk about or be asked about at the job interview.

The one-page resume in chronological format is the format preferred by most employers.

Once you get your resume, what do you do with it?
You will be using your resume to answer ads, as a tool to use in talking with friends and relatives about your job search, and, most importantly, in using the "direct approach" described in this book.

When you mail your resume, always send a "cover letter."
A "cover letter," sometimes called a "resume letter" or "letter of interest," is a letter that accompanies and introduces your resume. Your cover letter is a way of personalizing the resume by sending it to the specific person you think you might want to work for at each company. Your cover letter should contain a few highlights from your resume—just enough to make someone want to meet you. Cover letters should always be typed or word processed on a computer—never handwritten.

> Never mail or fax your resume without a cover letter.

1. Learn the art of answering ads.
There is an "art," part of which can be learned, in using your "bestselling" resume to reply to advertisements.

Sometimes an exciting job lurks behind a boring ad that someone dictated in a hurry, so reply to any ad that interests you. Don't worry that you aren't "25 years old with an MBA" like the ad asks for. Employers will always make compromises in their requirements if they think you're the "best fit" overall.

What about ads that ask for "salary requirements?"
What if the ad you're answering asks for "salary requirements?" The first rule is to avoid committing yourself in writing at that point to a specific salary. You don't want to "lock yourself in."

> What if the ad asks for your "salary requirements?"

There are two ways to handle the ad that asks for "salary requirements."
First, you can ignore that part of the ad and accompany your resume with a cover letter that focuses on "selling" you, your abilities, and even some of your philosophy about work or your field. You may include a sentence in your cover letter like this: "I can provide excellent personal and professional references at your request, and I would be delighted to share the private details of my salary history with you in person." If you are like most students, you may be too inexperienced to have much of a "salary history." Second, you could give a range. If you are an experienced or "older student" with a substantial work history, and if you feel you must give some kind of number, just state a range in your cover letter that includes your medical, dental, other benefits, and bonuses. You might state, for example, "my previous compensation, including benefits and bonuses, was in the range of $35,000-40,000."

Analyze the ad and "tailor" yourself to it.
When you're replying to ads, a finely-tailored cover letter is an important tool in getting your resume noticed and read. On the next page is a cover letter which has been "tailored to fit" a specific ad. Notice the "art" used by PREP writers of analyzing the ad's main requirements and then writing the letter so that the person's background, work habits, and interests seem "tailor-made" to the company's needs. Use this cover letter as a model when you prepare your own reply to ads.

Date

Mr. Arthur Wise
Chamber of Commerce of the U.S.
9439 Goshen Lane
Burke, VA 22105

Dear Mr. Wise:

I would appreciate an opportunity to show you in person, soon, that I am the energetic, dynamic salesperson you are looking for as a Membership Sales Representative of the Chamber of Commerce.

As you will see from my enclosed resume, I am a "newly minted" college graduate with a degree in Marketing, which I earned *cum laude*. Here are just three reasons why I believe I am the effective young professional you seek:

- *I myself am "sold" on the Chamber of Commerce* and have long been an admirer of its goal of forming a cohesive business organization to promote the well-being of communities and promote business vigor. As someone better known than I put it long ago, "the business of America is business." I wholeheartedly believe in the Chamber's efforts to unite, solidify, and mobilize American business. My father is an independent businessman and has been a Chamber member all his life, so I have grown up hearing about the Chamber and its honorable goals.

- *I am a proven salesperson* with a demonstrated ability to "prospect." Because of my natural sales ability, I was elected Membership Chairperson of my sorority and I led my organization in achieving the most successful membership drive in its history. I have been told that I "could sell a refrigerator to an Eskimo," and I am confident I could be highly effective in recruiting new members.

- *I am single and enjoy traveling and am eager to assist in the growth of Virginia and vicinity.* I am fortunate to have the natural energy, industry, and enthusiasm required to put in the long hours necessary for effective sales performance.

You would find me to be a friendly, good-natured person whom you would be proud to call part of the Chamber's "team."

I hope you will call or write me soon to suggest a convenient time when we might meet to discuss your needs further and how I might serve them. Please allow me an opportunity to show you in person that I am the enthusiastic and hard-working individual you are seeking.

Yours sincerely,

Your Name

Employers are trying to identify the individual who wants the job they are filling. Don't be afraid to express your enthusiasm in the cover letter!

2. Talk to friends and relatives.

Don't be shy about telling your friends and relatives the kind of job you're looking for. Looking for the job you want involves using your network of contacts, so tell people what you're looking for. They may be able to make introductions and help set up interviews.

About 25% of all interviews are set up through "who you know," so don't ignore this approach.

The "direct approach" is a strategy in which you choose your next employer.

3. Finally, and most importantly, use the "direct approach."

More than 50% of all job interviews are set up by the "direct approach." That means you actually send a resume and a cover letter to a company you think might be interested in employing your skills.

To whom do you write?

In general, you should write directly to the *exact name* of the person who would be hiring you: say, the vice-president of marketing or data processing. If you're in doubt about to whom to address the letter, address it to the president by name and he or she will make sure it gets forwarded to the right person within the company who has hiring authority in your area.

How do you find the names of potential employers?

You're not alone if you feel that the biggest problem in your job search is finding the right names at the companies you want to contact. But you can usually figure out the names of companies you want to approach by deciding first if your job hunt is primarily geography-driven or industry-driven.

In a **geography-driven job hunt,** you could select a list of, say, 50 companies you want to contact **by location** from the lists that the U.S. Chambers of Commerce publish yearly of their "major area employers." There are hundreds of local Chambers of Commerce across America, and most of them will have an 800 number which you can find through 1-800-555-1212. If you think Atlanta, Dallas, Ft. Lauderdale, and Virginia Beach might be nice places to live, for example, you could contact the Chamber of Commerce in those cities and ask how you can obtain a copy of their list of major employers. Your nearest library will have the book which lists the addresses of all chambers.

In an **industry-driven job hunt,** and if you are willing to relocate, you will be identifying the companies which you find most attractive in the industry in which you want to work. When you select a list of companies to contact **by industry,** you can find the right person to write and the address of firms by industrial category in *Standard and Poor's, Moody's,* and other excellent books in public libraries. Many web sites also provide contact information.

Many people feel it's a good investment to actually call the company to either find out or double-check the name of the person to whom they want to send a resume and cover letter. It's important to do as much as you feasibly can to assure that the letter gets to the right person in the company.

At the end of Part One, you will find some advice about how to conduct library research and how to locate organizations to which you could send your resume.

What's the correct way to follow up on a resume you send?

There is a polite way to be aggressively interested in a company during your job hunt. It is ideal to end the cover letter accompanying your resume by saying, "I hope you'll welcome my call next week when I try to arrange a brief meeting at your convenience to discuss your current and future needs and how I might serve them." Keep it low key, and just ask for a "brief meeting," not an interview. Employers want people who show a determined interest in working with them, so don't be shy about following up on the resume and cover letter you've mailed.

It pays to be aware of the 14 most common pitfalls for job hunters.

STEP THREE: Preparing for Interviews

But a resume and cover letter by themselves can't get you the job you want. You need to "prep" yourself before the interview. Step Three in your job campaign is "Preparing for Interviews." First, let's look at interviewing from the company's point of view.

What are the biggest "turnoffs" for companies?

One of the ways to help yourself perform well at an interview is to look at the main reasons why companies *don't* hire the people they interview, according to companies that do the interviewing.

Notice that "lack of appropriate background" (or lack of experience) is the *last* reason for not being offered the job.

The 14 Most Common Reasons Job Hunters Are Not Offered Jobs (according to the companies who do the interviewing and hiring):

1. Low level of accomplishment
2. Poor attitude, lack of self-confidence
3. Lack of goals/objectives
4. Lack of enthusiasm
5. Lack of interest in the company's business
6. Inability to sell or express yourself
7. Unrealistic salary demands
8. Poor appearance
9. Lack of maturity, no leadership potential
10. Lack of extracurricular activities
11. Lack of preparation for the interview, no knowledge about company
12. Objecting to travel
13. Excessive interest in security and benefits
14. Inappropriate background

Department of Labor studies since the 1950s have proven that smart, "prepared" job hunters can increase their beginning salary while getting a job in *half* the time it normally takes. (4½ months is the average national length of a job search.) Here, from PREP, are some questions that can prepare you to find a job faster.

Are you in the "right" frame of mind?

It seems unfair that we have to look for a job just when we're lowest in morale. Don't worry *too* much if you're nervous before interviews (top television personalities say they usually are, too). You're supposed to be a little nervous, especially if the job means a lot to you. But the best way to kill unnecessary fears about job hunting is through 1) making sure you have a great resume and cover letter and 2) preparing yourself for the interview. Here are three main areas to think about before each interview.

Do you know what the company does?

Don't walk into an interview giving the impression that, "If this is Tuesday, this must be General Motors."

Research the company before you go to interviews.

Find out before the interview what the company's main product or service is. Where is the company heading? Is it in a "growth" or declining industry? (Answers to these questions may influence whether or not you want to work there!)

Information about what the company does is in annual reports as well as newspaper and magazine articles. Just visit your nearest library and ask the reference librarian to guide you to materials on the company. Internet searches will also yield valuable information. At the end of Part One you will find many suggestions about how to research companies.

Do you know what you want to do for the company?

Before the interview, try to decide how you see yourself fitting into the company. Remember, "lack of exact background" the company wants is usually the *last* reason people are not offered jobs.

Understand before you go to each interview that the burden will be on you to "sell" the interviewer on why you're the best person for the job and the company.

Anticipate the questions you will be asked at the interview, and prepare your responses in advance.

How will you answer the critical interview questions?

Put yourself in the interviewer's position and think about the questions you're most likely to be asked. Here are some of the most commonly asked interview questions:

Q: *"What are your greatest strengths?"*
A: Don't say you've never thought about it! Go into an interview knowing the three main impressions you want to leave about yourself, such as "I'm hard-working, loyal, and an imaginative cost-cutter."

Q: *"What are your greatest weaknesses?"*
A: Don't confess that you're lazy or have trouble meeting deadlines! Confessing that you tend to be a "workaholic" or "tend to be a perfectionist and sometimes get frustrated when others don't share my high standards" will make your prospective employer see a "weakness" that he likes. Name a weakness that your interviewer will perceive as a strength.

Q: *"What are your long-range goals?"*
A: If you're interviewing with Microsoft, don't say you want to work for IBM in five years! Say your long-range goal is to be *with* the company, contributing to its goals and success.

Q: *"What motivates you to do your best work?"*
A: Don't get dollar signs in your eyes here! "A challenge" is not a bad answer, but it's a little cliched. Saying something like "troubleshooting" or "solving a tough problem" is more interesting and specific. Give an example if you can.

Q: "What do you know about this company?"

A: Don't say you never heard of it until they asked you to the interview! Name an interesting, positive thing you learned about the company recently from your research. Remember, company executives can sometimes feel rather "maternal" about the company they serve. Don't get onto a negative area of the company if you can think of positive facts you can bring up. Of course, if you learned in your research that the company's sales seem to be taking a nose-dive, or that the company president is being prosecuted for taking bribes, you might politely ask your interviewer to tell you something that could help you better understand what you've been reading. Those are the kinds of company facts that can help you determine whether you want to work there or not.

> Go to an interview prepared to tell the company why it should hire you.

Q: "Why should I hire you?"

A: "I'm unemployed and available" is the wrong answer here! Get back to your strengths and say that you believe the organization could benefit by a loyal, hard-working cost-cutter like yourself.

In conclusion, you should decide in advance, before you go to the interview, how you will answer each of these commonly asked questions.

Have some practice interviews with a friend to role-play and build your confidence.

STEP FOUR: Handling the Interview and Negotiating Salary

> A smile at an interview makes the employer perceive of you as intelligent!

Now you're ready for Step Four: actually handling the interview successfully and effectively. Remember, the purpose of an interview is to get a job offer.

Eight "do's" for the interview

According to leading U.S. companies, there are eight key areas in interviewing success. You can fail at an interview if you mishandle just one area.

1. *Do wear appropriate clothes.*
   You can never go wrong by wearing a suit to an interview.

2. *Do be well groomed.*
   Don't overlook the obvious things like having clean hair, clothes, and fingernails for the interview.

3. *Do give a firm handshake.*
   You'll have to shake hands twice in most interviews: first, before you sit down, and second, when you leave the interview. Limp handshakes turn most people off.

4. *Do smile and show a sense of humor.*
   Interviewers are looking for people who would be nice to work with, so don't be so somber that you don't smile. In fact, research shows that people who smile at interviews are perceived as more intelligent. So, smile!

5. *Do be enthusiastic.*
   Employers say they are "turned off" by lifeless, unenthusiastic job hunters who show no special interest in that company. The best way to show some enthusiasm for the employer's operation is to find out about the business beforehand.

6. *Do show you are flexible and adaptable.*

   An employer is looking for someone who can contribute to his organization in a flexible, adaptable way. No matter what skills and training you have, employers know every new employee must go through initiation and training on the company's turf. Certainly show pride in your past accomplishments in a specific, factual way ("I saved my employer $50.00 a week in my summer job by a new cost-cutting procedure I developed"). But don't come across as though there's nothing about the job you couldn't easily handle.

7. *Do ask intelligent questions about the employer's business.*

   An employer is hiring someone because of certain business needs. Show interest in those needs. Asking questions to get a better idea of the employer's needs will help you "stand out" from other candidates interviewing for the job.

8. *Do "take charge" when the interviewer "falls down" on the job.*

   Go into every interview knowing the three or four points about yourself you want the interviewer to remember. And be prepared to take an active part in leading the discussion if the interviewer's "canned approach" does not permit you to display your "strong suit." You can't always depend on the interviewer's asking you the "right" questions so you can stress your strengths and accomplishments.

Employers are seeking people with good attitudes whom they can train and coach to do things their way.

An important "don't"

Don't ask questions about salary or benefits at the first interview.

Employers don't take warmly to people who look at their organization as just a place to satisfy salary and benefit needs. Don't risk making a negative impression by appearing greedy or self-serving.

The place to discuss salary and benefits is normally at the second interview, and the employer will bring it up. Then you can ask any questions you like without appearing excessively interested in what the organization can do for you.

"Sell yourself" before talking salary

Make sure you've "sold" yourself before talking salary. First show you're the "best fit" for the employer and then you'll be in a stronger position from which to negotiate salary.

Interviewers sometimes throw out a salary figure at the first interview to see if you'll accept it. Don't commit yourself. You may be able to negotiate a better deal later on. Get back to finding out more about the job. This lets the interviewer know you're interested primarily in the job and not the salary.

Don't appear excessively interested in salary and benefits at the interview.

Now...negotiating your salary

You must avoid stating a "salary requirement" in your initial cover letter, and you must avoid even appearing **interested** in salary before you are offered the job.

Never bring up the subject of salary yourself. Employers say there's no way you can avoid looking greedy if you bring up the issue of salary and benefits before the company has identified you as its "best fit."

When the company brings up salary, it may say something like this: "Well, Mary, we think you'd make a good candidate for this job. What kind of salary are we talking about?"

Never name a number here, either. Give the ball back to the interviewer. Act as though you hadn't given the subject of salary much thought and respond something like this: "Ah, Mr. Jones, salary. . .well, I wonder if you'd be kind enough to tell me what salary you had in mind when you advertised the job?" Or ... "What is the range you have in mind?"

Don't worry, if the interviewer names a figure that you think is too low, you can say so without turning down the job or locking yourself into a rigid position. The point here is to negotiate for yourself as well as you can. You might reply to a number named by the interviewer that you think is low by saying something like this: "Well, Mr. Lee, the job interests me very much, and I think I'd certainly enjoy working with you. But, frankly, I was thinking of something a little higher than that." That leaves the ball in your interviewer's court again, and you haven't turned down the job, either, in case it turns out that the interviewer can't increase the offer and you still want the job.

Salary negotiation can be tricky.

Last, send a follow-up letter
Finally, send a letter right after the interview telling your interviewer you enjoyed the meeting and are certain (if you are) you are the "best fit" for the job.

Again, employers have a certain maternal attitude toward their companies, and they are looking for people who want to work for *that* company in particular.

A follow-up letter can help the employer choose between you and another qualified candidate.

The follow-up letter you send might be just the deciding factor in your favor if the employer is trying to choose between you and someone else.

A sample follow-up letter is shown on page 24. Be sure to modify it according to your particular skills and interview situation.

Researching companies and locating employers

Figuring out the names of the organizations to which you want to mail your resume is part of any highly successful job campaign. Don't depend on just answering the ads you read in printed or electronic form, waiting for the ideal job to appear in **newspapers or magazines,** many of which are published online. If you are geographically oriented and need to find work in a particular city or town, check out the Sunday advertisements in the classified sections which suit you best, such as "administrative" or "professional" or "technical." Also aggressively research possible employers. Here is some information which you can use in researching the names of organizations for which you might be interested in working.

In electronic and printed form, most libraries have a variety of information available on various organizations throughout the U.S. and worldwide. If your local library has computers, you will probably have access to a vast network of information. Many printed materials might be available only for use in the reference room of the library, but some may be checked out. Listed below are some of the major sources to look for, but be sure and check at the information desk to see if there are any books available on the specific types of companies you wish to investigate.

The Worldwide Chamber of Commerce Directory

Most chambers of commerce annually produce a "list of major employers" for their market area (or city). Usually the list includes the name, address, and telephone number of the employer along with information about the number of people employed, kinds of products and services produced, and a person to contact about employment. You can obtain the "list of major employers" in the city where you want to work by writing to that chamber. There is usually a small charge.

The *Worldwide Chamber of Commerce Directory* is an alphabetical listing of American and foreign chambers of commerce. It includes:

    All U.S. Chambers of Commerce (with addresses and phone numbers)
    American Chambers of Commerce abroad
    Canadian Chambers of Commerce
    Foreign Chambers of Commerce in principal cities worldwide
    Foreign Embassies and Consulates in the U.S.
    U.S. Consulates and Embassies throughout the world

Standard and Poor's Register of Corporations, Directors, and Executives

Standard and Poor's produce three volumes annually with information concerning over 77,000 American corporations. They are:

Volume 1—**Corporations.** Here is an alphabetical listing of a variety of information for each of over 77,000 companies, including:
- name of company, address, telephone number
- names, titles, and functions of several key officers
- name of accounting firm, primary bank, and law firm
- stock exchange, description of products or services
- annual sales, number of employees
- division names and functions, subsidiary listings

Volume 2—**Directors and Executives.** This volume lists alphabetically over 70,000 officers, directors, partners, etc. by name. Information on each executive includes:
- principal business affiliation
- business address, residence address, year of birth
- college and year of graduation, fraternal affiliation

Volume 3—**Index.**

Moody's Manuals

Moody's Manuals provide information about companies traded on the New York and American Stock Exchanges and over the counter. They include:

Moody's Industrial Manual

Here, Moody's discusses detailed information on companies traded on the New York, American, and regional stock exchanges. The companies are listed alphabetically. Basic information about company addresses, phone numbers, and the names of key officers is available for each company listed. In addition, detailed information about the financial and operating data for each company is available. There are three levels of detail provided:

Complete Coverage. Companies in this section have the following information:
- *financial information* for the past 7 years (income accounts, balance sheets, financial and operating data).
- *detailed description of the company's business* including a complete list of subsidiaries and office and property sites.
- *capital structure information,* which includes details on capital stock and long-term debt, with bond and preferred stock ratings and 2 years of stock and bond price ranges.
- *extensive presentation of the company's last annual report.*

Full Measure Coverage. Information on companies in this section includes:
- *financial information for the past 7 years* (income accounts, balance sheets, financial and operating data).
- *detailed description of company's business,* with a complete list of subsidiaries and plant and property locations.
- *capital structure information,* with details on capital stock and long term debt, with bond and preferred stock ratings and 2 years of stock and bond price changes.

Comprehensive Coverage. Information on companies in this section includes:
- *5 years of financial information* on income accounts, balance sheets, and financial and operating ratios.
- *detailed description of company's business,* including subsidiaries.
- *concise capital structure information,* including capital stock and long term debts, bond and preferred stock ratings.

Moody's OTC Manual
Here is information on U.S. firms which are unlisted on national and regional stock exchanges. There are three levels of coverage: complete, full measure, and comprehensive (same as described above). Other Moody's manuals include: *Moody's Public Utility Manual, Moody's Municipal and Government Manual,* and *Moody's Bank and Finance Manual.*

Dun's Million Dollar Directory
Three separate listings (alphabetical, geographic, and by products) of over 120,000 U.S. firms. There are three volumes:
Volume 1—The 45,000 largest companies, net worth over $500,000
Volume 2—The 37,000 next largest companies
Volume 3—The 37,000 next largest companies

U.S. industrial directories
Ask your librarian to guide you to your library's collection of industrial directories. Almost every state produces a manufacturing directory, for example, and many libraries maintain complete collections of these directories. You may find information on products and the addresses and telephone numbers of industrial companies.

Thomas' Register of Manufacturers
16 volumes of information about manufacturing companies.
Volumes 1-8—Alphabetical listing by product.

Volumes 9-10—Alphabetical listing of manufacturing company names, addresses, telephone numbers, and local offices.

Volumes 11-16—Alphabetical company catalog information.

Information About Foreign Companies

If you'd like your next job to be overseas or with an international company, you can find much helpful information in the library. You approach these companies in the same way as you would approach U.S.-based companies.

Directory of Foreign Manufacturers in the U.S.

Alphabetical listing of U.S. manufacturing companies which are owned and operated by parent foreign firms. The information provided includes the name and address of the U.S. firm, the name and address of the foreign parent firm, and the products produced.

Directory of American Firms Operating in Foreign Countries

Alphabetical listing of the names, addresses, chief officers, products, and country operated in of U.S. firms abroad.

International Firms Directory

This lists foreign corporations.

Hoover's Handbook of World Business

This lists corporations in Asia and Europe.

Principal International Businesses

This is a comprehensive directory of international businesses.

Information Available From The Internet

Information about companies is widely available through the Internet. You can use all the search engines to help you in your search for company information and company website addresses. To avoid giving you information which would be hopelessly out of date by the time you read this book, we will simply suggest that you maintain your up-to-date resume on a disk and be prepared to e-mail it to companies when you visit their websites. If you go to the search engines, typing in words like "employment" and "jobs" and actual company names should help you begin your journey toward the latest information and most interesting sites on the worldwide Web.

Many people are aware of the importance of having a great resume, but most people in a job hunt don't realize just how important a cover letter can be. The purpose of the cover letter, sometimes called a **"letter of interest,"** is to introduce your resume to prospective employers.

"A Picture Is Worth a Thousand Words."

As a way of illustrating how important the cover letter can be, we have chosen to show you on the next two pages the cover letter and resume of a young person seeking her first job in the teaching field. If the employer received only her resume without a cover letter, this promising young teacher would look like a cook and restaurant worker! A busy principal would probably not be motivated to dial her telephone number to suggest an interview time. In her case, the cover letter is probably more important than the resume she has been asked to submit. What the cover letter allows her to do is to explain that she worked as a cook, closing manager, and cashier full time while going back to school to earn her college degree. This puts her work experience in a different perspective.

The cover letter is the critical ingredient in a job hunt such as Marcia Vivero's because the cover letter allows her to say a lot of things that just don't "fit" on the resume. For example, she can emphasize her commitment to the teaching profession and stress her talent for teaching mathematics to people who find the subject difficult.

One of the things that sets her apart from other new graduates in her field is that she is a mature professional who, at age 27, is accustomed to a demanding work schedule. She's no "old lady" but she is five years older and wiser than the typical 22-year-old college graduate. In the high-stress profession which high school teaching is often considered to be, many principals will perceive of her age and experience as a positive factor.

Although the general rule is that women do not mention how many children they have in their resume and cover letter, there are exceptions to every rule, and Ms. Vivero breaks that rule for a good reason. She points out that she is a mother and would bring to the classroom an in-depth understanding of different learning styles.

Finally, the cover letter gives her a chance to stress the outstanding character and personal values which she feels will be a positive influence on the high school students to whom she wishes to teach mathematics.

You will see on the next two pages that the cover letter gives you a chance to "get personal" with the person to whom you are writing whereas the resume is a more formal document. Even if the employer doesn't request a cover letter, we believe that it is *always* in your best interest to send a cover letter with your resume. The aim of this book is to show you examples of cover letters designed to blow doors open so that you can develop your own cover letters and increase the number of interviews you have. In subsequent pages, you will read advice about formatting your cover letters.

Date

Exact Name of Principal
Exact Title
School Name
School Address
City, State Zip

Dear Exact Name: (or Dear Principal if you don't know the Exact Name)

With the enclosed resume, I would like to introduce myself and initiate the process of being considered for a position as a Mathematics Teacher in your high school.

As you will see from my resume, I recently graduated from the University of Rhode Island with a B.S. degree in Mathematics which I earned **magna cum laude**. I am especially proud of graduating with honors since I was combining a rigorous academic curriculum with a demanding work schedule which involved handling a variety of managerial, accounting, and customer service responsibilities.

Although I graduated in May 2000 with my B.S. degree, I am 27 years old and offer considerable experience in working with children of all ages. Since I am a wife and mother, I would bring to the classroom much understanding of the varying learning styles of children. I feel I would be skilled in classroom behavior management, and I would offer a maturity which younger college graduates might not have. I am a responsible individual known for my well-organized work habits and disciplined style.

I am deeply committed to a career in the teaching profession, and I intend in my spare time to earn my Master's degree in Mathematics and then a Ph.D. I am a highly motivated hard worker, and I feel my own strong values could be an inspiration to high school students. Although I have earned my degree in Mathematics with high honors, I am fully aware of how difficult mathematics is for many people, and I excel in translating abstract concepts into understandable language.

If you can use a vibrant young teaching professional who could enhance the fine reputation of your school, I hope you will contact me to suggest a time when I could make myself available for a personal interview. I can provide outstanding personal and professional references.

Sincerely,

Marcia Vivero

MARCIA VIVERO

1110½ Hay Street, Providence, RI 28305 • (910) 483-6611 • preppub@aol.com

OBJECTIVE	To contribute to a high school that can use a dedicated mathematics teacher who is attuned to the varied learning abilities and styles which students bring to the classroom.
EDUCATION	Earned B.S. degree in **Mathematics,** University of Rhode Island, Providence, RI, May 2000.

- Graduated **Magna Cum Laude** with a GPA of 3.754.
- Received the Certificate of Excellence and was named to the Chancellor's List.
- Excelled academically while working part-time to finance my college education.

Graduated from Eastern Senior High School, Pawtucket, RI, 1992.
- Participated in track and intramural sports.

EXPERIENCE

CLOSING MANAGER, COOK, CASHIER. Chuck's Chicken & Barbecue, Providence, RI (1993-present).
- Was singled out to handle a variety of management responsibilities, and became known for my trustworthiness and cheerful disposition while simultaneously earning my college degree **with honors.**
- Refined my interpersonal skills working with all types of customers and with other employees.
- Trained other employees; assigned tasks to junior employees and supervised their work.
- Expertly operated a cash register, and was known for my accuracy in handling large amounts of cash; trained other employees to use the register.
- As Closing Manager, was responsible for closing the store at the end of the business day; accounted for financial transactions and oversaw end-of-the-day maintenance and security matters.
- Was frequently commended for my gracious style of dealing with the public and for my courteous approach to customer service.

COMPUTER OPERATOR/CLERICAL AIDE. Clear Lake Elementary School, Pawtucket, RI (summer 1992).
- In the summer after my high school graduation, excelled in an office position handling numerous responsibilities related to record keeping for students in summer school.
- Operated a computer in order to input data and maintain records.
- Filed and typed as needed.
- Was known for my attention to detail and accuracy when handling large volumes of work under tight deadlines.

PERSONAL

Have aspirations to earn my Master's degree in Mathematics, and believe I could be a great asset to the teaching profession. Can provide outstanding references. Have taught in Bible School Programs. Believe all students can learn, and am skilled at communicating difficult mathematics concepts to students who find math difficult.

Addressing the Cover Letter: Get the exact name of the person to whom you are writing. She could address the letter to all high school principals in her area.

First Paragraph: The first paragraph explains why you are writing.

Second Paragraph: Here you have a chance to talk about your most distinguishing feature.

Third Paragraph: In the third paragraph, you can bring up your next most distinguishing qualities. Sell yourself!

Fourth Paragraph: Here you have another opportunity to reveal qualities or achievements which will impress your future employer.

Final Paragraph: She asks the employer to contact her. Make sure your reader knows what the "next step" is.

Alternate Final Paragraph: It's more aggressive (but not too aggressive) to let the employer know that you will be calling him or her. Don't be afraid to be persistent. Employers are looking for people who know what they want to do.

Date

Exact Name of Person
Exact Title of Person
Company Name
Address
City, State Zip

Dear Sir or Madam:

With the enclosed resume, I would like to make you aware of my strong desire to become a part of your elementary teaching staff.

As you will see from my resume, I recently earned my Bachelor of Science in Education (B.S.E.) degree at the University of Georgia. Since it has always been my childhood dream to become a teacher, my college graduation was an especially meaningful event in my life.

As you will see from my resume, I recently completed a teaching internship as a first grade student teacher, and I successfully assumed all the duties of a first grade teacher. During those two months, under the guidance of an experienced educator, I wrote and completed my own professional growth and development plan, and I also planned and implemented a classroom and behavior management program.

In my previous two-month internship as a kindergarten student teacher, I performed with distinction in planning and implementing creative lessons, communicating with teaching professionals and parents, and working with the children. You will notice from my resume that I have expressed my true love for children through my summer and part-time jobs while in college. For four years, I was a nanny for a professional family and in that capacity I cared for three triplet newborns as well as two older children. It is an understatement to say that I refined my time management skills in that part-time job!

If you can use a highly motivated young professional with unlimited personal initiative as well as strong personal qualities of dependability and trustworthiness, I hope you will contact me to suggest a time when we might meet to discuss your needs. I can provide excellent personal and professional references, and I am eager to apply my strong teaching skills and true love for children in an academic institution which emphasizes hard work and a commitment to the highest learning goals.

Sincerely,

Melanie Thompson

Alternate final paragraph:
I hope you will welcome my call soon when I contact you to try to arrange a brief meeting to discuss your needs and how my talents might help you. I appreciate whatever time you could give me in the process of exploring your needs.

Date

Three blank spaces

Exact Name of Person
Title or Position
Name of Company
Address (number and street)
Address (city, state, and zip)

Address

Dear Exact Name of Person: (or Dear Sir or Madam if answering a blind ad)

Salutation

One blank space

I would appreciate an opportunity to talk with you soon about how I could contribute to your organization through my proven accounts management, customer service, and public relations skills. Mr. Thomas Crane of your Atlanta office has strongly suggested that I send you my resume acquainting you with my abilities.

You will see from my resume that I began working with Revco when I was 16 years old; I continued my employment with Revco while attending college and was promoted to Pharmacy Technician while earning my Bachelor of Business Administration degree. After college graduation, the university where I earned my degree recruited me for a job in its admissions office, and I excelled in handling a wide variety of administrative and public relations tasks.

Most recently I have worked full time as an Account Representative while going to school at nights and on the weekends to earn my M.B.A., which I received in May 2000. I was handling key accounts worth more than $2 million annually for my employer and was being groomed for rapid promotion into a higher management position.

Body

I have, however, relocated permanently to the LaFayette area because I recently married and my husband owns and manages his own business in this area. I am seeking an employer who can use a highly motivated individual with very strong communication, sales, customer service, and public relations skills. Because I earned both my undergraduate and graduate degrees while excelling in demanding professional positions, I have acquired excellent organizational and time management skills which permit me to maximize my own productivity.

If you can use a self-starter who could rapidly become a valuable part of your organization, I hope you will contact me to suggest a time when we might meet to discuss your needs and how I might serve them. I can provide excellent personal and professional references.

One blank space

Sincerely,

Louise Patton

Signature

cc: Thomas Crane

cc: Indicates you are sending a copy of the letter to someone

**Two Different Cover Letters
for Two Different Types of
Employers: How to target
your resume to specific
employers by using your
cover letter.**

This young student
tailors her jobhunting
approach to specific
employers by using two
different cover letters.

Dear Exact Name of Person: (or Dear Sir or Madam if answering a blind ad):

With the enclosed resume, I would like to make you aware of my interest in exploring employment opportunities with your organization.

As you will see from my resume, I recently completed a B.A. degree in Industrial Relations from the University of South Carolina at Columbia. After college graduation, I completed a graduate-level mini-MBA program which consisted of a rigorous curriculum emphasizing accounting, marketing, finance, operations management, and organizational behavior.

In the jobs I have held in the summers both as a teenager and college student, I have learned to deal with the public in a poised and gracious manner. On one occasion, I was offered an opportunity to work at an elite, world-famous restaurant, and I was commended on my ability to professionally interact with a VIP clientele. In another summer experience, I was chosen as a Congressional Intern by Congressman Nathan Roberts from South Carolina and I played a role in solving problems for his constituents while also scheduling White House tours and performing a variety of administrative duties. I also refined my customer service and public relations skills in jobs as a tennis instructor, hostess and waitress, and bank teller.

Cover Letter #1: The first cover letter targets employers in private industry and profit-making companies.

If you can use a self-confident and versatile young professional within your organization, I hope you will contact me to suggest a time when we might meet. I am single and will relocate and travel according to your needs, and I can provide outstanding personal and professional references at the appropriate time.

Dear Exact Name of Person: (or Dear Sir or Madam if answering a blind ad):

With the enclosed resume, I would like to make you aware of my interest in exploring employment opportunities with your staff. I am particularly interested in a career in public service, and I am confident I could make valuable contributions to your goals.

Cover Letter #2: The second cover letter targets employers in the public sector, specifically senators and congressional representatives in Washington, D.C.

After recently completing a B.A. degree in Industrial Relations from the University of South Carolina at Columbia, I completed a graduate-level mini-MBA program with a rigorous curriculum emphasizing accounting, marketing, finance, operations management, and organizational behavior. My computer skills are excellent, and I am proficient with Microsoft Office, WordPerfect, MS Works, and other programs and software.

You will notice from my resume that I worked as a Congressional Intern for Congressman Nathan Roberts one summer, and that is when I realized that I wanted to make a career out of public service. While working for the Congressman, I played a key role in solving numerous problems of his constituents, and I sharpened my ability to analyze problems quickly and negotiate solutions. In my other summer jobs as a bank teller, tennis instructor, receptionist, waitress, and hostess, I refined my ability to deal with the public in a gracious and poised fashion. I offer highly refined written and oral communication skills.

If you can use a hard-working and highly intelligent young professional who could become a valuable addition to your staff, I hope you will contact me to suggest a time when we might meet to discuss your needs. I am single and would willingly work the long and irregular hours which I know are often required in the political arena. I thank you in advance for your time, and I hope I shall have the pleasure of meeting you.

NANCY DUNN

1110½ Hay Street, Fayetteville, NC 28305 • preppub@aol.com • (910) 483-6611

OBJECTIVE   To benefit an organization that can use an outgoing and articulate young communicator who offers strong communication, organizational, sales, and marketing skills.

EDUCATION   Completed **B.A. degree in Industrial Relations**, University of South Carolina at Columbia, May, 2000; was named to Dean's List.
Completed **graduate-level mini-MBA program** following college graduation at the Columbia Business Institute, Columbia, SC, May-June 2000.

COMPUTERS   Proficient with Microsoft Office, WordPerfect, MS Works, Netscape, and offer a proven ability to rapidly master new software applications and programs.

EXPERIENCE   **ADMINISTRATIVE ASSISTANT.** Quality Constructors, Columbia, SC (1999-present). In a part-time job while earning my college degree, was involved in a wide variety of duties which required excellent written and oral communication skills.
- Interfaced with banks, appraisers, and designers while accumulating data for housing starts.
- Maintained continuous communication with subcontractors regarding daily tasks and scheduling in order to facilitate the smooth and on-time completion of jobs.
- Assisted in preparing the paperwork for submitting homes to begin construction.

WAITRESS. The Captain's Den, Columbia, SC (Summer, 1999). Was offered an opportunity to work at this elite, world-famous restaurant; was part of the team providing fine dining in a five-star restaurant.

TELLER. Southern National Bank, Macon, GA (Summer, 1998). During this summer job, worked as a roving teller in numerous branches filling in for vacationing employees.
- Learned to adapt rapidly to changing management styles and different personalities in the various branches.
- Earned a reputation as an efficient and versatile worker as I performed clerical and administrative duties and interacted with the public in resolving problems related to their personal and business finances.
- Utilized computers daily for data entry and to perform various banking functions.

CONGRESSIONAL INTERN. Office of Congressman Nathan Roberts, Washington, DC (Summer, 1997). Was responsible for scheduling White House tours while interacting with constituents to help resolve their problems and concerns.
- Sharpened my ability to analyze problems quickly and negotiate solutions.
- Performed clerical and administrative duties utilizing a computer for word processing.

Other experience (summer jobs):
HOSTESS & WAITRESS. D's Restaurant, Myrtle Beach, SC (Summer 1996). Gained poise and confidence in dealing with the public.
TENNIS INSTRUCTOR. Country Club of the South, Atlanta, GA (Summers 1994-95). Was a popular instructor of tennis; taught children.

PERSONAL   Personal interests include sports, fishing, and piano. Outstanding references upon request.

Date

Exact Name of Person
Title or Position
Name of Company
Address (number and street)
Address (city, state, and zip)

Dear Exact Name:

I am writing to express my appreciation for the time you spent with me on December 9, and I want to let you know that I am sincerely interested in the position of Account Representative which you described.

As you described to me what you are looking for in an Account Representative, I had a sense of "déjà vu" because even at my young age I have always stepped into situations which required creativity, resourcefulness, and strong problem-solving skills. For example, when I worked for Congressman Nathan Roberts one summer, I took over many tasks previously performed by the Congressman's staff, which freed up vital staff members to handle tasks of a more strategic nature. All the employers for whom I have worked have told me that I am eligible at any time for rehiring, and I have been strongly encouraged to consider entering the management trainee programs at the restaurants where I have excelled in summer jobs.

I am skilled at developing effective working relationships with fellow workers and customers, and I am confident that I would thrive on the challenge of solving customers' business problems. I like your company's motto that you "provide business solutions" and I want to be a part of your team.

You will notice from my resume that I excelled academically while earning my college degree. I am confident that the same highly motivated nature which helped me excel academically would facilitate my becoming a valuable member of your sales team. I am confident that I have much to offer, but I am humbly aware of how much I have to learn in a new industry. It would be a pleasure to work for a company on the fast track, and I feel I could contribute significantly to your profitability. I would welcome being trained to do things your way, and I can assure you that I would, on my own initiative, seek out opportunities to become a top producer. I will look forward to hearing from you soon, and thanks again for your time.

Yours sincerely,

Nancy Dunn

All-Purpose Cover Letters and Cover Letters for People Seeking Their First Job in Their Field

In this section you will find cover letters which are "cousins" of each other. In general, the cover letters in this section are written for people who need a very creative and resourceful cover letter. Most of these cover letters are designed to help people launch a career after graduation.

The All-Purpose Cover Letter: In a job hunt, the all-purpose cover letter can be a time saver because it can serve as a "standard" or "model" or "template" which you can use each time you send out your resume. You may wish to modify it from time to time, but the all-purpose cover letter is there, already written, often in your computer, when you see an ad you want to answer or when you identify an employer whom you wish to contact in order to explore suitable opportunities for someone of your skills and abilities.

Seeking First Job in Field: Most people know the frustration of not having any experience in the field in which they are seeking employment. There are particular techniques that should be used when writing a cover letter to try to obtain the first job in one's field. This type of cover letter "builds a bridge" to a new field. In this section you will see several examples of cover letters that be used in versatile ways.

Using the Direct Approach: As we said earlier, most people find it useful to have a cover letter "model" in their computer so that all they have to do is change the name and address on the top of the letter each time they send it out. This allows you to get out a cover letter quickly when you learn of a suitable opportunity.

Follow-up Letter: Research has shown that those who send a follow-up letter after an interview dramatically increase their chances of getting the job. It seems that frequently employers end up with two equally strong candidates for the job. The one who sends a follow-up letter, such as the one on the facing page, will often be the beneficiary of the job offer. See the follow-up letter on page 24.

Exact Name of Person
Title or Position
Name of Company
Address (number and street)
Address (city, state, and zip)

SEEKING FIRST JOB IN FIELD

Sociology and Social Work graduate emphasizes his internship and peer mentor experience.

Although this individual is in a Management Trainee position (notice he omits mentioning the industry in which he is currently working), he is yearning to obtain a position in the field for which he obtained a college degree. He is trying to come across as a young professional committed to making a difference in his chosen field, not just making a living in any type of work.

Dear Exact Name of Person: (or Sir or Madam if answering a blind ad)

With the enclosed resume, I would like to make you aware of my interest in being considered for employment within your organization in any capacity in which you could utilize my versatile knowledge related to human resources and human services as well as my communication skills, management abilities, and computer operations knowledge.

Since graduation I have been excelling in a job as a Management Trainee but I am seeking a position in which I can utilize my education in sociology and social work. You will see from my resume that I completed a social work internship at Walker Senior High School where I earned a reputation as a highly motivated individual who was most effective in working with at-risk juveniles. Indeed, as an upperclassman during my junior and senior years at Michigan State University, I served as a Peer Mentor helping incoming freshmen transition into college life. Through my experience as a Peer Mentor and as a Social Work Intern, I gained insights into the particular problems faced by first-generation college students and by low-income students.

In a part-time job while earning my degree, I refined my counseling and interviewing skills as a Counselor at the V.A. Medical Center.

While in college I had several field experiences relevant to social work and sociology. In one situation I functioned as a Home Assistant, working with Thomas A (mentally challenged) adults and assisting those consumers in acquiring more independence and mastery of their everyday activities. In another situation as an Autism Therapist, I worked with an autistic child in a private home.

I hope you will give me an opportunity to talk with you in person because I am sure that my personal qualities and professional skills could enhance your organization's goals. Thank you in advance for your consideration.

Sincerely,

Leo Martelli

Date

Exact Name of Person
Title or Position
Name of Company
Address (number and street)
Address (city, state, and zip)

Dear Exact Name of Person: (or Sir or Madam if answering a blind ad)

SEEKING FIRST JOB
IN FIELD

With the enclosed resume, I would like to initiate the process of being considered for employment within your organization.

As you will see from my resume, I will receive on May 10 a Bachelor of Arts degree in English with a minor in French and Writing, and I have excelled academically. I have worked as a Staff Writer for my college newspaper, and I have become skilled at composing copy that requires little editing and in meeting tight deadlines. I have also tutored students in both English and French.

In an internship as an Advertising Copywriter with a respected and award-winning advertising agency, I created copy for the agency's web page, wrote a newsletter aimed at children, and compiled a portfolio of sample ads which was received quite favorably by my supervisor. In a summer job with a magazine in Arizona, I worked in the distribution and circulation part of the business and became a valuable part of the magazine's staff within a short period of time.

Although I have limited hands-on experience simply because I am 20 years old, I can assure you that I am an accomplished writer. I have been published in Tapestries and in The National Book of Poetry. My life experiences have been quite diverse as I have traveled extensively worldwide including in Europe and Africa as well as South America. I lived and worked in India last summer.

I can provide outstanding personal and professional references at the appropriate time, and I can assure you that you would find me to be a hard-working, congenial individual who prides myself on always doing my best. If you can use a hard worker who could become a valuable part of your organization through my creativity and language skills, I hope you will contact me to suggest a time when I can make myself available for a personal interview at your convenience. Thank you in advance for your time.

Sincerely,

Madeline A. Pereira

English major is seeking job in publishing or advertising. You will see that she emphasizes her summer work experience, publishing credits, and extensive international travel. She is trying to project herself as an ambitious and talented young professional who has demonstrated a deep and abiding interest in the writing field.

Date

Exact Name of Person
Exact Title
Exact Name of Company
Exact Address
City, State Zip

Dear Sir or Madam:

With the enclosed resume, I would like to make you aware of my interest in your organization and to acquaint you with the considerable talents and skills I could put to work for you.

As you will see from my resume, I recently earned my B.A. degree in History from North Carolina State University, and I was offered a full-time management position immediately upon graduation with the company for which I had worked throughout college. In my current position, I manage a wide range of functional areas for a large cinema complex. My responsibilities include training and hiring employees, overseeing cash control and assuring accurate financial management, auditing a wide range of activities, and assuring outstanding public relations and customer service. While working for the company on weekends and during summers and other breaks throughout college, I was named Employee of the Month five times and I earned a reputation as a hard worker known for the highest standards of reliability, integrity, and initiative.

Although I am held in high regard in my current position and am being groomed for further promotion by the company's owners, I am interested in applying my management skills in a more traditional business environment. I can provide excellent personal and professional references at the appropriate time.

Since the cinema business is generally an afternoon and nighttime business, I am usually at work from 5 p.m. to midnight, so you would be able to reach me at home most mornings. Thursday is my regular day off, so I could make myself available to meet with you personally on any Thursday or perhaps on another day if arrangements were made well in advance. I feel certain that you will find me to be a dynamic young professional whose abilities could enhance your organization.

Sincerely,

James Ray Watkins

Date

Exact Name of Person
Title or Position
Name of Company
Address (number and street)
Address (city, state, and zip)

Dear Exact Name of Person: (or Sir or Madam if answering a blind ad)

SEEKING FIRST JOB IN FIELD

Media Journalism and English major is emphasizing his natural sales ability and leadership skills.
Especially in sales, employers will frequently offer employment to a young person with "the right stuff" in terms of personality and the "true grit" for sales success. This young professional is "selling" his raw talent, enthusiasm, and energy in addition to his intense desire to enter the media sales field.

    I would appreciate an opportunity to talk with you soon about how I could contribute to WKRG TV-3 as a Salesperson.

    As you will see from my enclosed resume, I am an experienced retail salesperson with a college background in Media Journalism and English. Although I have no previous experience in broadcast sales, I feel that my intelligence, educational background, and exceptional written and verbal communication skills would more than make up for any lack of practical experience.

    I have a strong history of success in leadership roles and in environments where I have excelled in selling my ideas and concepts to others. Beginning with my days as student body president of my high school, on through college volunteer activities requiring negotiating and communication skills, I have always been highly effective in getting my views across to others in a persuasive and effective manner while still displaying tact and an understanding of their views.

    One area that I did not mention on my resume but would like to point out now is that while I was in college, I was given an opportunity to write public service announcements and then represent a writing class by presenting them on the air on a new campus radio station.

    I believe that I have high levels of raw talent, enthusiasm, and energy that would translate into successful sales for your station and allow me to become a productive member of your sales force. I hope you will welcome my call soon to arrange a brief meeting at your convenience to discuss WKRG TV-3's present and future needs, and how I might serve them. Thank you in advance for your time.

Sincerely yours,

Rainey L. Crocker

Date

Exact Name of Person
Title or Position
Name of Company
Address (number and street)
Address (city, state, and zip)

Dear Exact Name of Person: (or Sir or Madam if answering a blind ad)

Electronics Graduate
With this cover letter, a
young Electronics
Technology graduate
with fiber optics
knowledge is seeking his
first full-time job in his
field.

With the enclosed resume, I would like to make you aware of my knowledge of and education in communications and fiber optic technology, and to express my strong interest in offering my skills to your company. I recently spoke with a former Lucent Technologies employee, Mr. Ti Wo-Chung, and he recommended that I forward my resume to your attention.

As you will see, I have just completed my Associate's Degree in Electronics Technology. My major area of concentration was Communications and Fiber Optics. I have worked with fiber optics previously while employed by Quantum Systems on a contract job in Seattle, WA, where we installed optical module boxes and fiber optic cable along the 5-mile perimeter of a military compound.

Though my previous work experience is not highly technical in nature, I think you will see that I have proven myself to be a hardworking and reliable employee as well as a capable supervisor. Now that I have finished my degree, I am anxious to utilize my knowledge of communications and fiber optics technology. My strong work ethic, education, and technical know-how would be assets to your organization.

If you can use a highly motivated, intelligent young communications professional with extensive fiber optics knowledge, I hope you will contact me to suggest a time when we might meet to discuss your needs and how I might serve them. I can provide outstanding personal and professional references.

Sincerely,

Tim Krepp

In this section, you will find resumes and cover letters of students.

The resumes of students must really "sell!"

This is not just a slogan in a book. One of the main motivating beliefs behind this book is that the resumes and cover letters of students must be more original and creative than the resumes and cover letters of ordinary job hunters. If a student can't generate excitement in his resume and cover letter, he or she has little chance of competing with experienced professionals.

How to use this book...

By deliberate design, this book has been developed as a manageable size so that its reader will have time to look over all of the resumes and cover letters. Visit the Table of Contents and you will find the resumes and cover letters shown in alphabetical order usually by major. But regardless of what you majored in, you can learn something from any resume in this book.

- Have you ever been a tutor (paid or nonpaid!!)? The resume on page 33 will show you how Page Jasanoff makes the most of her tutoring experience and uses it to illustrate her communication skills. Carol Mace's resume on page 55 also shows tutoring experience in a way that should make her look intelligent to potential employers.
- Wonder how to show off student teaching experience? See Janet McCue's resume on page 41.
- Have you ever been a Student Government President? You may have the type of leadership employers are seeking. Larry Burrough's resume on page 59 may give you some good ideas if you have strong "extracurriculars."
- Are you a somewhat "older" student, such as Mr. Charles Harding on page 63, who offers prior military experience to potential employers?
- Have you had internships or clinical rotations which you think could be shown off to your advantage? You can see Mr. Hideto Eguro's resume on page 75 and you can also see Mr. Mullen's resume on page 77. Regina Raftery's resume on page 141 also shows clinical rotations and Patricia Lane Wise's resume on page 165 shows experience gained as a Social Work Intern.
- Do you have a lot of volunteer experience in campus organizations which constitute important but unpaid work? You might want to look at Sybil Dawes' resume on page 85.

Learn from other students...

In conclusion, read as many resume and cover letters in this book as you can. You have achieved a great deal by completing, or nearing completion of, the academic or professional training program in which you have been involved. Inside these exciting pages, you will see the stories and profiles of students who have used these resumes to achieve professional success. You can learn something from every resume and cover letter in this book. And we sincerely hope you do.

Believe it or not, students often have an advantage over others in a job hunt. Many companies like to take "raw material" and teach people "from scratch" who haven't been trained by competitors.

Date

Exact Name of Person
Title or Position
Name of Company
Address (no., street)
Address (city, state, zip)

Dear Exact Name of Person: (or Dear Sir or Madam if answering a blind ad.)

    I would appreciate an opportunity to talk with you soon about how I could contribute to your organization through my education in accounting as well as through my excellent math skills, adaptability, and reputation as a fast learner.

    As you will see from my enclosed resume, I will receive my B.S. in Accounting from the University of North Carolina at Chapel Hill in December. I earned a full scholarship on the basis of my potential to excel academically and high SAT scores and have succeeded in maintaining a perfect 4.0 GPA throughout my college career. I was singled out to receive the Dean's Award for achieving the highest GPA of any student in the School of Business and Finance.

    My work history outside the accounting field reveals my high level of creativity, resourcefulness, and adaptability.

    Recently as a tutor in the university's writing center, I have been able to teach written communication skills and computer knowledge. My computer experience includes the most commonly used programs including Word, Lotus 1-2-3, and dBase IV, and I offer a proven ability to rapidly master new software and operating systems.

    I am a highly motivated individual with a reputation for outstanding communication, motivational, and organizational skills along a high level of enthusiasm and energy.

    I hope you will welcome my call soon to arrange a brief meeting at your convenience to discuss your current and future needs and how I might serve them. Thank you in advance for your time.

Sincerely yours,

Page Jasanoff

Alternate last paragraph:
    I hope you will call or write me soon to suggest a time convenient for us to meet and discuss your current and future needs and how I might serve them. Thank you in advance for your time.

PAGE JASANOFF

1110½ Hay Street, Fayetteville, NC 28305 • preppub@aol.com • (910) 483-6611

OBJECTIVE

To contribute to an organization in need of a mature professional who can offer a keen eye for detail and high level of initiative as well as an education in accounting, excellent math skills, and the enthusiasm and energy needed to achieve superior results.

EDUCATION

Bachelor of Science (B.S.) degree in Accounting, University of North Carolina, Chapel Hill, NC; December 2001.

- Received the Chancellor's Scholarship Award, a full scholarship given on the basis of my SAT scores and potential to excel academically.
- Have maintained a perfect 4.0 GPA throughout my college career.
- Was honored with the Dean's Award for achieving the highest GPA of any student in the School of Business and Economics.
- Earned acceptance in Delta Mu Delta National Honor Sorority in recognition of my academic excellence.
- Completed specialized course work including the following:

cost accounting	marketing	auditing
accounting theory	tax accounting	business law
money and banking	fund accounting	corporate finance

EXPERIENCE

TUTOR. University of North Carolina, Chapel Hill, NC (2000-present).
Instructed other students in the university's writing center where assistance was given in the areas of essay writing, conducting research, and using computers.
- Built on my own knowledge of Word and Lotus software programs by helping others increase their skills and familiarity with the software and equipment.

PIANIST. Grayson Methodist Church, Chapel Hill, NC (1994-present).
Offer my musical talents to provide the church congregation with piano music during regularly scheduled services and for practices as well as occasionally for funerals.
- Used my musical knowledge and creativity to write music after listening to tapes when the sheet music was not available for a particular song.

BOOKKEEPER. Harwicke & Klingel Accountants, Chapel, Hill, NC (1999-present).
Learned the value of being professional, tactful, and courteous helping out in this busy accounting firm for a month over the Christmas holiday while filling in for regular employees on vacation.
- Demonstrated that I am capable of quickly mastering a job with no formal training and with no one to show me the way things "should" be done.

SPECIAL SKILLS

Type 50 wpm.
Familiar with Word and have working knowledge of Lotus 1-2-3 and dBase IV.

LANGUAGES

Completely bilingual—speak, read, and write both English and German fluently.

PERSONAL

Well-organized individual with a creative flair. Offer a very outgoing and friendly personality. Enjoy helping others learn, live, and grow. Eager to tackle new challenges.

Date

Exact Name of Person
Title or Position
Name of Company
Address (no., street)
Address (city, state, zip)

Dear Sir or Madam:

With the enclosed resume, I would like to formally apply for the position of Laboratory Technician which you recently advertised in *"The San Diego Times."*

As you will see from my resume, I earned a Bachelor of Science degree from the University of California majoring in Biological Sciences. While earning my degree I gained extensive "hands-on" experience in biology, physics, and chemistry labs.

Through my experience in those laboratories, I became familiar with a wide range of laboratory equipment. I am comfortable using the microscope, preparing slides, working with a cell counting apparatus, utilizing an autoclave and incubator, and using an NMR Spectrometer. I have utilized loops and swabs to cultivate bacteria in petri dishes, and I am proficient in working with test tubes, pipettes, and measuring suction pipettes. With a reputation as a creative and hard-working young professional, I have constructed complex reflux apparatuses in order to obtain pure end products from a reaction.

You would find me to be a high-energy person who would enjoy contributing to your goals. I can provide outstanding personal, professional, and academic references upon your request.

I hope you will write or call me soon to suggest a time when we might meet in person to discuss your needs and how I might serve them. Thank you in advance for your time.

Yours sincerely,

Mary Erkelens

MARY ERKELENS

1110½ Hay Street, Fayetteville, NC 28305 • preppub@aol.com • (910) 483-6611

OBJECTIVE	I want to contribute to an organization that can use an enthusiastic and high-energy young professional who offers excellent mathematical skills and computer knowledge along with "hands-on" laboratory experience.
COMPUTER SKILLS	Experienced in using IBM/IBM-compatible and Macintosh computer systems with software including Word, Quicken, and Windows; rapidly master new hardware and software.
LABORATORY KNOWLEDGE	• Gained extensive laboratory knowledge in biology, chemistry, and physics. • In laboratory settings, have aided with medical procedures including blood work, anesthesia, animal euthanasia, as well as prep for surgery and x-ray. • Have learned how to prepare slides; was instructed in using lighting and magnification and both the oil/non-oil viewing of the slides. • Have created chemical compounds and analyzed them using chemical, reflux, cooling, heating, and evaporation techniques. • Have utilized gel electrophoresis to determine sample contents; have become skilled in titration experiments to determine amount of substance in a solution.
EDUCATION	Earned **Bachelor of Science** (B.S.) degree with a major in **Biological Sciences**, University of California, Irvine, CA, 2000. • Excelled in course work in genetics, cell biology, parasitology, psychobiology, molecular biology, and ecology as well as chemistry and organic chemistry. • Completed five biology labs, five chemistry labs, and two physics labs. In high school, was an honors student and excelled in advanced physics, chemistry, and calculus as well as three years of both Spanish and German.
LANGUAGES	Speak German and Spanish; can read/write both languages with moderate proficiency.
EXPERIENCE	**BIOLOGY STUDENT/LABORATORY TECHNICIAN.** University of California, Irvine, CA (1998-2000). Gained insight into laboratory operations while performing as a student in biology, chemistry, and physics labs in the process of earning my B.S. degree; completed in four years a rigorous degree program which many students take five years to finish. • While earning my degree, worked as a Receptionist/Administrative Assistant at the University of California's Human Resources Department. • Also worked in a sales job at Pet Haven, a pet store; frequently explained to customers how to use medications we sold; cared for dogs, cats, mice, rats, and snakes. **VETERINARY ASSISTANT.** University City Veterinary Clinic, San Diego, CA (1997). At a busy clinic, aided the vet in procedures which included prepping the animals for surgery by shaving and sterilizing the area, assisting with surgeries including spays and ovariohysterectomies, and performing minor surgeries for broken legs and internal injuries; also assisted in taking X-rays. • Collected and prepared samples and created slides which I viewed under the microscope to determine presence of parasites; used a combination chemical/centrifuge technique to check blood samples for feline leukemia. • Mastered the use of the fecal float method.
PERSONAL	Am a very creative person who enjoys the research, analysis, and problem solving that goes on in a laboratory. Have been fortunate in having a strong academic family background which has given me feelings of security, stability, and confidence. Enjoy horseback riding.

Date

Exact Name of Person
Title or Position
Name of Company
Address (no., street)
Address (city, state, zip)

Biology

Dear Exact Name of Person: (or Dear Sir or Madam if answering a blind ad.)

If you have worked in a family-owned business, don't discount the skills and knowledge you obtained by working there. Notice that the Experience section on Mr. Coopland's resume is comprised entirely of jobs he performed in his family's motel business. Even though he is seeking a job in the scientific field, his work experience in another field helped him gain valuable experience that potential employers will appreciate.

I would appreciate an opportunity to talk with you soon about how I could contribute to your organization through my education in biology and experience in small business management.

As you will see from my enclosed resume, I will receive my bachelor's degree in Biology from The University of South Carolina at Columbia in December. I have completed more than 300 hours as a Lab Technician in biology, chemistry, and organic chemistry labs at USC and earlier while studying Organic Chemistry at Bradley University.

Through my experience in helping build a family-owned business to increased profitability, I have gained valuable exposure to bookkeeping and finance, customer service, maintenance and groundskeeping, and public relations. During the past eight years, beginning while I was still in high school and part-time throughout my college years, I have been involved in making decisions and advanced with the business as profits increased at a 20% growth rate over the last five years.

I am a fast learner with knowledge of several languages. Through my adaptability, friendly personality, and initiative I have always been able to quickly earn the respect and admiration of people from employees, to peers, to members of the public.

I hope you will welcome my call soon to arrange a brief meeting at your convenience to discuss your current and future needs and how I might serve them. Thank you in advance for your time.

Sincerely yours,

George Coopland

Alternate last paragraph:
I hope you will call or write me soon to suggest a time convenient for us to meet and discuss your current and future needs and how I might serve them. Thank you in advance for your time.

GEORGE COOPLAND

1110½ Hay Street, Fayetteville, NC 28305   •   preppub@aol.com   •   (910) 483-6611

OBJECTIVE

To contribute to an organization through my education in biology, my experience in small business management, as well as my exposure to public relations, customer service, and financial/accounting functions.

EDUCATION

Bachelor's degree in Biology, The University of South Carolina at Columbia, SC, December 2001.
Studied Organic Chemistry, Bradley University, Bradley, SC.

TRAINING

Completed 100 hours as a Lab Technician in university laboratory settings such as:
    Chemistry lab and biology lab — USC-SC
    Organic chemistry lab — Bradley University

EXPERIENCE

Gained experience in all phases of small business operations and made important contributions to the growth of a family-owned motel, Days Inn, Columbia, SC, in this track record of advancement:
MANAGER. (1998-present). Refined my managerial skills and learned to oversee the work of others while becoming familiar with the financial aspects of taking care of the company's bookkeeping activities.

- Quickly learned the details of handling financial activities and prepared the daily figures for the accountants and wrote checks to pay various operating expenses.
- Was praised for decision-making skills and ability to develop ideas which led to increased profitability and smoother daily operations.
- Made suggestions which helped ease the transition to a new name after the motel had operated as the Columbia Motor Inn for several years.
- Refined my interpersonal communication skills dealing with a wide range of customers and employees.
- Have been recognized as a key figure in the motel's record of annual increases in income— over the past five years the business has seen a 20% increase.

DESK CLERK and **REPAIRMAN.** (1997). Advanced to take on a more public and active role in day-to-day operations as a front-desk clerk responsible for providing helpful and courteous service to customers and handling large sums of money.

- Maintained the swimming pool which included seeing that the proper chemical balances were reached and that the pool was clean and safe to use.
- Displayed my versatility by doing painting, roofing, and minor electrical repairs on air conditioning systems and TVs which resulted in extending the usefulness of appliances and reduced the need for outside repairs.

MAINTENANCE WORKER/GROUNDSKEEPER. (1996-97). While still in high school, began helping with building maintenance, minor repairs, and lawn maintenance.

Highlights of other experience: As a **Patient Care Volunteer** at the VA Hospital, Columbia, SC (1996), helped the nursing staff in emergency room care such as transporting patients and assisting in preliminary check-ups.

- Learned how to operate vital computer systems and hook up equipment such as heart monitors and blood sugar checking devices as well as preparing records.

COMPUTERS

Am proficient in using MS Word, WordPerfect, and Windows for word processing and recordkeeping. Excellent personal and professional references on request.

Date

Exact Name of Person
Exact Title
Exact Name of Company
Address
City, State, Zip

Dear Exact Name of Person: (or Dear Sir or Madam if answering a blind ad):

With the enclosed resume, I would like to make you aware of my education and background in the fields of science and medicine as well as my highly developed analytical, technical, and problem-solving skills and extensive laboratory experience.

As you will see, I have earned a Bachelor of Science in Biology with a minor in Chemistry from Ball State University, where I graduated with honors, maintaining a cumulative GPA of 3.5. For the past year, I have also worked as a tutor for first-year biology students, conducting individual sessions twice weekly and leading a classroom discussion with all sixteen of my students once per week.

In earlier positions as a Laboratory Technician and Medical Assistant, I honed my growing technical skills while using my knowledge of medical, biological, and laboratory theory and technique in a practical working environment. Experienced in taking vital signs and updating medical charts, performing phlebotomies, and conducting laboratory tests to include complete blood counts (CBCs) and drug screens, I am also proficient in the safe and accurate operation of most common laboratory equipment.

If you can use a skilled laboratory technician with highly-developed analytical and technical skills, I hope you will welcome my call soon when I try to arrange a brief meeting to discuss your goals and how my background might serve your needs. I can provide outstanding references at the appropriate time.

Sincerely,

Kathleen Gallagher

Alternate Last Paragraph:
I hope you will write or call me soon to suggest a time when we might meet to discuss your needs and goals and how my background might serve them. I can provide outstanding references at the appropriate time.

KATHLEEN GALLAGHER

1110½ Hay Street, Fayetteville, NC 28305 • preppub@aol.com • (910) 483-6611

OBJECTIVE	To benefit an organization that can use an articulate and intelligent young professional with exceptional technical and analytical skills who offers a strong educational background and experience with scientific and medical testing in laboratory and medical clinic environments.

EDUCATION

Bachelor of Science in **Biology** with a minor in Chemistry, Ball State University, Muncie, IN, 2000; **graduated with honors**, maintaining a **3.5 cumulative GPA**.

- Recognized for academic performance by my induction into Beta Beta Beta National Honor Society for Biology majors and the State Science Club.
- President of the Indian Trail Head Start Parent Committee.
- Studied a wide range of challenging courses related to science and medicine, including:

Cellular and Molecular Biology	Principles of Genetics	Microbiology
General Chemistry I & II	Comparative Anatomy	Radiation
Organic Chemistry I & II	Animal Development	Trigonometry
Histology & Microtechniques	Principles of Biology	Biochemistry
Vertebrate Physiology	Medical Terminology	Psychology
Analytical Chemistry	Child & Adolescent Development	

CERTIFICATIONS & TRAINING

Certified in CPR and First Aid through the Indiana Community Action Program. Familiar with OSHA guidelines and regulations, as well as the use and proper disposal of chemicals, specimens, and instruments; skilled at recording and maintaining data.

TECHNICAL SKILLS

Skilled in the use of the following types of laboratory equipment:

gel electrophoresis plates	autoclave	digital & manual scales
chemical fume hoods	centrifuge	spectrometer
electron & dissecting microscopes	pH meters	micropipettes and large pipettes

EXPERIENCE

BIOLOGY TUTOR. Ball State University, Muncie, IN (1999-2000). Provided instruction and assistance to first-year students in the Biology program, teaching Principles of Biology and Zoology in one-on-one sessions and in a weekly classroom discussion.

- Provided tutoring for 16 students in twice-weekly sessions addressing the problems of the individual student; led a weekly classroom discussion attended by all my students.

LABORATORY TECHNICIAN and **RECEPTIONIST.** Alpha Plasma Center, Muncie, IN (1998). Admitted donors to the center, recording vital signs (height, weight, temperature, and blood pressure) and performing a complete blood count (CBC) on each donor before they were allowed to donate plasma.

- Assisted the on-site physician with performing physicals; trained other laboratory technicians/receptionists in center policies and donor admission/approval procedures.

MEDICAL ASSISTANT. Primary Care Plus, Muncie, IN (1997-1998). Provided a variety of medical and laboratory assistance at this local urgent care center; recorded patients vital signs and assisted physicians and physician's assistants.

- Performed eye and ear screens, drug screens, and EKGs, as well as performing phlebotomy and blood work, to include CBCs; assisted in performing X-rays.

COMPUTERS

Familiar with operating systems and software including Windows and Microsoft Office.

PERSONAL

Excellent personal and professional references are available upon request.

Exact Name of Person
Exact Title
Exact Name of Company
Address
City, State, Zip

Biology Teaching

Dear Exact Name of Person: (or Dear Sir or Madam if answering a blind ad):

A great cover letter helps someone "get to know you." Notice that this cover letter is personal and revealing. She helps the reader gain insight into why she chose Biology Teaching as a field, and she reveals some of her strong personal qualities. Remember this in a cover letter: You're not interviewing for the job yet, you're simply trying to come across as someone who would be nice to meet.

With the enclosed resume, I would like to make you aware of my interest in teaching biology at your school. I have earned my B.S. in Biology Teaching and recently completed a highly successful student teaching assignment at a high school in Wyeth, GA. I was commended by the teacher who supervised me for my exceptional creativity and for my willingness to tackle and follow through on difficult assignments.

My interest in teaching biology developed while I was serving my country in the U.S. Army, where I was trained as a Laboratory Technician. In order to gauge the depth of my interest in the field, I became a Volunteer with the Red Cross at an Army hospital. When I decided to leave military service and enter the civilian work force, I explored opportunities for earning my Biology Teaching degree and I chose Bainbridge College. You will notice from my resume that I worked nearly 30 hours a week in a demanding job throughout my college career.

Because I am slightly older than the average college graduate, I feel I have a degree of maturity which could be most beneficial in a high school classroom. Since I was myself the first person in my family to graduate from college, I am confident that I could be a powerful motivator to youth who are unsure of their goals in life. I am a highly motivated individual and I believe in leading by example.

If you can use a well-trained individual who offers outstanding communication skills along with a proven ability to work well with others, I hope you will contact me to suggest a time when we might meet to discuss your goals. I can provide outstanding references at the appropriate time.

Sincerely,

Janet McCue

JANET McCUE

1110½ Hay Street, Fayetteville, NC 28305 • preppub@aol.com • (910) 483-6611

OBJECTIVE	To offer my strong desire to teach and work with young people by applying my degree in the science field as well as my creativity, motivational skills, knowledge of computer operations, and practical experience with a variety of laboratory procedures.
EDUCATION	**Bachelor of Science, Biology Teaching,** Bainbridge College, Bainbridge, GA, 2000.

- Named to the Chancellor's List in recognition of academic achievements in maintaining a GPA of 3.8 or higher.
- Excelled in specialized coursework including:

methods of teaching	analytical chemistry	histology
anatomy and physiology	medical terminology	biochemistry
probability and statistics	human development	Spanish
computers in education — emphasis on Lotus 1-2-3, Word, Report Card		

- Held membership in the Science Club.

EXPERIENCE

STUDENT TEACHER. Georgia Board of Education, Wyeth, GA (2000). Instructed a diverse student population at Wyeth High School while teaching Biology I and Biology II to ninth through 12th grade students.

- Applied active learning techniques while motivating students to participate in class activities and open themselves to learning.
- Implemented positive classroom management strategies to encourage proper behavior and respect for others.
- Utilized planning and organizational skills in carrying out classroom support activities including completing interesting and thorough lesson plans as well as preparing test materials and monitoring testing.
- Earned the teacher's respect for my true concern for the students, willingness to tackle hard assignments, and ability to follow through on any project taken on.
- Displayed creativity and initiative in the development of informative bulletin boards.

CASHIER. Taco Bell, Bainbridge, GA (1997-2000). Refined time management skills and displayed a high level of self-motivation while working 30 hours a week.

- Known for my dedication to providing high quality customer service, was entrusted with training new employees and setting an example for them to follow.

LABORATORY ASSISTANT. The American Red Cross, Germany (1995-96). As a volunteer in the chemistry department lab of a U.S. Army hospital in Germany, logged in and separated blood specimens and then ran them through the SMA-18 machine which analyzed specimens for 18 separate chemical tests.

- Assisted in drawing blood from patients and doing electrolyte testing.

Highlights of earlier experience as a LABORATORY TECHNICIAN, U.S. Army:

- Processed urine specimens for military personnel throughout the Pacific while screening for illegal substances including heroin, cocaine, barbiturates, and amphetamines.
- Conducted drug screening procedures at a facility which supported Army, Navy, and Air Force personnel based in the Philippines, Japan, Korea, and Hawaii.
- Assisted a doctor doing research on high blood pressure and the effects of high altitude.

PERSONAL

Am an open water-certified SCUBA diver; received Red Cross certification in CPR and life-saving techniques. Offer empathy for the problems and tough choices facing young people.

Date

Ms. Elaine Hendrickson
Director of Undergraduate Admissions
University of Vermont
123 Mossman Building
Burlington, VT 89023

Broadcast Journalism

Dear Ms. Hendrickson:

When you write a cover letter, it's a good idea to focus on up to three things that you wish to emphasize. In the case of Mr. Hakken, he wants to emphasize his leadership in student activities. You will notice that, although he majored in Broadcast Journalism and has had an internship in that field, he is seeking employment outside broadcast journalism.

I would appreciate an opportunity to talk with you soon about how I could contribute to the university as the Assistant Director of Admissions through the application of my outstanding communication skills and reputation as a personable, persuasive, and articulate professional.

Throughout my years as a student at the University of Vermont, I have been very active in a wide variety of campus activities and have contributed leadership to various student activities. The recipient of numerous honors and awards for my academic accomplishments, public speaking abilities, and contributions to the university community, I feel that I would be a strong representative for the university and able to relate effectively with incoming students. As you will see from my enclosed resume, I built a reputation as a talented speaker and scholar/athlete during my high school years and have continued to be known as a dedicated young professional who gives unselfishly of my time and talents.

I offer a reputation as an outstanding motivational speaker and have often been called on to make presentations to young people and encourage them to develop personal goals and strive to excel through strong morals and high personal standards. I am certain that I would be a productive and results-oriented admissions counselor who would motivate university students by setting an example for them to follow.

I hope you will call or write me soon to suggest a time convenient for us to meet and discuss your current and future needs and how I might serve them. Thank you in advance for your time.

Sincerely,

George Hakken

GEORGE HAKKEN

1110½ Hay Street, Fayetteville, NC 28305 • preppub@aol.com • (910) 483-6611

OBJECTIVE

To benefit an organization that can use a persuasive and articulate speaker with the ability to deal with people of all ages and socioeconomic levels to an organization that can use a young professional known for drive as well as integrity and high moral standards.

EDUCATION

B.A., **Broadcast Journalism,** University of Vermont, Burlington, VT, 2000.
- **Activities:** Refined communication and time management skills in these activities:
  Member of the Student Advisory Committee, 2000
  Member of the Student Activity Fees Committee, 1999-2000
  President of the Black Society Gospel Choir, 2000
  Freshman delegate to the Student Government, 1997
- **Honors and Awards:** Recipient of numerous honors and awards including the following:
  NBS Gospel Choir Anointed Spiritual Leader Award, 2000
  Department of Communication and Theater Outstanding Speaker Award, 2000
  Special Support Services Certificate of Achievement in Academic Activities, 2000
  New Generation Campus Ministries Integrity Award, 1997-99

COMMUNITY INVOLVEMENT

As a volunteer with the Burlington Pregnancy Center, speak to high school students about the importance of setting high personal goals including in the matter of sexual abstinence. Served meals to the poor and homeless for the Burlington Urban Ministries and received a Certificate of Appreciation from the Vermont Radio Reading Service (1999-present).

EXPERIENCE

While attending college full time, learned the value of hard work in summer and holiday jobs which were often simultaneous and included the following:
SALES ASSOCIATE. S & K Famous Brands, Burlington, VT (summers and holidays, 1997-present). Excelled in providing quality customer service at two different locations of this fine men's clothing store: measured customers and assisted with inventories.

BROADCASTING INTERN. WKIS 87.9-FM Radio Station, University of VT, Burlington (summer 1999). Assisted the news director of this National Public Radio Station by rewriting local stories which had appeared in that day's *Vermont Times* and acting as general assignment reporter for the "Sandhills Today" radio show.
- Covered political ad entertainment activities throughout the region.
- Worked with equipment including reel-to-reel player/recorders, cartridge machines, tape and CD players, and computers.
- As a **Volunteer Disc Jockey,** (summers and holidays 1997-2000), played traditional and contemporary jazz music as well as announcing news.

CAMP COUNSELOR. Camp Haystack, Metarie, VT (summers 1995-98). During two years as a Senior Camp Counselor and earlier years as a Junior Counselor, supervised 12 six through 13-year-old day camp participants.
- Set an example of how to respect yourself and others while encouraging a sense of cooperation and fair play during games, meal times, and other activities.

SPECIAL SKILLS

Offer computer knowledge related to the Windows operating system, and software including Word, dBase, Lotus 1-2-3, and E-mail as well as experience with calculators.

PERSONAL

Earned numerous awards as a high school scholar-athlete: placed on the Mid-South 4A all Conference Academic All-American Team, and lettered in basketball three years.

Date

Exact Name of Person
Exact Title
Exact Name of Company
Address
City, State, Zip

Dear Exact Name of Person (or Dear Sir or Madam if answering a blind ad):

With the enclosed resume, I would like to make you aware of my interest in advancing into the position of Production Supervisor with Samsonite, Inc.

As you are aware and as you will see from my resume, I have loyally served the company's needs since 1998, when I began as a Heat/Treat Operator. After six months, I was promoted to Set-Up/Lead Person, and I have been commended for my leadership ability and management potential while serving in this role. I am known for my meticulous attention to detail, my continuous emphasis on safety and quality control, and my ability to work well with others. I have become the individual to whom others turn when they want to troubleshoot difficult problems, and I have established excellent working relationships with the supervisor, group leader, as well as with the five operators for whom I provide oversight.

In my spare time, I am completing my Bachelor's degree in Business Administration, and I have only four courses remaining until I receive that degree.

As you will also see from my resume, I have been accustomed to hard work and management responsibilities since I was a child. While in junior high, high school, and college, I worked summers in supervisory capacities on a 550-acre farm, and I supervised up to 60 migrant workers involved in harvesting tobacco, cotton, and soybeans. I also gained supervisory experience in high school working as a Parts Manager and Shop Floor Supervisor for Car-Plus, an automotive repair shop and NAPA Certified Auto Care Center, where I supervised up to eight mechanics.

I hope you will give me the opportunity to meet with you in person to discuss my interest in the position of Production Supervisor. I am confident that my natural leadership ability, technical troubleshooting skills, and management experience could be beneficial to Samsonite, and it is my strong desire to continue my employment with the company in a position of increased responsibility.

Yours sincerely,

John Purvis

JOHN PURVIS

1110½ Hay Street, Fayetteville, NC 28305 • preppub@aol.com • (910) 483-6611

OBJECTIVE   To benefit an organization that can use a hard-working and dedicated young professional with proven supervisory and management skills along with experience in quality assurance, safety, maintenance management, production control, and problem solving.

EDUCATION   Completing four remaining courses for **Bachelor of Science degree in Business Administration (B.S.), Lincoln College, Lincoln, IL;** am completing these courses in my spare time (degree to awarded in 2001).
- Played football for Lincoln College, fall 1997.

EXPERIENCE   **Have been excelling in the following track record of promotion with Samsonite, Inc., Lincoln, IL:**
1998-present: SET-UP/LEAD PERSON. Have been commended for my leadership ability on numerous occasions while setting up 36 air and hydraulic presses and providing oversight for five operators as they continuously inspect to assure that specifications are maintained.
- Troubleshoot difficult problems; once, when the Applications Engineer could not establish the correct weight in a particular cavity, I worked continuously for five hours to resolve the problem with the result that the part left the pressroom on time.
- Perform SPC checks; set up machines daily and produce the first part; then oversee operators in their inspection process.
- Am considered the leader on the second shift, and am the individual to whom others turn when they have difficult technical problems.
- Handle jobs for the Group Leader as requested; seek his guidance on problems which are occurring and do my best to resolve problems.
- Was assigned to work on a sensitive, high-priority part for six months because the company needed its most quality-conscious and efficient workers on this project.

April 1998-August 1998: HEAT/TREAT OPERATOR. Was promoted to the job above based on my outstanding work performance and management potential. Worked in continuous heat treat with belt furnaces, ovens, etc. Set oven temperatures and operated furnaces.

PARTS MANAGER & SHOP FLOOR SUPERVISOR. Car-Plus, Inc., Lincoln, IL (1994-98). While in high school, began working for this automotive repair shop and NAPA Certified Auto Care Center; was placed in supervisory positions at a young age, and supervised up to eight mechanics.
- Was crosstrained in numerous areas of the business including accounting, bookkeeping, payroll, and inventory control. Ordered parts and controlled stock.
- Teamed up with a Lincoln College professor to produce a professional PowerPoint presentation for the upcoming racing season which resulted in an $85,000 sponsorship being provided for a world-known race car driver.

FARM MANAGER. Lincoln Farms, Lincoln, IL (summers 1992-97). Worked in the summers in junior high, senior high, and college and advanced into a position in which I was supervising 60 migrant workers on a farm of 550 acres which produced tobacco, cotton, and soybeans.

COMPUTERS   Microsoft Word, MS-Works, PowerPoint, WordPerfect, Lotus 1-2-3, Windows, DOS

PERSONAL   Can provide outstanding personal and professional references. Professional, well-organized, cooperative, reliable, and trustworthy. Work well under pressure. Proficient in handling diverse tasks simultaneously. Highly motivated hard worker who thrives on responsibility.

Date

Exact Name of Person
Title or Position
Name of Company
Address (no., street)
Address (city, state, zip)

Business Administration

Dear Exact Name of Person: (or Dear Sir or Madam if answering a blind ad.)

Although this young
professional could
probably cash in his
degree for a position at
a higher level now that
he is a college graduate,
he is taking the
opportunity to explore
his options outside the
industry in which he has
worked. He emphasizes
that his current
employer wants him,
though, because every
employer is seeking to
hire the people that
other companies are
after.

    I would appreciate an opportunity to talk with you soon about how I could contribute to your organization through my background in sales and management as well as through the outstanding planning, organizational, communication, and problem-solving skills that have made me very valuable to my current employer.

    As you will see from my resume, I have excelled for the last seven years in a "track record" of promotion within the K-Mart Corporation, where I began working at the age of 17. While excelling in my full-time job, I simultaneously obtained my B.S. degree in Business Administration and also found time to donate my time to charities including the Special Olympics. In May 2000, I was promoted to manage the electronics department at one of K-Mart's largest stores, and I am being groomed for entry into the company's formal Management Training Program after completing six months as a department manager.

    Although I respect the K-Mart Corporation greatly and enjoy my challenging management responsibilities, I am writing to your organization because I am attracted to your company's fine reputation and respected product line. I feel I could make valuable contributions to your bottom line through my strong sales and management skills, and I would enjoy an opportunity to meet with you to explore the possibility of putting my experience and talents to work for your company. I can provide outstanding personal and professional references; I am single and will travel and relocate according to your needs.

    I hope you will welcome my call soon to arrange a brief meeting at your convenience to discuss your current and future needs and how I might serve them. Thank you in advance for your time.

Sincerely yours,

Michael Seligson

Alternate last paragraph:
I hope you will call or write me soon to suggest a time convenient for us to meet and discuss your current and future needs and how I might serve them. Thank you in advance for your time.

MICHAEL SELIGSON

1110½ Hay Street, Fayetteville, NC 28305 • preppub@aol.com • (910) 483-6611

OBJECTIVE   To contribute to the bottom line of an organization that can use a resourceful young manager who offers proven abilities in sales, personnel supervision, and operations management and who also offers excellent planning, organizational, communication, and problem-solving skills.

EDUCATION   **B.S. degree in Business Administration**, the University of Nebraska-Lincoln, Lincoln, NE, June, 2000.
- Completed this degree while excelling in my full-time job in retailing.
- A member of Air Force ROTC, received the prestigious ROTC Award of Merit for leadership potential and academic excellence; was appointed to leadership positions which involved managing 40 people; completed the six-week Officer Training program.

EXPERIENCE   *Began with K-Mart when I was 17 years old, and have been promoted into increasingly responsible positions; am being groomed for entry into the formal Management Training Program after I complete six months as a department manager.*
- Have been appointed to serve on key corporate committees including the Promotional Committee, Hiring Committee, Safety Team, and Support Team (a support team is authorized to make management decisions).

DEPARTMENT MANAGER, ELECTRONICS. K-Mart in Lincoln, NE (2000-present). Was promoted to this position in May, 2000, and am responsible for training, motivating, scheduling, and supervising eight employees.
- Work with dozens of vendors to negotiate terms of trade, select merchandise, develop marketing plans, and determine pricing policy.
- Develop special promotions to create consumer demand for electronics products; implement modular set-ups.
- Am continuously in the process of strategic planning; plan for seasonal events and set/ order special features.
- Improved the appearance of the department by organizing the risers, flagging merchandise, and assuring that every item is properly labeled.
- Have utilized my extensive computer knowledge to develop a more informed staff and to boost sales of computers and computer accessories.
- Am respected for my excellent problem-solving and decision-making skills.

SALES CLERK, ELECTRONICS. K-Mart on Second Street (1995-2000). Used my computer knowledge to boost sales while stocking counters, setting features, operating the cash register, ordering merchandise, and maintaining a perpetual inventory system.
- On my own initiative, developed several new measures that established better security and which reduced theft and pilferage.
- Became known for my exceptionally strong customer service skills.

SALES CLERK, LAWN & GARDEN CENTER AND PET CENTER. K-Mart on Second Street (1994-95). While providing excellent customer service, discovered ways of preventing loss from plants dying and from exterior theft; set up modulars; ordered merchandise.

COMPUTERS   Knowledge of Windows and MS DOS, Microsoft Word, PowerPoint, Lotus 1-2-3, dBase.

PERSONAL   Can provide outstanding personal and professional references. Will relocate. Am known for my ability to get along well with anyone.

Date

Exact Name of Person
Title or Position
Name of Company
Address (number and street)
Address (city, state, and zip)

Dear Exact Name of Person: (or Sir or Madam if answering a blind ad.)

This is a slightly older
student, since she
served in the Air Force
prior to earning her
college degree. Although
this cover letter and
resume are designed to
be all-purpose so that
she can approach
numerous industries,
she has her eye on the
medical field.

With the enclosed resume, I would like to introduce you to the considerable administrative, supervisory, and operations management skills I could put to work for you.

As you will see, I earned my B.S. degree in Business Administration with a 3.4 GPA after serving my country in the U.S. Air Force for four years. While in the Air Force, I was handpicked for a job in Korea where I worked closely with the Red Cross and other relief agencies in locating military personnel working throughout Asia. My final job in the U.S. Air Force was as Administrative Supervisor at the Fitzsimmons Army Medical Center in Colorado, where I trained and managed personnel clerks in a major medical center.

In addition to my B.S. degree, I hold an A.S. degree in Medical Administration and I completed numerous courses while in the military related to medical record keeping, coding, and terminology.

I offer excellent computer skills including experience with Windows 2000 and proficiency with software including Excel, Word, WordPerfect 6.1, and Lotus 1-2-3. In my job in Korea working with the Red Cross I maintained an extensive database, and I became proficient in database maintenance.

You would certainly find me in person to be a warm individual known for my cheerful nature and professional style. I can provide outstanding personal and professional references at the appropriate time, and I hope you will contact me if you can use my versatile skills and talents.

Sincerely,

Seung Sokolsky

SEUNG SOKOLSKY

1110½ Hay Street, Fayetteville, NC 28305   •   preppub@aol.com   •   (910) 483-6611

OBJECTIVE   To contribute to an organization that can use a skilled professional with extensive customer service, supervisory, and operations management experience.

EDUCATION   Earned **Bachelor of Science (B.S.) degree in Business Administration**, Lawrence University, Appleton, WI, 2001.
- Excelled academically; achieved a 3.4 GPA and graduated cum laude.

Received **Associate of Arts (A.A.) degree in Medical Administration**, Community College of the Air Force, 1996.
- Graduated magna cum laude with a 3.7 GPA.

Completed courses and training programs sponsored by the U.S. Air Force related to:

office administration	human resources management
computer operations	personnel management
medical recordkeeping	training administration

SPECIAL SKILLS   Skilled in utilizing Windows; proficient with Word, Excel, and Lotus 1-2-3.
- Experienced in setting up/utilizing spreadsheets.
- Proficient in medical transcription and medical office administration.

EXPERIENCE   *Have dedicated myself primarily to earning my college degree while also working in temporary and part-time assignments including these (1996-present):*
RESEARCHER & LIBRARY ASSISTANT (part-time work study position). Veterans Administration Medical Center, Appleton, WI (1999-2001). In this part-time work study position which I held while completing my college degree, conducted research on medical topics for interlibrary loans while typing correspondence and maintaining files.

ADMINISTRATIVE ASSISTANT & FULL-TIME COLLEGE STUDENT. Appleton, WI (1997-2001). While pursuing my B.S. in Business Administration, worked for Workforce Temporary Agency in various offices and businesses on a temporary basis.
- Handled switchboards; maintained office records including medical records; performed data entry utilizing various computer hardware and software.

Served my country with distinction in the U.S. Air Force and was promoted into administrative and supervisory positions ahead of my peers while earning a reputation as a dedicated and hard-working young professional:
ADMINISTRATIVE SUPERVISOR. Fitzsimmons Army Medical Center, Aurora, CO (1995-96). In this large medical center, trained and supervised four personnel clerks in all aspects of their duties including typing, filing, and maintaining personnel records.
- Developed and implemented training schedules.
- Admitted patients into the hospital and transcribed medical records.
- Learned medical coding and refined my knowledge of medical terminology.

PERSONNEL ADMINISTRATOR. 19th Personnel Replacement Detachment, Seoul, South Korea (1992-95). Trained, motivated, and managed six personnel while functioning in a highly visible position which required me to work with top Red Cross officials in locating military personnel working throughout Asia; maintained a database.
- Was praised by the Red Cross for my resourcefulness and diplomacy.

PERSONAL   Can provide outstanding references. Known as a very outgoing and enthusiastic professional who prides myself on attention to detail and organizational skills.

Exact Name of Person
Title or Position
Name of Company
Address (number and street)
Address (city, state, and zip)

Business Management

Dear Exact Name of Person: (or Sir or Madam if answering a blind ad.)

There aren't many resumes that can support a section called Community Involvement but Ms. Schwartz wants to reveal her extensive civic involvements. She doesn't mind verbalizing some of her views related to the environment, since she is seeking an employer that is environmentally responsible.

I would appreciate an opportunity to talk with you soon about how I could contribute to your organization through the application of my versatile experience and knowledge in the areas of sales and marketing as well as finance operations and business management.

As you will see from my resume I earned my B.A. in Business Management from Lehigh University in 2000. My leadership abilities and communication skills led to my election by the student body to hold a seat as a Student Government Senator, and I was then selected by the organization's president to serve on the Campus Hearing Board where my sound judgment and ability to listen to both sides and make fair decisions was valuable.

I am a highly self-motivated individual who can handle pressure and deadlines and manage time for maximum productivity and efficiency. While earning my degree and maintaining a 3.5 GPA, I worked often in simultaneous jobs, managed a home and raised four children, and was active in PTA and local politics. I am a community-minded person who enjoys working with others to achieve team objectives.

I am certain that I can provide a company or organization with sound abilities in multiple areas which range from financial management, to human resources and personnel administration, to marketing and sales. Known as an energetic and enthusiastic professional, I excel in motivating others and organizing complex activities.

I hope you will welcome my call soon to arrange a brief meeting to discuss your current and future needs and how I might serve them. Thank you in advance for your time.

Sincerely,

Maxine Schwartz

Alternate last paragraph:
I hope you will call or write me soon to suggest a time convenient for us to meet and discuss your current and future needs and how I might serve them. Thank you in advance for your time.

MAXINE SCHWARTZ

1110½ Hay Street, Fayetteville, NC 28305 • preppub@aol.com • (910) 483-6611

OBJECTIVE

To offer experience in areas requiring communication, sales, training, and marketing skills as well as knowledge of financial and inventory control to an organization that can use a detail-oriented professional with an ability to handle pressure, deadlines, and challenges.

EDUCATION

B.S., Business Management, Lehigh University, Bethlehem, PA, 2000.
- Completed my degree in three years and maintained a 3.5 GPA while working in three jobs (often simultaneously), being an active member of three different PTAs, and raising four children.
- Elected by the student body as a Student Government Senator, was appointed by the organization's president to serve on the Campus Hearing Board.

COMMUNITY INVOLVEMENT

Have been active in community affairs including being personally invited by Bethlehem County Commissioner Nelson to serve on his campaign committee.
- Played an important part in efforts which resulted in the commissioner being elected despite several polls predicting he would lose.
- Spearheaded a successful campaign to stop trains from carrying nuclear waste through the town of Bethlehem: approached local and state-level elected figures and sports figures, distributed petitions, attended environmental seminars, and held rallies to make people aware of the potential for disaster; my leadership led to a grant for $300,000 from the Department of Energy!

EXPERIENCE

Financed my education and refined my time management and organizational abilities while holding these often-simultaneous jobs, taking care of a home and family, participating in community affairs, and attending college:
PUBLIC INFORMATION ASSISTANT. Lehigh University Student Activities Office Bethlehem, PA (1998-00). Provided support services for faculty, staff, students, and campus visitors while controlling inventory for the student supply store and ordering merchandise; supervised and scheduled student employees.
- Became familiar with a wide range of services available on the campus such as where to find out class schedules and locations of facilities.
- Provided management insight which allowed this service facility to operate at a profit.
- Was respected by students as someone in authority who was always cheerful and ready to help with problems; became a source of advice on where to find reasonably priced housing, food, and transportation.
- Represented the university to potential new students and recruited six young adults.

NIGHT MANAGER. Bo's Supermarkets, Bethlehem, PA (1998-99). Gained exposure to using computers and provided supervision for at least 12 employees while handling additional functional areas such as scheduling, collections, and inventory control.
- Learned to take care of the financial activities while preparing daily sales reports.

SALES REPRESENTATIVE and **BOOKKEEPER**. Southeastern Wood Technology, Bethlehem, PA (1994-98). Learned how cabinetry is made and how to operate woodworking tools while providing administrative support by ordering materials, preparing bids, preparing receipts for customers, and making determinations on the profitability of potential jobs.

PERSONAL

Attended several workshops and seminars sponsored by local colleges which emphasized listening, leadership, teaching, and problem-solving skills. Am a creative thinker.

Date

Exact Name of Person
Exact Title
Exact Name of Company
Address
City, State, Zip

Chemistry Graduate

Dear Exact Name of Person: (or Dear Sir or Madam if answering a blind ad):

This young chemistry
graduate offers some
experience as a
research assistant. It's
not often that one can
graduate and have
experience in one's field,
but this fortunate
individual found a
summer and part-time
job that helped her
refine her technical skills
while she was
completing her degree.

With the enclosed resume, I would like to make you aware of my exceptional technical abilities as well as my background as a motivated and experienced chemist who offers experience in research and development, troubleshooting, and quality assurance for a variety of latex polymer compounds.

As you will see from my resume, I have a Bachelor of Science in Chemistry from Drake University in Des Moines, IA. In addition to exceptional computer skills, I am also experienced in the operation of numerous state-of-the-art laboratory apparatuses, including HPLC, Nuclear Magnetic Resonance (NMR), MS-GC, IR, and UV-VIS, as well as Gas Chromatography and other tests used for identification purposes.

While completing my education, I excelled as a Research Assistant at a large international chemical company. As a member of the Applications team, I have performed quality assurance, testing, and evaluation of various latex polymers used in commercial paint applications and made several successful presentations related to projects to which I was assigned. My supervisors lauded me for displaying "initiative and creativity" in problem-solving, and I have met or exceeded all of my individual performance goals.

I am in the process of permanently relocating to my home state of California in order to be closer to family and friends. I feel that there is a good "fit" between my knowledge and skills and your company's needs. I hope you will welcome my call soon, when I try to arrange a brief meeting to discuss your goals and how my background might serve your needs. Thank you in advance for your time and professional courtesies.

Sincerely,

Laura Ann Feldhahn

LAURA ANN FELDHAHN

1110½ Hay Street, Fayetteville, NC 28305 • preppub@aol.com • (910) 483-6611

OBJECTIVE

I want to contribute to an organization that can use an experienced young chemist with exceptional technical, communication, and organizational skills who offers a background in research and development, production, and quality assurance.

EDUCATION

Bachelor of Science in **Chemistry**, Drake University, Des Moines, IA, 2000.
- Received the Outstanding Graduate Research Award for 2000.

Completed three years towards my Bachelor of Science in Chemistry at Iowa State University prior to transferring to Drake University.
- Awarded a scholarship after being named Miss Iowa State University, 1998; was selected as representative to the Miss Iowa State Scholarship Pageant.

TECHNICAL & COMPUTER SKILLS

Experienced in operation of various state-of-the-art laboratory instrumentation for chemical analysis, such as **HPLC**, **Nuclear Magnetic Resonance (NMR)**, **MS-GC**, **IR**, and **UV-VIS**. Familiar with many popular operating systems and software, including Windows, Microsoft Word, Excel, PowerPoint, and Access; Local Area Networks (LAN) and Internet applications; WordPerfect; Quattro Pro.

AFFILIATIONS

Member, Student Chemist's Society.
Serve on the Rules and Procedures Site Safety Committee (SOP).
Oversee Quality Control for the Environmental Chamber.

EXPERIENCE

RESEARCH ASSISTANT. UCAR Emulsion Systems (Union Carbide), Des Moines, IA (Summers and part-time during college, 1998-2000). Based on the recommendation of the Chairman of the Department of Chemistry, was selected for this job performing research and development, formulation, troubleshooting, and product improvement for numerous developmental latex polymers used in commercial paint applications.
- Functioned as a resource to the Applications team during the development of both the low VOC semi-gloss and Branched Ester Ethylene Vinyl Acetate (BEEVA) projects.
- Prepared presentations on Ethylene Vinyl Accil, using Microsoft PowerPoint and other software.
- Assessed raw materials for cost efficiency and to identify and implement improvements in product performance; evaluated the Total Solids, Glass Transition, and MFT for various latex polymer formulations.
- Completed detailed evaluations of commercial paint products in order to benchmark products against current performance objectives.
- Served on Y2K team for the Applications and CTCH areas, inventorying and evaluating all equipment to determine vulnerability to Y2K-related failures.
- Described as "an integral part of the Applications team," was cited in an appraisal for displaying "a great deal of initiative and creativity" and "constantly trying new methods to produce better results."

ASSISTANT TO THE RESEARCH CHEMIST. Iowa State University, Des Moines, IA (Summers, 1996-97). Assisted in researching compounds containing fluorine and performing laboratory tests related to this element.
- Utilized chemical compounds containing carbon-fluoride linkages as building blocks in the construction of larger molecules; performed Nuclear Magnetic Resonance (NMR) and Gas Chromatography testing for identification purposes.

PERSONAL

Excellent personal and professional references are available upon request.

Exact Name of Person
Title or Position
Name of Company
Address (number and street)
Address (city, state, and zip)

**Chemistry Graduate Hoping
for Position in
Pharmaceutical Industry**

Knowing that experience
as a Mentor and Tutor
would look good on a
resume, this professional
sought out opportunities
to refine her
communication skills in
those jobs. She also
points out that she was
elected President of her
sorority.

Dear Exact Name of Person: (or Sir or Madam if answering a blind ad.)

With the enclosed resume, I would like to initiate the process of being considered for employment within your organization. I am a May 2001 graduate of the College of Notre Dame with an excellent scientific education along with superior technical writing skills, experience in laboratory analysis and instrumental analysis, as well as some knowledge of medicinal chemistry.

While earning my B.S. in Chemistry, I excelled in courses including Medicinal Chemistry, which focused on modern pharmaceuticals, and Instrumental Analysis. I am skilled in operating equipment and devices including fluorescence spectrometers, atomic mass spectrometers, UV/VIS molecular absorption spectrometers, high performance liquid chromatography (HPLC), Gas chromatography (GC), as well as IR/Raman spectrometers, NMR, and FTIR.

At college, I was a popular tutor of Chemistry and Calculus, and I acted as a Mentor for 11 Engineering and Science students. During the summers while earning my college degree, I worked in technical environments which taught me much about teamwork. In the summer of 1998, I worked on an assembly line assembling, inspecting, and packing electrical control panels. In the summer of 1997, I worked as a Procedure Writer for an electric company, where I developed and revised Defense Waste Processing Operations Procedures with special emphasis on chemical processing procedures. In the summer of 1996, I worked as a Production Assistant.

You would find me in person to be a warm and congenial individual who relates well to others and who offers excellent communication skills. While mentoring other Engineering and Science students, I frequently mediated disputes and trained students to utilize conflict management techniques. Known for my natural leadership skills, I served as President of my sorority and led the sorority to a major membership increase. At the same time, however, I take my greatest pleasure in performing analytical tasks ranging from analyzing drinking water to agricultural samples.

If you can use a sharp and astute young chemistry graduate who offers excellent analytical and communication skills, I hope you will contact me to suggest a time when we might meet in person. I am flexible and able to relocate according to your needs. Thank you in advance for your time.

Yours sincerely,

Carol Mace

CAROL MACE

1110½ Hay Street, Fayetteville, NC 28305 • preppub@aol.com • (910) 483-6611

OBJECTIVE   To contribute to an organization that can use a dedicated young professional with an excellent scientific education along with superior technical writing skills, experience in laboratory analysis and instrumental analysis, as well as some knowledge of medicinal chemistry.

EDUCATION   Earned **B.S. degree in Chemistry,** College of Notre Dame, Belmont, CA, 2001.
- Recipient of the U.S. Achievement Academy Collegiate Award; nominated by faculty.
- Authored a senior paper entitled *"The Effects of Proton Conductivity."*
- Coursework included Medicinal Chemistry which focused on modern pharmaceuticals.
- Coursework also included Instrumental Analysis, and my skills include operating:

Fluorescence Spectrometers	UV/VIS Molecular Absorption Spectrometers
IR/Raman Spectrometers	High Performance Liquid Chromatography (HPLC)
NMR	FTIR
Atomic Mass Spectrometer	Gas Chromatography (GC)

- Am skilled in utilizing chart recorders and multimeters.
- Elected President of my sorority, Zeta Phi Beta, and led sorority to a major increase in membership while becoming recognized as a vibrant and enthusiastic leader.

COMPUTERS   Highly proficient with Excel, MS Word, PowerPoint, WordPerfect, Lotus, and ZPlot.

EXPERIENCE   **ENGINEERING & SCIENCE MENTOR** and **CHEMISTRY & CALCULUS TUTOR.** College of Notre Dame's Program for Educational Enrichment and Retention, Belmont, CA (1999-2001). Earned a reputation as an articulate communicator and inspiring young leader while introducing first-year engineering and science students to different opportunities in the PEER Program.
- Taught students to solve problems; tutored students in calculus and chemistry.
- Utilized my natural tact and ability to develop consensus while mediating disputes among students; trained the students themselves in conflict management techniques.
- Mentored 11 engineering and science students who looked to me as their "Team Leader."

SALES ASSOCIATE. Volume Services, Belmont, CA (1998-99). Was frequently commended for my ability to handle the public in a gracious manner while selling food and drinks during home games at the College of Notre Dame; handled various administrative tasks including controlling an inventory of perishable items and other supplies.
- Developed balance sheets for different food stands; supervised the contract groups and vendors who operated the stands; gained experience in financial management and financial control while developing balance sheets.

Other experience (summers):
PRODUCTION ASSISTANT. Cutler-Hammer, San Diego, CA (summer 1998). Assembled, inspected, and packed various sizes of electrical control panels while ensuring that the production line was always stocked with needed supplies.

PROCEDURE WRITER. Electric River Company, Elkton, CA (summer 1997). Developed and revised Defense Waste Processing Operations Procedures with special emphasis on chemical processing-related procedures; edited procedures to ensure they addressed human factors; conducted research for data critical to success of the procedures.

PRODUCTION ASSISTANT. Black & Decker, San Diego, CA (summer 1996). Tested commutators for power drills, and ensured they were heat and wear resistant; on my own initiative, prevented a bad batch of commutators from being used in power drills.

Date

Exact Name of Person
Exact Title
Exact Name of Company
Address
City, State, Zip

Dear Exact Name of Person: (or Dear Sir or Madam if answering a blind ad):

With the enclosed resume, I would like to make you aware of my desire to explore employment opportunities with your organization. I am completing my Bachelor of Science degree in Communications from Winona State University and feel I have much to offer an organization.

As you will see from my resume, I have worked up to 30 hours a week during college in jobs which provided me an opportunity to partially finance my college education. In one job as a Waiter I have enjoyed working as a part of a small team committed to delivering top-notch customer service. I have simultaneously worked in another job as a Sales Representative.

You will also notice from my resume that I worked every summer during college as a Counselor and then as Activities Manager for a church camp. I became a respected role model not only for young campers but also for other counselors and program staff.

I offer strong communication, sales, and interpersonal skills. In college, I utilized those skills while serving my fraternity in numerous capacities which involved acting as a spokesman and serving as an organizer and manager of special events. I possess a gift for motivating and leading others.

If you can use a dedicated young professional with a strong desire to excel in all I do, I hope you will contact me to suggest a time when we can meet to discuss your needs. I can provide excellent personal and professional references.

Sincerely,

James LaHaye

JAMES LaHAYE

1110½ Hay Street, Fayetteville, NC 28305 • preppub@aol.com • (910) 483-6611

OBJECTIVE   I want to contribute to an organization that can use an outgoing young professional who offers considerable sales skills and proven management potential along with a desire to serve the public and work with others in achieving top-quality results.

EDUCATION   **Bachelor of Science in Communications,** Winona State University, Winona, MN, 2000; major was in Applied Communications and minor was in General Business.
- Have been active as a campus leader and in intramural sports.
- Served as **Social Chairman,** Delta Zappa Fraternity, 1997-98; and as **Communications Chairman,** 1999-2000. Was selected by the President for these positions because of my outstanding organizational and management skills. Managed numerous projects which involved managing a budget and planning events for hundreds of people.
- Functioned as **Captain** of the intramural championship soccer team, 1999-2000.
- Was nominated as **Homecoming King** by Delta Zappa Fraternity, 1999.
- Was named Interfraternity Council (IFC) Representative, 1997-98.

Graduated from Winona High School, MN, 1995.
- On the varsity soccer team, lettered in the sport and was named **All-Conference.**
- Was named **Captain** of the varsity soccer team in my senior year.
- Lettered in baseball in my junior and senior years.

COMPUTERS   Windows operating systems and Microsoft Word, Works, Excel.

EXPERIENCE   **WAITER.** Winona Inn, Winona, MN (1999-present). Work up to 30 hours weekly in order to partially finance my college education while completing my Bachelor's degree.
- Have become known for my reliability and excellent customer service skills.
- Have learned to work effectively as part of a small team committed to delivering top-notch customer service and quality food service.
- Also work as a **Sales Representative** and **Landscape Assistant** for a landscaping company; have become known for my strong sales skills as well as my creativity in solving landscaping problems and implementing effective designs.

Was promoted in the following track record of advancement by Camp Knowles, Highstead, MN, during my summer employment over four consecutive summers:
Summers, 1997 and 1998: ACTIVITIES MANAGER. Was promoted to this job as a member of the program staff; continuously developed and implemented ideas for new programs in order to stimulate campers while strengthening their social and physical skills.
- Became skilled in leading large groups of people and in developing programs which appealed to different age groups ranging from elementary, to junior high, to senior high.
- Planned the camp's daily sports program which included kickball, three ball, volleyball, soccer, and numerous "made-up" games.
- On my own initiative, built new soccer goals which greatly enhanced the enjoyment of this sport.
Summers, 1995 and 1996: COUNSELOR. Excelled in leading ten one-week sessions of camp for elementary school children, junior high campers, senior high campers, and handicapped campers; became a respected part of the counseling staff, and was a role model not only to young campers but also to other counselors.

PERSONAL   Am an effective communicator and naturally outgoing individual. References upon request.

Date

Exact Name of Person
Title or Position
Name of Company
Address (no., street)
Address (city, state, zip)

**Communications and
Political Science**

Notice the bullets on the
resume that point out
accomplishments related
to leadership,
communication skills,
and sports honors.
Although he went back
to school after serving in
the Marine Corps, he
worked in leadership
roles and part-time
capacities while in
college.

Dear Exact Name of Person: (or Dear Sir or Madam if answering a blind ad.)

With the enclosed resume, I would like to make you aware of my interest in exploring employment opportunities with your organization.

As you will see from my resume, I have earned a degree in Communications and Political Science while achieving recognition as a scholar and athlete. My extensive involvement in sports has taught me how to work as part of a team of highly motivated individuals in pursuit of a common goal.

While excelling academically, I held important leadership positions during my college career. I was twice elected Student Body President, and I gained valuable experience in solving problems, mediating issues, and expressing the views of students to administrators. I am known for my strong communication skills which I am certain I could utilize for the benefit of my employer.

You will notice that I previously served my country in the U.S. Marine Corps. I credit my military experience with teaching me valuable techniques related to discipline and self-control which I later used in college in managing my time for maximum productivity.

I hope you will welcome my call soon to determine if there is a time when we could meet in person so that I could show you that I am a highly motivated, ambitious person who could become a valuable part of your team. Thank you in advance for your time.

Sincerely yours,

Larry Burroughs

LARRY BURROUGHS

1110½ Hay Street, Fayetteville, NC 28305 • preppub@aol.com • (910) 483-6611

OBJECTIVE   To offer exceptional communication and motivational skills to an organization that can use an enthusiastic, energetic, and talented natural leader who works well with people of all ages, educational levels, and socioeconomic levels.

EDUCATION   **Bachelor's degree in *Communications* and *Political Science*,** Keystone College, La Plume, PA, May 2001.
- Maintained an overall 3.2 GPA with 3.7 GPA in my major subjects.
- In recognition of my academic accomplishments, placed on the Dean's List four times.
- Have been honored as a Varsity Scholar-Athlete every semester.
- Won the Arthur Ashe, Jr., Sports Scholar Award for 1999.
- Chosen on the basis of my skills in communicating with and motivating others, was selected to serve as a guest commentator for a 2000 congressional forum.
- Emceed a fund raising event for the local Boys and Girls Clubs of America in 2000.
- Earned numerous awards as a four-year varsity letterman in football: was an honorable mention for the 1999 *Football Gazette* All-American team.
- Named the "Unsung Hero All-American" for the 2000 *College Football Chronicle*.
- Was one of only five college students selected nationwide for CNN internships for the spring of 2000; performed production work on the network's "World Report" segments.
- Wrote two essays featured in *"Issues,"* a student publication which grew from an idea expressed in a journalism class to a slick student-written and produced magazine.
- Wrote and presented the convocation speech for the 1999-2000 school year.

EXPERIENCE   *Refined time management, leadership, and communication skills while simultaneously earning honors as a scholar-athlete-student leader, Keystone College, La Plume, PA.*
STUDENT AIDE. (1998-present). Supervised 10 other students during weight training and off-season maintenance of the football facilities as well as by tutoring them.
- Improved equipment storage procedures by devising a better system.

RESIDENT ADVISOR. (1998-present). Provide supervision for dormitory residents in order to ensure that living quarters are safe and clean so that students can learn and progress in a healthy environment.
- Applied maturity and life experiences as an "older" student to help me while counseling and giving guidance to younger students with academic or social problems.

STUDENT GOVERNMENT PRESIDENT. (1999-present). Was twice elected to this highest office in student government to represent the interests of the members of the student body and serve as liaison to the Board of Trustees.
- Displayed the ability to speak out tactfully and ensure productive dialog when problems or questions arose.

U.S. MARINE. U.S. Marine Corps, various locations (1995-1998). Received numerous honors and awards for my accomplishments while serving with distinction during a period which included combat in Panama and in the Middle East; applied mechanical skills as a Tracked Vehicle Repairman.
- Was recognized with three prestigious medals.

PERSONAL   Am a bright, articulate young professional who enjoys meeting challenges head on. Have a reputation as an enthusiastic and energetic individual who is physically and mentally tough.

Date

Exact Name of Person
Title or Position
Name of Company
Address (no., street)
Address (city, state, zip)

Dear Exact Name of Person: (or Dear Sir or Madam if answering a blind ad.)

Can you use a dynamic and highly motivated young professional who offers a track record of outstanding sales and managerial results based on hard work, enthusiasm, and persistence?

As you will see from the resume I am enclosing, I worked full-time while earning my B.S. degree at Trinity University. In every job I have held—ranging from warehouse co-manager, to shift supervisor, to painter—I have prided myself on doing every task to the best of my ability.

I feel my highly motivated nature and enthusiastic personality are especially suited to sales situations, and you will also see from my resume that I have excelled in selling both life and health insurance products as well as pest control services. In one job as an Insurance Salesman for Bankers Life & Casualty in charge of a territory including Dallas, TX, and surrounding counties, I rapidly became skilled at prospecting for customers, telemarketing, overcoming objections, and closing the sale. I excelled in that and other jobs while attending college full time.

I offer a mature understanding of what it takes to succeed in sales, and I am aware that discipline, patience, and persistence are critical. I believe I demonstrated those qualities at a young age when I achieved the Eagle rank in Boy Scouts, an accomplishment which few attain.

I hope you will welcome my call soon to determine if there is a time when we could meet in person so that I could show you that I am a highly motivated, ambitious person who could become a valuable part of your team. Thank you in advance for your time.

Sincerely yours,

Jack Wolford

JACK WOLFORD

1110½ Hay Street, Fayetteville, NC 28305   •   preppub@aol.com   •   (910) 483-6611

OBJECTIVE   To contribute to an organization that can use a dynamic and results-oriented young professional who offers proven sales, marketing, and communication skills along with an enthusiastic and highly motivated nature that always persists until a job is done.

HONORS   Achieved Eagle Scout rank; this is the highest award in Boy Scouts and is attained by only 2% of those who join Scouts.
- Elected President, Vocational Industrial Clubs of America (DECA), in high school.
- Elected Vice President, Pi Kappa Phi Fraternity, in college.
- Elected Philanthropy Chairman for Pi Kappa Phi Fraternity.

EDUCATION   **B.S. degree**, Community Services, Trinity University, San Antonio, TX, 2001.
- Worked full-time in the jobs described below in order to finance my college education.
Graduated from Southern Senior High School in San Antonio, TX, 1997.

LICENSES   Licensed in TX to sell Life and Health Insurance; Licensed pest controller in TX.

EXPERIENCE   **PAINTER**. ABLE Custom Paint, San Antonio, TX (2000-01). Worked full time in this job while putting myself through college; was known for my professional attitude and expert workmanship on both industrial and residential sites.
- Frequently provided leadership to inexperienced crews.

SHIFT SUPERVISOR. H.P.R.G., Inc., San Antonio, TX (1999-2000). While financing my college education, worked up to 15 hours a week at a local pool hall/bar within walking distance from my college campus; handled management responsibilities including supervising waitresses on the shift, overseeing the serving of alcohol within strict legal guidelines, and accounting for all money made on my shift.

SALES REPRESENTATIVE. Orkin Pest Control, Dallas, TX (1998). After obtaining my pest control license, excelled in selling pest control services based on the professional inspections I conducted.
- Gained experience in selling a service and in communicating the technical details of pesticides and chemicals in language which the general public could understand.
- Rapidly became one of the company's most productive sales representatives.
- Demonstrated my ability to step into an industry with which I was unfamiliar and quickly transform myself into a valuable employee.

INSURANCE SALESMAN. Bankers Life & Casualty Company, Dallas, TX (1997-1998). After studying for and obtaining my Life and Health Insurance License, quickly became one of the company's top sales performers.
- Was in charge of a territory including Dallas, TX, and surrounding counties.
- Learned techniques in selling financial services and in explaining abstract concepts to people; refined skills in prospecting for customers, telemarketing, overcoming objections and closing the sale as well as in servicing customers.

Other experience: For an automobile dealership and a carwash, detailed cars in high school.

PERSONAL   Excel at dealing with people on the telephone and in person. Am skilled at building rapport with people of all backgrounds. Believe that my enthusiastic nature is an asset.

Date

Exact Name of Person
Title or Position
Name of Company
Address (number and street)
Address (city, state, and zip)

This is an example of a
resume and cover letter
targeted specifically to
the computer industry.
Notice that this individual
served in the U.S. Army
and then went back to
college, so he used the
G.I. Bill to finance his
college education.

Dear Exact Name of Person: (or Sir or Madam if answering a blind ad.)

I would appreciate an opportunity to talk with you soon about how I could contribute to your organization through my degree in Computer Programming as well as through my technical computer skills and proven background of expertise in training program development and management.

With a reputation as a talented instructor, technical writer, and specialist in planning and developing course requirements, I was promoted ahead of my peers to leadership positions in the U.S. Army. Since leaving military service I have completed degree requirements for an Associate in Applied Science (A.A.S.) degree from Cortland Technical Community College, NY. My skills include repairing and upgrading computers, programming in various languages, and utilizing DOS, Windows, and UNIX operating systems.

I hope you will welcome my call soon to arrange a brief meeting to discuss your current and future needs and how I might serve them. Thank you in advance for your time.

Sincerely,

Charles Harding

Alternate last paragraph:
I hope you will call or write me soon to suggest a time convenient for us to meet and discuss your current and future needs and how I might serve them. Thank you in advance for your time.

CHARLES HARDING

1110½ Hay Street, Fayetteville, NC 28305 • preppub@aol.com • (910) 483-6611

OBJECTIVE

To offer my education and skills related to computer analysis, design, and programming; systems administration/networking; and equipment repair/upgrade coupled with my experience in performance-based computer instruction and training management.

EDUCATION & TRAINING

Completed **Associate in Applied Science degree in Computer Programming,** Cortland Technical Community College, NY, November 2000.
- Completed specialized course work including the following:

systems analysis	operating systems	UNIX
financial accounting	network technology	statistics
database managementdata communications		data access

- Excelled in more than 6,600 hours of courses emphasizing training development and management as well as a Spanish language course.
- Completed rigorous Special Forces training.

COMPUTERS

Experienced in repairing, upgrading, and networking IBM-compatible PCs with Windows and UNIX operating systems using software including:

Windows 2000	WordPerfect	MS Word
dBase	Micro Focus	Novell Netware
Visual BASIC	Harvard Graphics	COBOL

EXPERIENCE

FULL-TIME STUDENT. Cortland Technical Community College, NY (1998-2000).

Advanced to the rank of Sergeant in the U.S. Army:
TRAINING PROGRAM MANAGER. Ft. Campbell, KY (1994-97). Handled activities ranging from supervising six people carrying out short- and long-term training management, to assisting in the development of one- and two-year training plans, to developing and consolidating weekly training schedules for one company in an Airborne Special Forces Group.
- Conducted weekly training meetings which focused on problem solving, directing the best utilization of resources, and keeping a senior executive informed of events.
- Coordinated administrative and medical support and resources for an 83-person company with an extensive inventory of communications equipment and 11 trucks.

SENIOR INSTRUCTOR and **OPERATIONS MANAGER.** Ft. Bragg, NC (1990-94). As senior course developer and administrator for numerous types of courses, provided subject matter expertise for the U.S. Army's Special Warfare Center and School.
- Monitored the performance of eight classroom instructors teaching groups of 20 students in dozens of different specialized areas.
- Taught performance-based instruction and the lecture method of instruction in a two-week Instructor Training Course which produced effective professional instructors.
- Served as Senior Instructor for the Training Developer Course in which instructors were taught how to develop training products in their specialized areas.
- Wrote instructional material for numerous courses and reviewed more than 150 training documents for sound doctrine and made recommendations for changes.
- Implemented a software program that facilitates training management by tracking expenses, generating calendars, and automating training resources.

PERSONAL

Was entrusted with a **Top Secret** security clearance. Was honored with one Humanitarian Service, one Meritorious Service, and two Commendation Medals.

Date

Exact Name of Person
Title or Position
Name of Company
Address (no., street)
Address (city, state, zip)

Computer Science

Dear Exact Name of Person: (or Dear Sir or Madam if answering a blind ad.)

Here we have another example of a student with previous military experience. He has a Computer Expertise section on his resume since he figures one of his key areas of strength is his computer knowledge.

With the enclosed resume I would like to introduce you to the strong computer skills and software knowledge which I could put to work for you.

With a degree in Computer Science, I offer previous experience as a Computer Operator while serving in the U.S. Navy. In fact, my military experience revealed that I have a knack for computer technology, as I rapidly mastered the software used by the Navy at a central operations center. Even prior to earning my B.S. degree at Emory, I excelled in numerous technical training programs. I was entrusted with one of the nation's highest security clearances: Top Secret.

Throughout my life, I have become known for my resourcefulness and creativity. I am eager to combine my strong computer knowledge with my innate problem-solving ability in order to benefit a company that can use a highly motivated hard charger.

I hope you will welcome my call soon to determine if there is a time when we could meet in person so that I could show you that I am a dedicated and ambitious person who could become a valuable part of your team. Thank you in advance for your time.

Sincerely yours,

Adam Henke

ADAM HENKE

1110½ Hay Street, Fayetteville, NC 28305 • preppub@aol.com • (910) 483-6611

OBJECTIVE   To offer extensive knowledge of computer software operations and systems maintenance to an organization that can use a skilled young professional with an aptitude for quickly learning and applying new technology.

EDUCATION   **B.S. in Computer Science,** Emory University, Atlanta, GA; degree anticipated June, 2001.
&   Excelled in military training programs emphasizing the following:
TECHNICAL
TRAINING

basic electricity	records processing	tape libraries
quality assurance	basic test equipment	system design
system tape backup	system configurations	LAN hardware
peripheral operations	system error messages	system diagnosis
message format	communications security	radio/phone procedures

COMPUTER   Offer exceptional computer skills gained through formal training as well as application
EXPERTISE   including the following:

Windows 2000	DOS	WordPerfect
Harvard Graphics	Harvard FX	Picture Publisher
Word Scan	Novell	UNIX

Microsoft Office (entire package including Excel and Word)

EXPERIENCE   **FULL-TIME COLLEGE STUDENT.** Emory University, Atlanta, GA (1998-present). Attend Emory University in the Computer Science degree program.

Advanced on the basis of technical proficiency, natural aptitude, and attention to detail as a
DATA PROCESSING TECHNICIAN *in the U.S. Navy:*
SHIFT SUPERVISOR. The USS Guam, Norfolk, VA (1997). Was promoted to supervise operation of the specialized ADP system used to support supply and operational activities.
- Officially described as a "superb performer" and awarded a service medal and citation, was recognized for technical expertise and a positive attitude.

MEDIA LIBRARIAN. The USS Guam, Norfolk, VA (1996-97). In recognition of my attention to detail and knowledge, was given the responsibility of managing and keeping detailed records of an inventory of electronic data tapes generated by the SNAP system.
- Ensured a "discrepancy free" rating for the supply department in a major assessment of logistics operations which resulted in an overall 98.4% rating.
- Assisted in removing more than 450 excess ADP electronics items: as a result storage space was maximized and inventory control simplified.
- Was the supply department "Employee of the Month," February 1996.

COMPUTER OPERATOR. Office of Naval Intelligence, Suitland, MD (1993-95). Operated VAX 600, VAX 8810, Filenet system, and Network Control microcomputers at a central operations center.
- Was cited for expert handling of more than 50 "hot line" calls a day which required that all information was properly documented and transferred so that problems were solved and users achieved maximum production time.
- Officially described as "having unlimited potential," was praised for being industrious and self motivated and for setting the standard for my peers.

PERSONAL   Was entrusted with a Top Secret security clearance. Accurately type at least 45 words per minute. Am in excellent physical condition. High level of determination and initiative.

Date

Exact Name of Person
Exact Title
Exact Name of Company
Address
City, State, Zip

Dear Sir or Madam:

With the enclosed resume, I would like to make you aware of my desire to explore employment opportunities with your hotel.

As you will see from my resume, I have recently completed my degree in Computer Science. While earning my B.S., I excelled in all aspects of front desk management at hotels in New York and North Carolina. At two Days Inns in NY, I was extensively trained in auditing and office while learning to handle the full range of responsibilities which go into effective front desk management.

In my current job as Front Desk Supervisor, I handle all front desk responsibilities and am totally committed to the hotel's goal of achieving the highest standards of customer satisfaction. I also perform the audit every Sunday which requires me to balance all hotel accounts.

I am held in high regard by my current employer and can provide outstanding personal and professional references at the appropriate time. If you can use an astute and experienced hospitality industry professional with the proven ability to impact your bottom line in profitable ways, I hope you will contact me to suggest a time when we might meet to discuss your needs. Thank you in advance for whatever time and professional courtesies you can extend.

Sincerely,

Mary Ann Pilcher

MARY ANN PILCHER

1110½ Hay Street, Fayetteville, NC 28305　•　preppub@aol.com　•　(910) 483-6611

OBJECTIVE
To offer extensive knowledge of computer software operations and systems maintenance to an organization that can use a skilled young professional with an aptitude for quickly learning and applying new technology.

EDUCATION
B.S. in Computer Science, North Carolina State University, Raleigh, NC, 2001.

EXPERIENCE
FULL-TIME COLLEGE STUDENT. NCSU, Raleigh, NC (1998-present).
In my spare time, attend NC State in the Computer Science degree program.

FRONT DESK SUPERVISOR. The Western Hotel, Raleigh, NC (1999-present). For this 168-room hotel, am excelling at all aspects of this job which involves extensive responsibilities related to customer service for large accounts and individuals, accounting and auditing, billing, as well as training new front desk clerks.
- Currently begin work at 7 AM and handle the heavy volume of customer complaints and questions which occur between 7 AM and 10 AM.
- Work with large accounts to book blocks of rooms and coordinate special events; provide customer service in the booking process and provide liaison regarding any special banquets and events which are set up.
- Handle a wide range of responsibilities related to billing, accounting, and auditing; for two months acted at the hotel's auditor until the position was filled, and am continuing to perform the audit every Sunday which requires me to balance all hotel accounts.
- Handle the billing, and deal with coupons; prepare the ledger.
- Am totally committed to the hotel's policy of assuring customer satisfaction, no matter what, and routinely solve problems to assure guest satisfaction and repeat business.
- Book up to 150 rooms monthly while providing courteous and friendly customer service.
- Received numerous letters of appreciation because of my professionalism and dedication to the highest standards of customer support and assistance.

STORE MANAGER. KFC, Raleigh, NC (1998-99). After relocating from New York to North Carolina, accepted a job as a store manager with Kentucky Fried Chicken and managed a staff of 12.
- Emphasized adherence to the highest standards of cleanliness and sanitation, and led the store to receive an O.S.H.A. award for food service and management.
- Coordinated the store's certification by S.A.F.E. for safety and sanitation.

FRONT DESK REPRESENTATIVE. Days Inn, Ulster, NY (1995-97). For this 176-room Days Inn, played a key role in the hotel's receiving the Gold Star for superior customer service.
- Received extensive formal and on-the-job training related to auditing, customer service, switchboard operations, reservations and office work, and sales.
- Was frequently commended for my sunny disposition and outgoing personality, and excelled in all aspects of customer service.

FRONT DESK RECEPTIONIST. Days Inn, Albany, NY (1994-95). For this 125-room hotel, was trained in auditing and office while becoming skilled in reservations and customer service.

COMPUTERS
Highly computer proficient; can operate, design, and build computers.

PERSONAL
Am a highly self-motivated individual known for my professional attitude. In my spare time, enjoy classical music and the study of religions. Excellent references on request.

Date

Exact Name of Person
Exact Title
Exact Name of Company
Address
City, State, Zip

Counseling

Dear Exact Name of Person: (or Dear Sir or Madam if answering a blind ad):

This talented young woman is hoping to make a career as a guidance counselor at a public school. She has demonstrated her interest in her field by taking on volunteer positions and internships at organizations which have helped her gain insight into social services and counseling.

With the enclosed resume, I would like to make you aware of my desire to explore employment opportunities with your organization. I have recently completed my Bachelor's. degree in Counseling and offer strong communication and counseling skills.

As you will see from my resume, I have excelled in counseling positions in a camp environment, in a home for displaced children, and at the YMCA. While working as a Counselor at an orphanage, I became known for my creativity and program development skills. On my own initiative, I organized a store at the orphanage so that youth aged 9-19 could learn money-handling and budgeting skills. I was commended for my efforts which resulted in building self-esteem and a feeling of self worth.

In a job as a Case Manager at the YMCA, I worked as an intern with the Big Brothers/Big Sisters of Forest City. In that capacity, I organized an after-school program at Forest City Middle School designed to build self-esteem in children. The program I developed began with 10 children and grew to serve 40 children, and after my internship the program received formal funding so that it can continue. For my efforts and initiative, I received a certificate of appreciation.

As a teenager, I discovered my orientation toward the social work field while working as a Camp Counselor with children aged 6-13. In 1998, I also volunteered as Office Manager and Receptionist at the local women's shelter, where I developed a book of essays written by the homeless clients of this nonprofit organization.

If you can use a caring and enthusiastic young professional with a true desire to make a difference in the lives of others, I hope you will contact me to suggest a time when we might meet to discuss your needs. I can provide excellent references.

Sincerely,

Brownie Sullivan

BROWNIE SULLIVAN

1110½ Hay Street, Fayetteville, NC 28305   •   preppub@aol.com   •   (910) 483-6611

OBJECTIVE
I want to contribute to an organization that can use an outgoing young professional who offers strong communication skills and proven management potential along with a desire to serve the public and work with others in achieving top-quality results.

EDUCATION
Bachelor of Science degree in Counseling, Waldorf College, Forest City, IA, 2000.
- Activities included Resident Advisor, Resident Hall Association, Spencer Hall Council **President,** Ki Alpha Phi **President,** Counseling Club, Social Work Club, Omega Chi Delta Historian, Waldorf Playmakers, Puppetry Association.

Training: Professional training included Teaching Parent Model and PC Essentials.

COMPUTERS
Windows operating systems and Microsoft Word, Works, Excel, WordPerfect, SPSS, Internet

EXPERIENCE
RESIDENT COUNSELOR. Baptist Home for Children, Forest City, IA (5/99-present). As a volunteer at this orphanage, provide training related to life skills for youth aged 9-19 while also implementing parent training; developed programs for each child which resulted in building self-esteem and a feeling of self worth.
- **Program Development:** On my own initiative, organized a store at the Baptist Home for Children so that children could earn money and learn skills in handling money and budgeting for their expenses; designed and managed the store's policies and procedures.

CASE MANAGER. YMCA, Forest City, IA (Spring 1999). As an Intern with the Big Brothers/ Big Sisters of Forest City, interviewed and placed prospective mentors and worked as the trusted "right arm" to the program manager.
- **Program Development:** Organized an after-school program designed to build self-esteem in children and worked closely with children making failing grades; the program at Forest City Middle School was widely praised and considered a success and I was praised for my creativity and professionalism. Began with 10 students and grew the program to 40 students. The program received funding after its pilot year and is being continued.
- **Award:** Received Certificate of Appreciation from the PTA.

HISTORIAN. Saint Simons Catholic Church, Forest City, IA (9/98-12/98). Developed a scrapbook which provided the school's first permanent record of its after-school program; planned photographic events and arranged photo opportunities with children, tutors, and staff.

OFFICE MANAGER & RECEPTIONIST. Women's Shelter of Forest City, Forest City, IA (1/98-5/98). While working as a volunteer, applied my creativity in developing a book of essays by the clients of this nonprofit organization serving battered women.
- **Social worker responsibilities:** Routinely handled duties of a social worker and counselor; processed intakes, made referrals to other agencies, supplied clients with clothing.

CAMP COUNSELOR. Carthage Summer Fun Camp, Carthage County, IA (6/95-7/97). Found many opportunities to express my creativity and resourcefulness while scheduling events, planning educational programs, and working with children aged 6-13.
- **Programming:** Planned a talent show for the children and nurtured their creativity.

SALES REPRESENTATIVE. Hecht's Department, Duluth, IA (12/91-2/95). Began working at the age of 13 and worked for four years part-time; was commended for bringing a youthful outlook into the department. Decorated windows, assisted customers, and handled money.

PERSONAL
Caring and nurturing professional who yearns to make a difference in the counseling field.

Date

Exact Name of Person
Title or Position
Name of Company
Address (number and street)
Address (city, state, and zip)

Criminal Justice

Dear Exact Name of Person: (or Sir or Madam if answering a blind ad.)

An enthusiastic attitude for her new field is one of the main points this young professional makes in her cover letter. She is mostly "raw material" and she is seeking an opportunity to enter the criminal justice field in an entry-level role.

I would appreciate an opportunity to talk with you soon about how I could contribute to your organization through my education in criminal justice and my personal qualities of honesty, self-reliance, compassion and empathy for others, and dedication to helping people in need.

One of my main interests is in finding a way to use my natural talents to help the victims of crime—I want to make the criminal justice system work from within so that people who have suffered as victims of a crime are not further abused by the very system that is supposed to help them. While excelling in my full-time job, I recently earned an Associate's degree in Criminal Justice at Denver Community College and hope to pursue a bachelor's degree in the near future.

I am a hard-working young professional who finds my greatest satisfaction in helping others. With a reputation as an honest person who will speak out for what I believe, I am convinced that I can offer a great deal to others through my life experience and education.

I hope you will welcome my call soon to arrange a brief meeting to discuss your current and future needs and how I might serve them. Thank you in advance for your time.

Sincerely,

Donna Ornstein

Alternate last paragraph:
I hope you will call or write me soon to suggest a time convenient for us to meet and discuss your current and future needs and how I might serve them. Thank you in advance for your time.

DONNA ORNSTEIN

1110½ Hay Street, Fayetteville, NC • preppub@aol.com • (910) 483-6611

OBJECTIVE

To offer my education in criminal justice and my reputation as an empathetic and compassionate individual to an organization that can benefit from my skills related to counseling, dealing with people of all ages and backgrounds, and my high level of self-motivation.

EDUCATION

Received an **Associate's degree in Criminal Justice,** Denver Community College, Denver, CO, 2000; graduated with a 3.4 GPA.
- Completed **Firearms and Defense Tactics Course** which included handling, carrying, and shooting all types of weapons as well as specialized course work in psychology, criminology, criminal investigations, corrections, and police supervision.
- Elected Secretary, Union for the Advancement of African-American Students.

ACTIVITIES & HONORS

Participated in extracurricular activities at Denver High School, Denver, CO.
- Elected *parliamentarian* of the forensics team, also was a member of the debate team
- Won the *first place award* for the category "original oratory" during a tournament.
- Graduated in the *Colorado Scholars Program* which meant taking advanced-placement classes. Was a member of the Honor Society

EXPERIENCE

MASTER CONTROL OPERATOR. WKZF-TV 40, Denver, CO (1998-present). Excelled in this full-time job while earning my Associate's degree; applied my organizational skills and ability to quickly learn new concepts and work methods ensuring that the television station is providing viewers with the highest possible quality of sound and picture while handling a range of sophisticated equipment.
- Learned to operate this equipment and handle activities ranging from adding commercial breaks at the proper time and of the proper length.
- Took care of support functions including receiving satellite feeds, dubbing commercials, typing logs, and running Emergency Broadcast System alerts.

DIETARY AIDE. Denver Care Center, Denver, CO (1997-98). Helped finance my education and learned the value of listening to people and dealing with them as individuals while helping with meal preparation and with social activities.
- Earned the honor of being the center's first "Employee of the Month."

Refined my communication and human relations skills while building this work history in summer jobs at the Jobs Training Service Center, Denver, CO.
RECREATION AIDE. (1996). Was given an opportunity to work with children from broken and/or poverty-stricken homes and to help them build their self-confidence while providing a safe environment in which they could play and be cared for during the summer vacation.

RECEPTIONIST. Kline Attorneys at Law, Denver, CO (1995). Earned a reputation as a self-motivated young person who was willing to work hard, could take constructive criticism gracefully, and who learned quickly while handling general office duties.

SPECIAL SKILLS

Through training and experience, am familiar with equipment and systems such as:
Computers: MS Word, WordPerfect and Lotus 1-2-3 and have taken a programming course
Communications: Emergency Broadcast System, satellite operations, TV transmitters
Office equipment: typewriters, copiers, computers, microfiche machines, cash registers, fax

PERSONAL

Am licensed in Broadcasting by the FCC (Federal Communications Commission).

Date

Exact Name of Person
Title or Position
Name of Company
Address (no., street)
Address (city, state, zip)

Dear Exact Name of Person: (or Dear Sir or Madam if answering a blind ad.)

I would appreciate an opportunity to talk with you soon about how I could contribute to your organization through my degree in Criminal Justice and strong interest in the fields of law enforcement and corrections.

I am a very mature and responsible young professional with a reputation for being articulate, hard-working, and good with people. A recent graduate from Adrian College, Adrian, MI, with a B.S. degree in Criminal Justice, I completed specialized course work which included law enforcement, criminal law, community-based corrections, and the legal aspects of the criminal justice system. Other classes in sociology, social problems, abnormal psychology, statistics, and computer science gave me a well-rounded base of knowledge. The degree program also gave me an opportunity to participate in two internships where I observed members of the Adrian Police Department on duty and which gave me a practical insight into the day-to-day operations of a metropolitan police department.

As you will see from the work experience described on my resume, I am no stranger to hard work. An enthusiastic, creative, and articulate individual, I have adapted to jobs which required customer service and sales abilities, attention to detail, as well as office operations and data processing skills.

Through my enthusiasm, motivational abilities, empathy, and compassion for others, I am confident I can make valuable contributions to an organization that seeks a professional with these qualities.

I hope you will welcome my call soon to arrange a brief meeting at your convenience to discuss your current and future needs and how I might serve them. Thank you in advance for your time.

Sincerely yours,

Juan Oropeza

JUAN OROPEZA

1110½ Hay Street, Fayetteville, NC 28305 • preppub@aol.com • (910) 483-6611

OBJECTIVE

To offer my strong interest in the field of law enforcement and my education in criminal justice to an organization that can use a mature young professional who offers strong computer, sales, and communication abilities.

EDUCATION

B.S. degree in Criminal Justice, Adrian College, Adrian, MI, 2000.
- Completed specialized course work including the following:

principles of sociology	crime and delinquency	law enforcement
contemporary social problems	the court system	community corrections
civil rights and the constitution	abnormal psychology	juvenile justice
criminal law	legal aspects of the criminal justice system	

INTERNSHIPS

Completed **two 40-hour Criminal Justice Internships** with the Adrian Police Department, Adrian, MI, fall, 1999 and spring, 2000.
- Was exposed to the day-to-day functions of the department and given an opportunity to ride in a patrol car observing police officers on duty.

EXPERIENCE

Refined my time management skills while gaining practical work experience and building a reputation as a detail-oriented and hard-working young professional in these jobs while also attending college full time:

SALES ASSOCIATE. Sam's Club, Adrian, MI (1997-present). Quickly earned promotion from Stocker to assist customers in the hard goods department which includes computers, electronics, sporting goods, pet supplies, and tools.
- Learned where a wide range of merchandise was located and became skilled in answering consumers' questions and helping them find what they needed.
- Provided pleasant, helpful telephone service to customers calling for information.
- As a Stocker, learned to use the computer to prepare price signs for merchandise and made sure grocery items were neatly and correctly stocked and properly priced.

WAREHOUSE WORKER. Nordic Warehouse, Inc., Kenansville, MI (1995-96). Gained experience in operating material-handling equipment including forklifts and power jacks as well as in activities including loading trucks, preparing items for cold storage, separating items into proper categories, and cleaning a warehouse.
- Used my attention to detail while taking careful and accurate tallies of items to be exported and items that had been imported.

SURVEYOR. U.S. Department of Agriculture, Kenansville, MI (summer 1994). Learned to work independently while being responsible for maintaining and operating a government vehicle and using my powers of observation and aerial maps to help locate fields of crops and inspect them for parasites.

COMPUTER KNOWLEDGE

Experienced in using Word, WordPerfect 5.0 and 5.1 for word processing on IBM-compatible PCs; was exposed to Lotus 1-2-3 and dBase in a computer science class.
Familiar with copy machines, electronic calculators, and 10-key adding machines.

LANGUAGE

Speak and read Spanish fluently; have a fair grasp of written Spanish.

PERSONAL

Am very enthusiastic, energetic, and creative. Truly like people and enjoy meeting and getting to know and help others. Offer strong problem-solving skills and a drive to succeed.

Date

Exact Name of Person
Title or Position
Name of Company
Address (no., street)
Address (city, state, zip)

Criminal Justice with Concentration in Police Studies

The key job on this individual's resume may be his Police Officer Intern position. He also devotes one paragraph on his cover letter to discussing that internship and what he gained from it.

Dear Exact Name of Person: (or Dear Sir or Madam if answering a blind ad.)

With the enclosed resume, I am formally expressing my desire to work in your organization, and I can assure you that I offer a solid commitment to the law enforcement and criminal justice field.

You will see from my resume that I excelled as a Chemical Specialist while serving my country in the U.S. Army prior to college. While acquiring expertise in the handling, storage, and disposal of toxic and hazardous substances, I was promoted ahead of my peers and selected to train other young people. It was during my time in the military that I decided to earn my degree in criminal justice and dedicate myself to a career in law enforcement. I believe my self control and calm temperament are well suited to police work.

After my honorable discharge in 1997, I enrolled at Seattle University and then completed my B.S. degree in Criminal Justice in only three years instead of the usual four years. I give much credit for my academic success to the disciplined work habits I learned while in military service.

Most recently I have excelled as a Police Officer Intern with the Seattle Police Department, and during that internship I became skilled in resolving domestic/personal disputes, conducting surveillance, handling auto accidents, retrieving stolen goods, writing up police documentation, and detecting illegal activities related to drugs, shoplifting, and other areas. Obviously this brief experience in law enforcement does not make me an "expert" in any area, but I hope you will conclude from my military and academic track record that I am committed to becoming an outstanding law enforcement professional.

Please be assured that I can provide outstanding personal and professional references. I can also assure you that you would find me in person to be an enthusiastic and dedicated young person who prides myself on being the best and doing the best at all times.

I hope you will welcome my call soon to arrange a brief meeting at your convenience to discuss your current and future needs and how I might serve them. Thank you in advance for your time.

Sincerely yours,

Hideto Eguro

HIDETO EGURO

1110½ Hay Street, Fayetteville, NC 28305 • preppub@aol.com • (910) 483-6611

OBJECTIVE
I want to work for an organization that can use a disciplined, hard-working, and resourceful young professional who offers skills related to law enforcement and the criminal justice field along with planning, management, and communication abilities transferable to any field.

EDUCATION
Bachelor of Science (B.S.) degree in Criminal Justice with Concentration in Police Studies, Seattle University, Seattle, WA, 2000.
* Completed this rigorous degree program in only three years by applying my hard-working nature as well as the disciplined habits I learned in military service.
* In the computer lab, gained familiarity with Lotus 1-2-3, WordPerfect, and dBase.

As a military professional, completed basic training; then excelled in the Army's Chemical School studying chemical warfare and decontamination; also completed training as a Drug and Alcohol Abuse Counselor.

EXPERIENCE
POLICE OFFICER INTERN. Seattle Police Department, Seattle, WA (Spring, 2000). Gained experience in many aspects of police work in this internship; was commended for demonstrating excellent judgment and exhibiting a patient approach to public relations and problem solving while working in hostile and often dangerous situations.
* *Police documentation:* Wrote citations while handling the normal duties of a police officer; learned to complete police reports and other documentation.
* *Personnel protection/transport:* Transported mental patients to and from hospitals.
* *Domestic disputes:* Refined my skills in handling domestic/family problems.
* *Stolen goods:* Retrieved stolen vehicles and coordinated their disposition.
* *Auto accidents:* Learned how to handle all aspects of auto accidents from arranging for medical help to writing up all the documentation required at accident scenes.
* *Illegal drugs:* Became knowledgeable of procedures used to detect the sale and use of illegal drugs and to apprehend suspects.
* *Property protection:* Became skilled in dealing with shoplifters and trespassers.
* *Surveillance:* Learned surveillance techniques; attended Community Watch meetings.

ADMINISTRATIVE ASSISTANT. V.A. Hospital, Seattle, WA (July 1997-August 1999). While excelling in this work-study job to finance my college degree, became skilled in completing medical forms and paperwork particular to the medical field.
* Scheduled students for work study interviews and other administrative duties.
* Answered telephones in a personnel placement operation.

ALCOHOL/DRUG ABUSE COUNSELOR. V.A. Hospital, Seattle, WA (May 1995-January 1997). Was cited for my compassionate personality and kind nature while dealing with people experiencing multiple personal problems; screened and counseled veterans abusing alcohol and drugs and determined appropriate treatment remedies.

SALES REPRESENTATIVE. Office Max, Seattle, WA (June 1994-November 1994). Learned how to order and control inventory while buying/selling furniture from companies in the region.

CHEMICAL SPECIALIST. U.S. Army, Ft. Bragg, NC, and Ft. McClellan, AL (1992-94). Gained expertise in the handling and disposal of toxic and hazardous substances while participating in numerous field exercises and projects in the chemical field.

PERSONAL
Am an energetic individual who has a positive outlook. Remain calm in stressful situations.

Date

Exact Name of Person
Title or Position
Name of Company
Address (no., street)
Address (city, state, zip)

Doctor of Pharmacy

After earning his degree with extensive academic honors, this young professional is now ready to market his skills and communicate the clinical rotations and clerkships which helped him refine his skills.

Dear Exact Name of Person: (or Dear Sir or Madam if answering a blind ad.)

With the enclosed resume, I would like to make you aware of my desire to utilize my Doctor of Pharmacy degree for the benefit of your organization.

In the process of completing my Doctor of Pharmacy degree, I excelled in several fourth year clinical rotations which enhanced my clinical knowledge and management abilities. After completing a rotation in geriatrics, I was specially requested to return for a second rotation by the medical professionals with whom I worked. You will also see that I completed two rotations at pharmacies in New York as well as a clinical rotation at the Veterans Administration Hospital.

You would find me in person to be an outgoing individual who prides myself on my ability to remain poised in all customer service situations. I can provide outstanding personal and professional references, and I would cheerfully relocate and travel extensively according to your needs.

I hope you will call or write me soon to suggest a time convenient for us to meet and discuss your current and future needs and how I might serve them. Thank you in advance for you time.

Sincerely yours,

Joseph Edward Mullen

JOSEPH EDWARD MULLEN

1110½ Hay Street, Fayetteville, NC 28305 • preppub@aol.com • (910) 483-6611

OBJECTIVE
I want to contribute to an organization that can use a skilled health care professional who offers an extensive background as a pharmacist along with a strong bottom-line orientation.

EDUCATION
Doctor of Pharmacy, Daemen College School of Pharmacy, Amherst, NY, 2000.
- Graduated *magna cum laude*.
- Elected officer in Phi Delta Chi Pharmacy Fraternity; inducted into Pre-Med-Allied Health Honor Society; Epsilon Pi Eta Honor Society; Phi Eta Sigma Honor Society.
- Named to Dean's List, President's List; awarded Presidential Scholarship.
- Member of Phi Delta Chi Pharmacy Fraternity; Christian Pharmacist Fellowship.
- Active in student life and community organizations: participated in annual Phi Delta Chi fundraiser for Daemen Creek Elementary School and battered women's shelter; as a tutor at Boose Creek Elementary School, participated in health fair.

EXPERIENCE
FOURTH YEAR CLINICAL ROTATIONS & CLERKSHIPS:
- **Geriatrics (two rotations):** Methodist Retirement Community, Amherst, NY and Southeastern General Hospital, Adlee, NY, Jan-June 2000. Gained knowledge of geriatric patients.

- **Community Pharmacy:** Revco Drugs, Amherst, NY, Dec 1999. Gained experience in all aspects of the operation of a community pharmacy; learned techniques related to receiving and processing Rx orders; dispensing and checking prescriptions; counseling patients; and billing third party payers.

- **Ambulatory Medicine:** Merck Permanente, Amherst, NY, Nov 1999. Worked closely with physicians and mid-level practitioners and provided clinical pharmacy services; refined my skills in basic physical assessment; drug utilization reviews; and clinical pharmacy practice including patient chart reviews, interpretation of lab results, development of drug regiments, patient counseling, and kinetics service.

- **Drug Information:** Daemen College Drug Information Center, Sep 1999. Received requests for information concerning drugs and drug therapy from physicians, pharmacists, and nurses; searched primary, secondary, and tertiary sources for information, to include computerized databases and online sources; compiled information into concise answers.

- **Community Pharmacy:** Rite Aid, Adlee, NY, Aug 1998. Gained experience in all aspects of the operation of a community pharmacy; completed a school project in which data was collected and counseling given to patients concerning drug-drug interactions.

- **Internal Medicine:** Veteran's Administration Hospital, Amherst, NY, Jun 1998. Monitored inpatients on a general medicine ward; member of a medical team consisting of an attending physician, a medical resident, an intern, and a student. Monitored patients through attending rounds, medical charts, and computerized databases.

PERSONAL
Outstanding references. Completed 16 hours of training in primary compounding.

Date

Exact Name of Person
Title or Position
Name of Company
Address (no., street)
Address (city, state, zip)

Dear Exact Name of Person: (or Dear Sir or Madam if answering a blind ad.)

I would appreciate an opportunity to talk with you soon about how I could contribute to your organization through my proven abilities related to customer service, sales, management, and finance.

In the process of completing my B.S. degree in Economics with concentrations in Banking and Finance, I worked during the summers and Christmas seasons and held part-time jobs throughout the school year. While juggling those part-time jobs with a rigorous academic curriculum, I also found time to become a respected campus leader and was elected Treasurer of my residence hall in my junior year and President in my senior year. Although I am just 21 years old, I have been told often that I am "mature beyond my years." I am known for my responsible and hard-working nature.

In one summer job as an Assistant to a Financial Analyst with Merrill Lynch, I gained exposure to the operations of the stock market and acquired hands-on experience in working with customers of various financial services and financial instruments. I obtained my current job as Customer Service Representative with Blockbuster Video because the company created a position for me in Dalton when I moved from Albany, where I had become a valued employee and was a major contributor to achieving the fourth highest Christmas sales volume of all stores in the chain. I have been encouraged by both Merrill Lynch and Blockbuster to seek employment there after college graduation, and I feel certain I could become a valued part of your organization within a short period of time, too.

You would find me in person to be an outgoing individual who prides myself on my ability to remain poised in all customer service situations. I can provide outstanding personal and professional references, and I would cheerfully relocate and travel extensively according to your needs.

I hope you will call or write me soon to suggest a time convenient for us to meet and discuss your current and future needs and how I might serve them. Thank you in advance for you time.

Sincerely yours,

Daryl Urbanowicz

DARYL URBANOWICZ

1110½ Hay Street, Fayetteville, NC 28305 • preppub@aol.com • (910) 483-6611

OBJECTIVE
To contribute to an organization that can use a hard-working young professional who offers proven leadership ability and management potential along with a congenial personality, outstanding communication skills, and an ability to relate well to anyone.

EDUCATION
Bachelor of Science (B.S.) degree with a major in **Economics** and concentrations in **Banking** and **Finance**, Dalton College, Dalton, GA, 2001.
- Worked part-time during the school year as well as every summer and Christmas season in order to finance my education; became a highly valued employee of every organization in which I worked and can provide outstanding references.
- Was a popular and respected campus leader; was elected **President** of my residence hall, Bryant Hall, in my senior year and **Treasurer** of Bryant Hall in my junior year.
- Active member of the Economics/Finance Club and the Illusions Modeling Club.

COMPUTERS
Familiar with MS Word, WordPerfect, Lotus 1-2-3 and PowerPoint.
- Offer an ability to rapidly master new software and operating systems.

EXPERIENCE
CUSTOMER SERVICE REPRESENTATIVE. Blockbuster Video, Dalton and Albany, GA (1997-present). Worked in the Albany Blockbuster Store part-time while going to college and was commended for playing a key role in helping the Albany store achieve the fourth highest sales volume in the chain during the 2000 Christmas season; when I transferred to Dalton College to complete my degree in economics, Blockbuster Video persuaded me to stay with the company and found a similar spot for me in Dalton.
- Handle thousands of dollars daily utilizing computer-assisted cash registers.
- Train new personnel hired by the company; earned a reputation as a polite and gracious individual while assisting dozens of people daily in video selection.
- Have been told I have a bright future in management with Blockbuster Corporation; have been encouraged to enter the company's management trainee program.

RESIDENCE MANAGER. Bryant Hall at Dalton College, Dalton, GA (1998-present). In a part-time job simultaneous with the one above, work closely with the dorm director to ensure the efficient administration of this residence hall housing 400 students.
- Supervise the conduct and activities of students living the dorm, and pride myself on setting an example for them in terms of my own morals and actions.
- Solved a wide range of maintenance and administrative problems while also counseling students with financial matters and personal problems ranging from depression and loneliness to poor academic performance and insufficient motivation.
- Acquired experience in mentoring others, most of whom were older than I am.

ASSISTANT TO FINANCIAL ANALYST. Merrill Lynch, Albany, GA (Summer 1997). Was the "right arm" of a financial analyst with this worldwide investment company; prepared documents designed to persuade potential clients to transact business with Merrill Lynch, and also processed and filed accounts of current customers.
- Gained insight into how selling and customer service occur within a brokerage firm.
- Scored very high on a mock test administered by my supervisor to test my knowledge of stock market issues and facts.
- Was commended for my hard work and financial aptitude, and was encouraged to seek employment with Merrill Lynch upon college graduation.

PERSONAL
Am skilled at remaining calm and courteous in all customer service situations.

Date

Exact Name of Person
Title or Position
Name of Company
Address (no., street)
Address (city, state, zip)

Economics

Dear Exact Name of Person: (or Dear Sir or Madam if answering a blind ad.)

Student resumes often have lengthy Education sections, since much of the experience and many of the honors thus far are related to the academic environment.

I would appreciate an opportunity to talk with you soon about how I could contribute to your organization through my education and knowledge in the area of economics.

In the process of completing my B.S. degree in Economics, I worked in a variety of jobs which permitted me to refine my communication and interpersonal skills. I enjoy helping others and you will notice that many of my summer and part-time jobs were in the social service and mental health field. I have learned the disciplines involved in teamwork, and I am eager to apply my hard-working nature within a professional team.

You will notice that I have been the recipient of numerous sports honors. Even in high school, I received the MVP award and was considered the star of the women's volleyball and basketball teams. In college, too, I earned numerous awards for athletic abilities and was named an All-American in two sports. I have learned much about people on the playing field and basketball court, and I am confident I can apply that knowledge for the benefit of my employer.

I can provide outstanding personal and professional references, and I would cheerfully relocate and travel extensively according to your needs.

I hope you will call or write me soon to suggest a time convenient for us to meet and discuss your current and future needs and how I might serve them. Thank you in advance for you time.

Sincerely yours,

Elizabeth Adams

ELIZABETH ADAMS

1110½ Hay Street, Fayetteville, NC 28305   •   preppub@aol.com   •   (910) 483-6611

OBJECTIVE   To offer my ability to manage time and human resources as well as my organizational and planning skills and attention to detail to an organization that can use a fast learner who excels in relating to people from diverse backgrounds, ages, and socioeconomic levels.

EDUCATION   Earned a **Bachelor's degree in Economics** from Hendrix College, Conway, AR, 2001; graduated **cum laude**.
- Was honored with a **Chancellor's Award of Merit** in recognition of my accomplishments in sports, academics, and family activities.
- Nominated by my peers, was elected **President of the Economics and Finance Club**; managed all funds for the Economics and Finance Club while also planning, implementing, and overseeing fundraising activities.
- Earned **numerous awards** for athletic abilities as a member of the university's basketball and volleyball teams.
- Was named to the **All-Conference Teams,** honored as **Most Valuable Player,** and an **All-American** in both sports.
- Participated in a work-study program in a university office where my responsibilities included typing tests and research papers while gaining strong computer skills.
- Was nominated **"Woman of the Year"** in sports.

EXPERIENCE   *Gained experience in positions where "people skills" and the ability to manage time and deal with problems professionally and calmly were of major importance while attending school full-time and working in demanding summer jobs to partially finance my education:*

YOUTH PROGRAM ASSISTANT. Workforce Temporary Agency, Conway, AR (summer, 2000). Worked as part of a team of professionals providing care for three mentally handicapped children while ensuring that daily care was provided according to policies.

MENTAL HEALTH TECHNICIAN. P.C. Contract Management Services, Conway, AR (summers, 1999 and 1998). Provided direct care to five mentally handicapped adults with an emphasis on implementing and carrying out behavior plans and behavior modification techniques.
- Taught self-help and independent living skills as well as maintaining documentation on each client's progress or lack of visible progress.
- Protected the well-being and legal rights of my clients.

HABILITATION TECHNICIAN. MSC of Arkansas and Procomm, Bitsburg, AR (summer, 1997). Provided direct care to profoundly mentally retarded clients; handled the expense accounts used in operating the group homes these clients lived in.
- Applied my knowledge of the legal rights of this class of clients and provided support for them so that their well being and legal rights were protected.
- Transported clients for and from activities such as recreational and social outings as well as medical and counseling appointments.

COMPUTERS   Windows operating system with software including WordPerfect, Lotus, and MS Word.

ATHLETIC   Graduated from Concordia Senior High School, Concordia, MI, 1997.
HONORS
- Was the "star" of both the women's basketball and volleyball teams.
- Won the MVP Award for the Concordia District schools, 1996.

PERSONAL   Am a highly self disciplined individual who always strives to give my greatest effort.

Date

Exact Name of Person
Title or Position
Name of Company
Address (no., street)
Address (city, state, zip)

Dear Exact Name of Person: (or Dear Sir or Madam if answering a blind ad.)

With the enclosed resume, I would like to make you aware of the considerable engineering knowledge and management potential which I could put to work for you.

While earning my degree in Engineering, I have had the opportunity to become familiar with numerous software programs. Before enrolling in Widener University, I excelled academically in high school while also holding numerous leadership positions.

I was recently honored by being selected for a prestigious work-study assignment which involves assisting a prominent engineering faculty member with research related to his consulting work. I can provide outstanding references from numerous college professors who will attest to my intellect and creative problem-solving approach.

I hope you will call or write me soon to suggest a time convenient for us to meet and discuss your current and future needs and how I might serve them. Thank you in advance for you time.

Sincerely yours,

Regina Davis

REGINA DAVIS

1110½ Hay Street, Fayetteville, NC 28305　•　preppub@aol.com　•　(910) 483-6611

OBJECTIVE

To offer a reputation as a bright, articulate, and intelligent quick learner to an organization that can benefit from my attention to detail as well as from my communication, time management, and interpersonal skills.

EDUCATION

Pursuing **B.S. in Engineering,** Widener University, Chester, PA; degree to be awarded 2001.
- Have completed specialized course work which has included:

calculus I, II, and III	statistics	graphic communications
FORTRAN	English	differential equations
physics	chemistry	psychology

- Was elected to membership in Phi Eta Sigma Freshman Honor Society.
- Maintaining 3.9 GPA.

Graduated from Chester Senior High School, Chester, PA, 1997.
- Participated as a volunteer for Special Olympics activities.
- Graduated from high school a year early and completed Advanced Placement course work in literature, U.S. history, European history, calculus, and physics as well as taking two years of computer applications courses.
- Was on the "Uppermost" yearbook staff.
- Played soccer three years.
- Was a cheerleader two years.
- Placed on the National Honor Society two years and on the National Junior Honor Society one year.
- Held membership in Future Business Leaders of America (FBLA) three years.

EXPERIENCE

FULL-TIME STUDENT. Widener University, Chester, PAC (1998-present). Attend college full time in pursuit of a Bachelor's degree in Engineering.
- While excelling academically, volunteer my time extensively with organizations including Habitat for Humanity and the local women's shelter.
- Became an active part of the presidential campaign of Al Gore.
- Have been selected for a prestigious work-study assignment which involves assisting a prominent engineering faculty member with research related to his consulting work

INSTRUCTOR/ADMINISTRATIVE ASSISTANT. Champion Cheer Gym, Chester, PA (1997-present). Handle a variety of general office and receptionist duties while also teaching cheerleading classes.
- On my own initiative, developed marketing materials and organized their distribution to prospective new members; this campaign resulted in a membership increase of 22%.

CASHIER. I-95 Amoco, Mallary, PA (1995-1997). Accepted cash and credit card payments from customers in this family business while attending high school.

PERSONAL

Am known as a hard worker with a high degree of initiative, drive, and self-motivation. Have a reputation for honesty and dependability. Excellent references on request.

Date

Rene Acosta
Principal
Central Middle School
1616 Ireland Drive
Port Huron, MI 48060

English and Media Journalism

A background in sales may not seem the best for teaching, but this young professional is aware of the shortage of teachers and has developed a strong desire to enter the teaching profession. She has been very active in college, and much of the Experience section on her resume showcases her leadership ability and involvements in organizations.

Dear Sir or Madam:

With the enclosed resume, I would like to initiate the process of formally applying for a lateral-entry teaching position in your school system.

You will see from my resume that I hold a BA degree in English and Media Journalism and was named to the Dean's List for academic achievements. In a part-time job as a reporter with the *Times Herald*, I am utilizing my strong writing and editing skills but I feel I would be best suited to a situation in which I could teach skills and concepts in English, language arts, and journalism to middle school or high school students. As a means of partially financing my college education, I tutored students throughout my college career. I am a seasoned public speaker and offer a proven ability to enthusiastically and articulately present academic material in well developed lesson plans.

Since my professional goal is now to embark upon public school teaching as a career, I would intend to pursue coursework which would lead to formal teaching certification.

As a high school student, I was known as one of the area's outstanding young leaders and was elected president of the Port Huron Northern High School student body. I was also active in student government when I went to college. I enjoy working with youth, and you will see from my resume that I have volunteered my time as a young adult to Big Sister programs, Special Olympics planning committees, and teen organizations. I am confident that I could become a strong positive role model for youth, and I am positive I could help youth grow in academic excellence, social maturity, professional skills, and emotional well being.

Please consider me for any lateral-teaching position you may have in the English, language arts, journalism, or social studies area, and I would be very happy to learn what would be the next step for me to take in formally pursuing a teaching position for the next calendar year.

Sincerely yours,

Sybil Dawes

SYBIL DAWES

1110½ Hay Street, Fayetteville, NC 28305 • preppub@aol.com • (910) 483-6611

OBJECTIVE   To contribute to an organization through my strong communication skills as well as through my creativity, intelligence, and interpersonal relations skills.

EDUCATION   Earned a **Bachelor of Arts (B.A.) degree in English and Media Journalism,** Austin College, Sherman, TX, 2000.
- Excelled in specialized course work such as:

    Introduction to Public Relations   Editing and Writing

    Writing for Radio and Television   Article and Feature Writing
- Was named to the Dean's List for my academic achievements.

EXPERIENCE   **SALES ASSOCIATE.** Belk Leggett, Sherman, TX (1998-2000). In this part-time job used to finance my college education, gained a strong base of experience in retail sales and support activities for this major regional department store while also taking care of stocking and customer service.
- Selected to attend regular marketing department seminars, added practical knowledge of marketing techniques to expand on what I had learned in college.
- Applied my enthusiastic and energetic personality while contributing to the creation of a good working atmosphere among my colleagues as well as with the public.
- In a simultaneous part-time job as a **REPORTER** with the *Times Herald,* am refining my writing and editing skills.

Refined my time management skills attending college full time while participating in numerous community service and volunteer activities:

COMMITTEE MEMBER. Delta Sigma Theta Sorority, Inc., Sherman, TX (1999-present). Participate in activities designed to promote economic, educational, and political growth as well as international awareness and physical/mental health among community members.
- Played a key role in planning, organizing, and carrying out the first Special Olympics Games hosted by the university.

"BIG SISTER" PROGRAM VOLUNTEER. Project LIFE, Powell Elementary School, Sherman, TX (1997-99). Provided an 11-year-old girl with one-on-one attention and a positive role model by helping her learn better study habits and build confidence and self-esteem.

STUDENT GOVERNMENT MEMBER. Student Government Association, Austin College, Sherman, TX (1997-00). Represented the freshman class during activities which included organizing fund raising events, social events, and class trips while working as a team player within the student government association.
- Learned how to conduct contract negotiations following university policy.
- Was instrumental in planning the first freshman class trip in eight years.

Highlights of other experience: Earned several awards for community involvement and leadership in high school activities: received a $1,000 academic scholarship along with recognition by such groups as the Kiwanis Club and Parks and Recreation Department.
- Was Student Body President at Port Huron Northern High School, Port Huron, MI.

COMPUTERS   Am experienced in using MS Word for word processing applications.

PERSONAL   Am a creative individual with a positive attitude. Offer a high level of energy and enthusiasm. Believe I have a gift for using words to create beauty and positive images.

Date

Exact Name of Person
Exact Title
Exact Name of Company
Address
City, State, Zip

English Degree with Goal of Teaching

Don't worry about how a job like "driver" will look on your resume. Prospective employers know that it is honest work, and they admire an individual who had to work to put herself through school.

Dear Exact Name of Person: (or Dear Sir or Madam if answering a blind ad):

With the enclosed resume, I would like to introduce you to my educational background and versatile experience as well as to express my interest in receiving consideration for a teaching position in your school system.

As you will see from my resume, I received my B.A. in English from Alverno College in 2001. While attending college, I continued to refine my time management and organizational skills while also working and holding volunteer positions. Presently polishing my communication skills in a fast-paced food service environment, I have become known for my ability to deal with customers and co-workers while completing twice the normal number of deliveries in a shift.

One of my proudest accomplishments was a tutoring project involving a fourth grade student. The student had been diagnosed with Attention Deficit Disorder (ADD) and was struggling to maintain a D average in school. I provided him with the guidance and motivation which allowed him to increase two full letter grades to a B average. In addition to preparing lesson plans, I also oversaw him as he completed assigned schoolwork and helped him prepare for tests to be taken in his regular classroom.

While in college, I also served as a radio news reader providing services for the blind. I read selected news articles and other materials to the listening audience and was known for my ability to speak clearly and plainly so that listeners could understand what was being read on the air. I am confident that through my reputation as an articulate and intelligent young professional, I have refined the skills and knowledge which would allow me to be effective in the classroom. With a degree in English and my strong interest in reading literature, history, and philosophy, I believe I would be most effective as an English teacher at the secondary school level.

If you can use an adaptable young professional who can handle pressure and deadlines and who is known for high levels of drive and initiative, I hope you will welcome my call soon when I try to arrange a brief meeting to discuss your goals and how my background might serve your needs. I can provide outstanding references at the appropriate time.

Sincerely,

Robyn Smith

ROBYN SMITH

1110½ Hay Street, Fayetteville, NC 28305 • preppub@aol.com • (910) 483-6611

OBJECTIVE

To contribute to a school system that can use an articulate and mature young professional who can offer a background of experience in positions requiring keen analytical skills, planning and organizational abilities, and a talent for instructing and educating others.

EDUCATION

Bachelor of Arts (B.A.) degree in English, Alverno College, Milwaukee, WI, 2001.
- Spent two summers abroad studying Literature.

COMPUTER KNOWLEDGE

Offer extensive knowledge of automated systems using Windows, Word, WordPerfect, and Lotus 1-2-3 using Macintosh and IBM-compatible PCs as well as proprietary systems developed for the food service industry.

EXPERIENCE

Developed excellent time management skills while attending college, volunteering, and working to help finance my education in jobs which have included the following:
CUSTOMER SERVICE SPECIALIST and **DRIVER.** Domino's Pizza, Milwaukee, WI (1998-present). Gained and am refining a variety of skills in dealing with the public and co-workers while becoming known for my ability to prioritize tasks and deal with pressure and deadlines in a fast-paced environment.
- Completed twice the normal number of deliveries for the same time period through well-refined time management skills.
- Am known for my ability to deal with customers in a helpful and pleasant manner while taking phone orders accurately on a multiline phone system.
- Have become skilled in using computers and in handling large amounts of cash.

PRIVATE TUTOR. Milwaukee, WI (1998). Took a fourth grade student who had been making Ds in all school subjects and, through intense personal attention to his abilities and limitations, helped bring his grades up two full letter grades to a B average.
- Excelled in motivating a young child diagnosed with ADD (Attention Deficit Disorder) and in finding the methods for helping him learn how to focus and study so that his performance was greatly improved.
- Emphasized the improvement of skills in basic reading and arithmetic.
- Prepared lesson plans and assigned additional tasks designed to improve educational abilities as well as coping skills and ways to overcome his learning disabilities.

RADIO ON-AIR READER. S.E.N.C. Radio Reading Service, Alverno College, Milwaukee, WI (1996-98). Provided radio reading services for the blind as a volunteer reading selected news articles and other materials on the air.
- Was known for my ability to speak clearly and plainly so that radio listeners could understand the information which was being given to them on the air.
- Gained a feeling of pride in my skills and in my ability to be of service to the community.

SALES AND CUSTOMER SERVICE REPRESENTATIVE. Boulevard Pawn Shop, Milwaukee, WI (1995-96). Was cited for my time management and organizational skills while handling multiple duties such as assisting customers with their purchases, completing sales, maintaining stock, and providing security for large amounts of cash.

Highlights of earlier experience: Became recognized as a mature and skilled young professional while serving in the U.S. Navy.

PERSONAL

Feel that among my greatest strengths are my intelligence and adaptive reasoning skills.

Exact Name of Person
Title or Position
Name of Company
Address (no., street)
Address (city, state, zip)

Dear Exact Name of Person: (or Dear Sir or Madam if answering a blind ad.)

English Degree with Concentrations in French and Communications

Many students have held jobs as a waitress, and employers often value restaurant industry experience. They know it helps you refine your customer service and sales skills. Notice she has given herself job titles on the resume which include "fundraiser assistant."

I would enjoy an opportunity to talk with you soon about how my education, public relations and writing experience, and my sincere love of a professional challenge could benefit your organization.

Dedication, establishing a rapport, and attention to detail are, I believe, the keys to success when it comes to working in a customer-oriented industry. I have sought out—and excelled at—jobs requiring excellent interpersonal skills, earning a reputation as someone who quickly and courteously resolves tough customer service problems.

My work experience, described more fully in my resume, shows my initiative and dedication to hard work, as well as my willingness to go beyond the call of duty when required. My employers have commended my loyalty, commitment, and positive attitude.

Academically, I excelled while attending Ball State University in Muncie, IN. Not only did I graduate *cum laude,* but I passed my English honors thesis with flying colors, made Dean's List every semester, and was a member of the Gamma Beta Phi academic honor society. I am proficient in French and have studied and traveled extensively in France.

I hope you will call or write me soon to suggest a time convenient for us to meet and discuss your current and future needs and how I might serve them.

Sincerely,

Pamela Anderson

Alternate last paragraph:
I hope you will welcome my call soon to arrange a brief meeting at your convenience to discuss your current and future needs and how I might serve them. Thank you in advance for your time.

PAMELA ANDERSON

1110½ Hay Street, Fayetteville, NC 28305   •   preppub@aol.com   •   (910) 483-6611

OBJECTIVE

To benefit an organization in need of an enthusiastic, young professional knowledgeable and experienced in verbal and written communication, customer service, and travel, who also possesses a knack for creativity, problem-solving, and decision-making abilities.

EDUCATION

Bachelor of Arts degree in English, with concentrations in French and Communications, Ball State University, Muncie, IN, 2000.
- Graduated **cum laude** with a 3.51 GPA.
- Earned Dean's List honors every semester.
- Member of Gamma Beta Phi academic honor society.
- Received outstanding marks on both the written and oral examinations of my Senior Honor's English thesis.
- Related coursework included advanced classes in French Literature, customs and culture, and conversation.

Graduated from Muncie Academy, Muncie, IN, 1996.
Attended Anniston Academy preparatory school, Muncie, IN, 1993-95.

LANGUAGE

Proficient in French.

EXPERIENCE

Gained valuable customer-service and time-management experience working in a variety of jobs while simultaneously attending college full-time:
WAITRESS. Speckled Trout Restaurant, Muncie, IN (1997-00). Refined my ability for easily establishing a rapport with people from diverse cultural and socioeconomic backgrounds while acting as a server in this popular restaurant.
- Earned a reputation for resolving thorny customer-service problems in a courteous, timely manner while guaranteeing customers had a pleasant dining experience.
- Trained and supervised new employees.

SECRETARY. International Development and Domestic Company, Muncie, IN (Summer 1997). Polished my understanding of the value of teamwork answering phones and screening calls, while also performing typing, data entry, filing, and other general office functions.

FUNDRAISER ASSISTANT. Ball State University, Muncie, IN (1997). Learned the importance of never quitting as well as how to graciously accept "rejection" while soliciting alumni by telephone for donations to alumni development programs.

Gained exposure to the "real world" holding customer-oriented administrative and journalism positions while in high school:
ADMINISTRATIVE ASSISTANT. Deerfield Company, Muncie, IN (Summer 1995). Provided customer service, data entry, and general clerical functions while working for this area insurance company.

STAFF WRITER. *The Muncie Times,* Muncie, IN (1994). Excelled in an internship with this 150,000-circulation paper, and was hired for a summer reporting position after impressing my editors with my excellent writing ability.
- Gained valuable research and interviewing experience compiling and writing local interest and business features.

PERSONAL

Am a versatile professional who enjoys people. Can handle pressure and react logically to emergencies. Adapt easily to new situations. Enjoy learning new skills. Willing to relocate.

Exact Name of Person
Title or Position
Name of Company
Address (no., street)
Address (city, state, zip)

English Degree

This is an extremely versatile cover letter and resume, because Ms. Growald plans on approaching numerous employers in various fields. She has no idea what she wants to do, but she plans on seeking work that is meaningful and challenging.

Dear Exact Name of Person: (or Dear Sir or Madam if answering a blind ad.)

With the enclosed resume, I would like to make you aware of the considerable communication skills which I could put to work for you. As you will see, I hold a degree in English and offer highly refined verbal and written skills.

While earning my degree, I became a popular campus leader and served the student population in various roles. I was elected Treasurer of the university's Residence Hall Association, and I was also elected President of my residence hall. I was often complimented on my ability to interpret the views of others and present them in tactful and articulate ways. I am certain my strong communication skills could be valuable to an employer as well.

I pride myself on my attention to detail in all matters, and in a part-time job which I held to finance my college education, I provided small businesses with inventory services which helped them improve their efficiency and accountability. I was commended for achieving one of the lowest margins of errors ever produced in the company. I offer a strong bottom-line orientation.

If you can use an astute young professional with excellent work habits and a congenial attitude, I hope you will call or write me soon to suggest a time convenient for us to meet and discuss your current and future needs and how I might serve them.

Sincerely,

Sonya Growald

Alternate last paragraph:
I hope you will welcome my call soon to arrange a brief meeting at your convenience to discuss your current and future needs and how I might serve them. Thank you in advance for your time.

SONYA GROWALD

1110½ Hay Street, Fayetteville, NC 28305 • preppub@aol.com • (910) 483-6611

OBJECTIVE
To offer my newly minted degree, reputation for creativity, and strong interest in writing, editing, and proofreading to an organization in need of a hard-charging young professional known for the ability to motivate and guide others to achieve outstanding results.

EDUCATION
B.A., English, Bradley University, Peoria, IL, December 2000.
- Excelled in a degree program which included specialized course work such as:

business writing	creative writing	editing
proofreading	technical writing	copy writing

- Played a leadership role in campus residence hall activities and developed programs which led to improvements in the quality of life for dormitory residents.

SPECIAL SKILLS
Am familiar with computer hardware and proficient with software programs including Word and WordPerfect.
- Type between 50 and 60 WPM.
- Offer experience with office equipment such as 10-key adding machines and copiers.

EXPERIENCE
INVENTORY ANALYST. AccuCount Inventory Service, Peoria, IL (1999-present). In a part-time job which I held in order to partially finance my college education, applied my attention to detail and well organized nature while providing retail businesses with inventory services; through my meticulous work habits, maintained a margin of error of less than one percent.
- Was increasingly relied upon to consult with clients who used my employer's services.
- Have learned to be tolerant of others and work as a team member in a group with widely diverse backgrounds and educational levels.

HOME HEALTH AIDE. Medical Personnel Pool, Marysville, IL (1998). Offered companionship to the elderly and displayed maturity while taking full responsibility for the care of a person who was physically unable to be independent: provided 24-hour care five days a week by preparing meals and administering medications as well as transporting her to doctor's appointments and giving assistance during physical therapy.

Gained experience in student leadership at Bradley University, Peoria, IL:
TREASURER. Bradley University Residence Hall Association (1999). Established budget preparation guidelines which are still used: the association had allowed itself to break budgets and operate with deficits in the past.
- Received an outstanding service award in recognition of my creativity and organizational skills used to establish fund raising activities which compensated for budget problems and got the association out of debt.
- Provided 15 residence halls with guidance on fund raising and budget compliance.

RESIDENCE HALL PRESIDENT. James Hall (1997-98). Motivated the residents of my hall and encouraged them to show more school spirit and pride in their residence facility so that it became a better place to live and a leader in intercampus competitions.
- Was honored for giving one of the top 10 presentations at a state-wide conference: gave a program entitled "Let Your Fingers Do the Talking" which dealt with tolerance for the hearing impaired and the use of sign language.
- Planned successful programs for homecoming and parents' weekends while coordinating with representatives of the Boys and Girls Clubs for special activities.

PERSONAL
Offer a reputation for determination, persistence, and attention to detail. Would relocate.

Date

Exact Name of Person
Title or Position
Name of Company
Address (number and street)
Address (city, state, and zip)

English Degree with Minor in French and Writing

This English major, unlike the English major on the previous page, is quite specifically oriented toward advertising agencies. She emphasizes her strong written and oral communication skills as well as her natural creativity which she assumes will be valued in the environment of art agencies.

Dear Exact Name of Person: (or Sir or Madam if answering a blind ad.)

With the enclosed resume, I would like to initiate the process of being considered for employment within your organization.

As you will see from my resume, I will receive on May 10 a Bachelor of Arts degree in English with a minor in French and Writing, and I have excelled academically. I have worked as a Staff Writer for my college newspaper, and I have become skilled at composing copy that requires little editing and in meeting tight deadlines. I have also tutored students in both English and French.

In an internship as an Advertising Copywriter with a respected and award-winning advertising agency, I created copy for the agency's web page, wrote a 12-month newsletter aimed at children, and compiled a portfolio of sample ads which was received quite favorably by my supervisor.

In a summer job with a magazine, I worked in the distribution and circulation part of the business and became a valuable part of the magazine's staff within a short period of time.

Although I have limited hands-on experience simply because I am 21 years old, I can assure you that I am an accomplished writer. I have been published in *The National Book of Poetry*. My life experiences have been quite diverse as I have traveled extensively worldwide including in Europe and Australia as well as Central and South America.

I can provide outstanding personal and professional references at the appropriate time, and I can assure you that you would find me to be a hard-working, congenial individual who prides myself on always doing my best. If you can use a hard worker who could become a valuable part of your organization through my creativity and language skills, I hope you will contact me to suggest a time when I can make myself available for a personal interview at your convenience. Thank you in advance for your time.

Sincerely,

Jill Louis

JILL LOUIS

1110½ Hay Street, Fayetteville, NC 28305 • preppub@aol.com • (910) 483-6611

OBJECTIVE	To offer my exceptionally strong writing skills and creativity to an organization that can use a highly motivated self starter with outstanding analytical and research abilities.
LANGUAGES	Fluent in French with working knowledge of Spanish.
PUBLICATIONS	Have been published in *The National Book of Poetry.*
EDUCATION	**Bachelor of Arts degree in English** with a minor in French and Writing, Cornell University, Ithaca, NY; May 10, 2000.

- Excelled academically; achieved 3.4 GPA and named to President's and Dean's List.
- Served as Treasurer of Sigma Tau Delta, the International English Honors Society.
- Courses included computer design/layout, creative writing of fiction, writing for mass media, speech communications, advanced expository writing, and writing for magazines.

Previously completed undergraduate courses at Scoggins College, Anglebrook, FL.
- Elected **President** of the Christian Science organization on campus.

Graduated from Principia Upper School (high school), Ithaca, NY, 1994.
- Elected **Senior Class Vice President.**
- Was named to Who's Who Among American High School Students.
- Member, Varsity Tennis Team; served in honorary role as Senior Advisor.

EXPERIENCE	**ADVERTISING COPYWRITER.** Cameron Advertising and Associates, Ithaca, NY (Jan 1999-present). In an internship while completing my college degree, am excelling as a copywriter in the city's most prominent and award-winning advertising agency.

- Created copy for the agency's web page.
- Developed advertising for medical organizations and handled liaison with clients.
- Compiled a portfolio of sample ads which received favorable reviews from superiors.
- Became skilled in utilizing the Adobe and Quark Xpress computer programs.
- Have written a 12-month newsletter aimed at children.

STAFF WRITER. *Cornell Today,* Cornell University, Ithaca, NY (1998-present). For my university's weekly newspaper, am a regular contributor of stories pertaining to campus life and student concerns.
- Became skilled in meeting deadlines and composing copy that required little editing.

TUTOR. Cornell University, Ithaca, NY (1998-present). Am a tutor for English and French.

MAGAZINE INTERN. Florida Retirement Lifestyles, Anglebrook, FL (summer 1998). Became knowledgeable of magazine circulation and distribution working in this summer job.
- Utilized a computer to input data for mailings and the magazine's customer base.

RECEPTIONIST. Principia Upper School, Ithaca, NY (1996). In my senior year of high school, was commended for my poise and public relations skills while answering phones and handling people in a gracious manner.

COMPUTERS	Highly proficient with numerous popular software programs; offer expertise in utilizing Windows and Word; am knowledgeable of Adobe PageMaker and Quark Xpress.
PERSONAL	Have traveled extensively worldwide including in Europe and Australia.

Exact Name of Person
Exact Title
Exact Name of Company
Address
City, State, Zip

Dear Exact Name of Person (or Dear Sir or Madam if answering a blind ad):

With the enclosed resume, I would like to offer my education and experience to an organization that can use an articulate, self-motivated young professional with a newly minted degree and exceptional communication, time management, and organizational skills. I posses a strong work ethic and a versatile background of work experience and community service.

As you will see, I have just graduated Summa Cum Laude with a Bachelor of Science in Family & Child Development from the University of Central Oklahoma. Throughout my collegiate career, I maintained a near-perfect 3.9 GPA while working in several jobs simultaneously and volunteering my time to local organizations.

Most recently, I served as a Volunteer for Let's Start Talking, a six-week program in which I traveled to St. Petersburg, Russia with a group of missionaries and taught conversational English to classes of up to 20 students. This provided me with an invaluable opportunity to interact and communicate with people from other cultures while honing my communication skills and learning to adapt to change in the process of living and working in this busy Russian city. Previously as a Practicum Site Volunteer at the Renaissance Women's Center, I performed various administrative tasks and taught classes to prepare children and parents for the birth of a baby.

As a Waitress for Café 501, I provided the highest possible levels of customer service in a busy restaurant environment. I excelled in this position while also providing in-home care for three children, ages 3 months to 7 years as a Nanny and attending college full-time. I feel that my education, exceptional time management skills and strong work ethic would be a valuable addition to your organization.

If you can use an articulate, self-motivated young professional with strong personal initiative, I would appreciate your contacting me to suggest a time when we might to discuss your needs. I can assure you in advance that I have an excellent reputation and would quickly become a valuable asset to your organization.

Sincerely,

Anna Tobias

ANNA TOBIAS

1110½ Hay Street, Fayetteville, NC 28305 • preppub@aol.com • (910) 483-6611

OBJECTIVE   To benefit an organization that can use an articulate, self-motivated young professional with exceptional communication and time management skills, a newly-minted degree, and a strong work ethic.

EDUCATION   Graduated **Summa Cum Laude** with a **Bachelor of Science** degree in Family & Child Development from the University of Central Oklahoma, Edmond, OK, 2000.
- Maintained a 3.9 GPA while working several jobs simultaneously and donating my time to various volunteer activities.

Earned numerous scholarships and awards for academic excellence, including:

Minority Academic Scholarship   President's Honor Roll
Native American Honor Roll   Mortar Board Honor Society
Fee Waiver Scholarship   President's Partner's Scholastic Achievement Award

Received certifications in **CPR** and **First Aid** from the University of Central Oklahoma, Edmond, OK, 1998.
Childbirth Educator's Workshop, Renaissance Women's Center, Edmond, OK, 1997.

AFFILIATIONS   *In addition to other volunteer work, have been an active member of the following professional organizations:*
- Elected **President** of the Early Childhood Student Association, 1999-2000.
- Member, Student Association for the Education of Young Children, 1998-1999.
- Member, Oklahoma Early Childhood Student Association, 1997-1998.
- Member, Southern Early Childhood Student Association, 1997-1998.

EXPERIENCE   **VOLUNTEER.** Let's Start Talking, St. Petersburg, Russia (Summer, 1999). Taught conversational English to classes of more than 20 students while living abroad during this six-week volunteer program

VOLUNTEER (PRACTICUM). Renaissance Women's Center, Edmond, OK (1997-1998). Performed various administrative tasks and taught classes to prepare parents and their children for the birth of a new baby.
- Prepared curriculum and presented materials to classes of up to 20 people, including classes to assist children in coping with the birth of a sibling.
- Scheduled classes, assembled information packets, and performed various clerical and secretarial duties; operated a multi-line phone system and filed medical records.

NANNY. Edmond, OK (1996-1998). Provided daytime child care on a part-time basis while maintaining a 3.9 GPA, working a second job nights and weekends, and doing volunteer work at the Renaissance Women's Center.
- Planned and implemented educational and recreational activities for three children, ages 3 months to 7 years, including arts & crafts, reading, and games.
- Prepared nutritious meals for the children and transported them to and from various scheduled activities outside the home.

Other experience: Worked as a **Head Waitress** at Café 501.

PERSONAL   Outstanding personal and professional references are available upon request.

Date

Exact Name of Person
Exact Title
Exact Name of Company
Address
City, State, Zip

Finance

Dear Exact Name of Person (or Dear Sir or Madam if answering a blind ad):

Notice in the
Education section how
this young
professional shows off
a team project which
has helped him refine
his analytical,
problem-solving, and
strategic thinking
skills.

With the enclosed resume, I would like to make you aware of the knowledge related to finance which I could put to work for you.

While completing my B.S. degree in Finance, I played a key role as a member of a team which analyzed the Harley-Davidson company and made strategic and operational recommendations for the company and industry as a whole. I have earned a reputation as an insightful analyst and problem-solver and I am certain I could make a significant contribution to the bottom line of a company that can use an astute young financier.

In jobs which I held to finance my college degree, I worked in several roles within Macy's Department Store, where I excelled in handling responsibilities as a Loss Prevention Detective, Supervisor, and handler of cash accounting. Although Macy's has strongly encouraged me to remain with the corporation after college graduation and seek internal promotions, I have decided to explore other opportunities.

I can assure you in advance that I have an excellent reputation and would quickly become a valuable asset to your organization. Please contact me if my considerable abilities interest you, and I will gladly make myself available for a personal interview at your convenience.

Sincerely,

David Yuen

DAVID YUEN

1110½ Hay Street, Fayetteville, NC 28305 • preppub@aol.com • (910) 483-6611

OBJECTIVE   To offer my education in finance and analytical, sales, and communication skills to an organization that can benefit from my strong interest in financial planning and banking as well as my personal reputation for integrity, high moral standards, and a strong work ethic.

EDUCATION   Completing a **Bachelor's degree in Finance,** The University of Kentucky, Lexington, KY; degree expected spring 2001.
- Placed on the university's Dean's List in recognition of my academic accomplishments.
- Received an "A" on an intensive class project: performed a company analysis on Harley-Davidson including keeping records, analyzing price and volume data as well as technical data, gathering and analyzing information about the industry, and making determinations on the economic outlook for the company and industry.
- Completed specialized course work such as Finance 330 (principles of finance, stock valuation, options, etc.) and Finance 331 (real estate investing).

EXPERIENCE   *Learned to manage time wisely while maintaining at least a 3.4 GPA in my college career and excelling in demanding part-time jobs including this track record of accomplishments with Macy's Department Store, Lexington, KY:*
LOSS PREVENTION DETECTIVE. (1998-present). In only 18 months with the company, have progressed to the highest level available to a part-time employee based on my maturity, willingness to take on hard work, and communication skills.
- Increased apprehensions of shoplifters 50%, thereby greatly reducing losses from theft.
- Displayed the ability to remain calm and in control and act as an arbitrator under intense conditions.
- Provided security for the store premises, researched discrepancies in cash accounts, and generated surveillance programs.
- Learned the importance of confidentiality while guarding privileged information.

FRONT-LINE SUPERVISOR. (1998). Supervised approximately 50 employees in order to ensure that customers received the highest quality of service and satisfaction.
- Opened cash drawers and initiated changeovers while register contents were transferred as well as changing large denominations of bills for smaller ones as needed.
- Approved refunds, lay-a-ways, and purchases by associates.
- Conducted new employee orientation which included such areas as cash handling procedures, customer service techniques, and company policy.
- Was honored as **"Associate of the Quarter"** by management and other associates.

CASH OFFICE ASSOCIATE. (1997). Was given the opportunity to apply my knowledge gained in college in a real-life situation while handling day-to-day retail store office activities.

CASHIER. (1996). Became skilled in handling refunds and sales accurately and quickly while becoming responsible for large amounts of cash transactions.
- Was known for my ability to greet and assist customers as well as for my keen eye for possible cases of switching tickets and theft by customers.

TRAINING   Completed several seminars and training programs including a Lotus 1-2-3 workshop and loss prevention training (detecting losses, detaining suspects, and making reports).

PERSONAL   Keep up with stock market and read *"The Wall Street Journal"* regularly. Familiar with Windows, WordPerfect, and the Internet. Graduated from high school with honors.

Date

Exact Name of Person
Exact Title
Exact Name of Company
Address
City, State, Zip

Finance

Dear Exact Name of Person: (or Dear Sir or Madam if answering a blind ad):

This student is starting
early in her job search
by sending out
resumes several
months in advance of
college graduation.
Notice how the cover
letter communicates
that she is involved in
a team effort to
develop a business
plan for a new
business. Whether the
experience is paid or
nonpaid, employers
infer that you gain
skills from team
projects or
independent work
activities.

With the enclosed resume, I would like to make you aware of my interest in seeking employment opportunities with your company and to acquaint you with my background as an articulate, well-educated, and mature young professional.

As you will see from my resume, I will be graduating from the University of Toledo in December 2001 and will receive a B.S. in Finance. Recognized on the university's Dean's List for my academic accomplishments, I have excelled in specialized course work which has included marketing, financial, personnel, and accounting management. Additional classes have covered the areas of international business, entrepreneurial activities, Management Information Systems, and managerial negotiations.

This semester I am involved in a team effort to develop a business plan, including a complete financial analysis and financial projections as well as marketing plans, for a new business. Working together, we are developing plans and standards for a successful entrepreneurial effort.

Presently refining sales and customer service skills in a part-time job in retail sales, I have become effective at managing my time productively while attending college full time. While handling sales and financial transactions, I excel at providing courteous and helpful assistance to customers. In an earlier job, I became experienced in dealing with the public with patience and courtesy while operating photographic equipment, handling cash transactions, and taking inventories of supplies and equipment. I was rehired each year for this seasonal job on the basis of my maturity and "people skills."

If you can use a dependable, mature, and reliable young professional with a reputation as a good listener who enjoys helping others, I hope you will welcome my call soon when I try to arrange a brief meeting to discuss your goals and how my background might serve your needs. I can provide outstanding references at the appropriate time.

Sincerely,

Ming Kao

MING KAO

1110½ Hay Street, Fayetteville, NC 28305 • preppub@aol.com • (910) 483-6611

OBJECTIVE
To benefit an organization that can use an articulate, resourceful, and reliable young professional who offers a proven ability to deal effectively with people in team settings and business situations while also demonstrating initiative when working independently.

EDUCATION
B.A. in Finance, University of Toledo, Toledo, OH; December 2001.
- During fall semester 2000, am developing a Business Plan for my entrepreneurship course as part of a team; our project is to start a drive-through coffee shop and develop standards which could be copied by small business owners; the plan includes a complete financial analysis and financial projections.
- Have placed on the university Dean's List twice with a GPA above 3.5.
- Transferred from Toledo State University after changing my major.

Graduated from Toledo High School, Toledo, OH, December 1997.
- As a journalist for *The Bulldog* newspaper, produced copy for one of the state's largest high schools; was a sports reporter.
- Placed on the Honor Roll and was a member of the National Honor Society.
- Was a member of Tri Chi service society, the Spanish Club, and basketball team.

COMPUTERS
Working knowledge of Word, Excel, and Access.

LANGUAGES
Basic working knowledge of Spanish.

EXPERIENCE
SALES REPRESENTATIVE & CASHIER. The Shoe Department, Toledo, OH (1999-present). Am refining time management and customer service skills working approximately 26 hours a week for this chain store where my main responsibilities are to operate the automated cash register system, stock shoes and accessories, and assist customers in finding the correct fit and style.
- As a business major, have been applying my knowledge to make suggestions about changes which would allow the store to operate more efficiently and which are being considered for implementation by management.
- Upon college graduation, have been encouraged to consider the company's management training program but have decided to pursue other options.
- Am gaining valuable sales experience as well as an opportunity to make practical applications of what has been learned in the college classroom.

PHOTOGRAPHER and **CASHIER.** Bluebird Photography Studio, Cleveland, OH (seasonal work and summers). While still in high school, worked in a seasonal job taking children's portraits operating a stationary camera.
- Impressed the owners with my maturity and pride in the quality of my work and was rehired each year.
- Collected payments and operated a cash register.
- Took inventories of photographic and office supplies.

PERSONAL
Attend Sylvester Memorial Baptist Church; Youth Choir member. Am highly conscious of environmental issues. Offer a reputation as a good listener who enjoys helping others. Excellent personal and professional references are available upon request.

Exact Name of Person
Title or Position
Name of Company
Address (no., street)
Address (city, state, zip)

Fine Arts in Photography

Dear Exact Name of Person: (or Dear Sir or Madam if answering a blind ad.)

What can a nice girl with a Fine Arts degree in Photography do? The answer is, anything she puts her mind to! This talented and versatile student has worked hard to acquire skills in sales and program management, so she is making a multifaceted approach toward employers in the profit-making world as well as the arts and nonprofit community.

I would appreciate an opportunity to talk with you soon about how I could contribute to your organization through my specialized background in and enthusiasm for art education as well as my strong public relations and communication skills.

As you will see from my enclosed resume, I earned my B.F.A. (Bachelor of Fine Arts) degree from the Rochester Institute of Technology, Rochester, NY, with a concentration in photography and extensive coursework in gallery management. I am a highly competent and creative photographer. While earning my college degree, I excelled in jobs which helped me acquire experience in sales and operations management, and in one position I played a key role in organizing and implementing an arts education program which is considered a "model" for other communities.

Among my major personal strengths are my enthusiasm, creativity in both practical problem solving and in the artistic sense, as well as my ability to communicate verbally and in writing with people of all ages, social backgrounds, educational levels, and cultures or ethnic groups.

I hope you will welcome my call soon to arrange a brief meeting at your convenience to discuss your current and future needs and how I might serve them. I can provide outstanding personal and professional references which will attest to my reputation as a highly motivated self starter with boundless energy and enthusiasm. Thank you in advance for your time.

Sincerely yours,

Zelda Wilburn

Alternate last paragraph:
I hope you will call or write me soon to suggest a time convenient for us to meet and discuss your current and future needs and how I might serve them. Thank you in advance for your time.

ZELDA WILBURN

1110½ Hay Street, Fayetteville, NC 28305 • preppub@aol.com • (910) 483-6611

OBJECTIVE

To offer my reputation as a dynamic and creative young professional to an organization that can benefit from my strong interest in promoting the arts throughout the community, my education in fine arts with an emphasis on photography, and my problem-solving skills.

EDUCATION

Bachelor of Fine Arts (B.F.A.) degree in Photography, Rochester Institute of Technology (RIT), Rochester, NY, 2000.
- Excelled in specialized course work including the following:

fine art photography	applied photography	photomedia survey
contemporary art	gallery management	history of photography

SKILLS

Cameras: 35 mm, Bronica medium format, and 4 X 5 Calumet and Cambo
Other equipment: B & W enlargers and Bessler color enlargers; Broncolor, White Lightning, and Lowell Tungston lighting equipment; Copal ML2000, Saunders, and Omega enlargers; Copal MSL printer; Copal CFP6550 processor

EXPERIENCE

Have earned a reputation as a very creative thinker, fast learner, and skilled communicator in often-simultaneous jobs, internships, and volunteer positions requiring time management skills and dedication to reaching personal and professional goals.
PHOTO LAB TECHNICIAN. Photo Center, Rochester, NY (1998-present). Built on my strong educational background in photography and gained practical experience in the technical aspects of commercial photography as well as the day-to-day business side.
- Recognized as a mature and dependable individual, was selected to relieve the manager of certain daily responsibilities such as opening and closing the store.
- Assisted in activities ranging from processing film, to copying film and printing enlargements, to running the cash register, to customer service.

ART EDUCATION PROGRAM VOLUNTEER. The Rochester Museum of Art, Rochester, NY (1998-present). Assist in a project partially sponsored by the governor's early childhood initiative Smart Start: 52 trunks will be filled with resource materials, artifacts, and literature and used as aids for teachers and parents.

COMMUNITY ARTS PROGRAM INTERN. Art in Action for Kids, Rochester, NY (Summer, 1997). Cited by the director for "quickly grasping the complexities" of an arts in education program, contributed ideas which helped expand the program and make it a success while learning how non-profit organizations are structured.
- Was exposed to all aspects of this program which links more than 130 performing, visual, and literary artists with schools and which presented more than 3,300 workshops, performances, and artists in residence programs in 250 schools.
- Distributed press kits and supplementary materials to schools and other organizations.
- Used my photography skills to document various Young Audiences events.
- Volunteered as a **Gallery Assistant** for a visual studies workshop: gained experience in grant writing, preparing press releases, and assisting in curating exhibitions.

PHOTOGRAPHIC EQUIPMENT CLERK. RIT School of Printing, Art, and Sciences, Rochester, NY (Summer, 1996). Increased my knowledge of the technical aspects of photography while issuing equipment to students, providing technical information, monitoring darkrooms.

PERSONAL

Feel very strongly that one of my purposes in life is to expose the joy of art and creativity to as much of the community as possible. Am very empathetic and able to communicate.

Date

Exact Name of Person
Exact Title
Exact Name of Company
Address
City, State, Zip

German

Dear Exact Name of Person (or Dear Sir or Madam if answering a blind ad):

Just because you major in a subject like German doesn't mean you have to find a job using the language on a daily basis. This young professional will explore opportunities with airlines that fly to Germany, and she will also approach large companies in the hotel industry and cruise ship business.

With the enclosed resume, I would like to make you aware of my interest in exploring employment opportunities with your organization and introduce you to my talents and potential.

After graduating from McDonald High School where I was an active member of the band and played the saxophone and marching baritone, I went on to earn my Bachelor's degree in German at Butler University. During my youth from the age of three through the eighth grade, I lived in Germany and traveled extensively in Europe, and I speak and read German fluently. On several occasions I was chosen by one of my college professors to substitute-teach an advanced German class when he was engaged in consulting assignments.

Both during college and since college graduation, I have worked for a company at two of its locations in Indiana. I was credited with playing a significant role in increasing sales at the Greensboro store, and I have been strongly encouraged to enter the company's management training program. As a Sales Representative in contact with up to 75 potential customers daily, I have refined my ability to close a sale and earn the consumer's confidence. I have worked part-time since I was a teenager, and I believe my early work experiences in hospitality industry environments helped me acquire a poised and professional style of dealing with the public.

You would find me in person to be a congenial individual with an outgoing personality who genuinely enjoys interacting with others. Because of my considerable experience in living and traveling abroad, I am comfortable in situations which require me to make decisions quickly in unusual circumstances. My current employer has praised my ability to make prudent decisions and has identified me as a young professional with proven management potential and executive ability.

If my talents and skills interest you, I hope you will contact me to suggest a time when we might meet to discuss your needs. I am single and will cheerfully travel and/or relocate as your needs require.

Yours sincerely,

Verona Titlesworth

VERONA TITLESWORTH

1110½ Hay Street, Fayetteville, NC 28305 • preppub@aol.com • (910) 483-6611

OBJECTIVE	I want to contribute to an organization that can use an outgoing young professional who offers considerable sales skills and proven management potential along with a desire to serve the public and work with others in achieving top-quality results.

EDUCATION

Earned Bachelor of Arts (B.A.) degree in German, minor in Anthropology, Butler University, Indianapolis, IN, 2000.
- Was specially selected by a German professor to substitute-teach his advanced level German course in his absences due to consulting commitments.
- Volunteered some of my free time to Habitat for Humanity projects.
- Was a member, International Student Association.

Graduated from McDonald High School, Crawford, IN, 1996.
- Was an active band member; played the saxophone and marching baritone.

LANGUAGE & TRAVEL

Fluently speak and read German.
Have traveled extensively throughout Europe.
Very knowledgeable of German customs and culture; lived in Germany as a child.

COMPUTERS

Proficient with Windows operating systems and Microsoft Word software.
- Gained familiarity with numerous programs through a course I took in college called "Toolbook Multimedia 3.0."

EXPERIENCE

SALES REPRESENTATIVE. Piercing Haven, Indianapolis, IN (1998-present). Began with the company in a part-time sales position while in college, and have always ranked in the top third of sales producers in the company; after college graduation, was offered a full-time position, and am being strongly encouraged to enter the company's management trainee program.
- Supervise up to two sales clerks, and have trained numerous sales professionals on effective techniques related to closing the sale and customer service.
- Have been trained to perform minor jewelry repair.
- Was credited with playing a key role in the growth of sales.
- Have been entrusted with the responsibility of opening and closing the store as one of the responsible "key holders."
- Have become skilled at conducting comprehensive inventories.
- Refined my teaching and communication skills in this business which places me in daily contact with up to 75 customers of ear piecing services; the company's services must be explained precisely with a view to clarifying medical and legal issues related to piecing while earning the consumer's confidence and closing the sale.

WAITRESS (part-time while in college). Libby Hill Restaurant, Indianapolis, IN. Worked up to 25 hours a week at a family restaurant, and became known for my sunny disposition and professional style of interacting with customers.

CASHIER (part-time while in high school). MacDonalds Restaurant, Crawford, IN. Learned to work well with others and refined my time management skills.

PERSONAL

Work well in environments which require an individual who is able to make prudent decisions in unusual circumstances. Am a positive individual with an upbeat personality. Can provide outstanding personal and professional references. Will travel or relocate.

Exact Name of Person
Exact Title
Exact Name of Company
Address
City, State, Zip

Government

Dear Exact Name of Person: (or Dear Sir or Madam if answering a blind ad):

Not everyone wants to put an Objective on the resume. In Ms. Brinson's case, she jumps right into her educational background. This young professional is oriented toward the public sector and will approach municipalities for junior-level management positions.

With the enclosed resume, I would like to make you aware of my background in criminal justice and government studies which I would like to put to work for your benefit.

As you will see from my resume, I excelled in demanding public roles while earning my college degree. As an active member of the Republican Party, I worked for Congressman Degrow from Michigan and acted as the link between the Congressman's office in Lansing and his Washington, D.C. office. After excelling in that position, I was recruited to be the Special Assistant to the Executive Director of the Michigan Republican Party's Victory 2000 efforts. I have established an excellent network of contacts in Lansing as well as in Washington, and I am certain I could benefit a municipality such as yours through my ability to quickly identify the key decision makers in any given situation.

If you can use a hard-working young professional with outstanding problem-solving and decision making skills, I hope you will welcome my call soon when I try to arrange a brief meeting to discuss your goals and how my background might serve your needs. I can provide outstanding references at the appropriate time.

Sincerely,

Angela Brinson

ANGELA BRINSON

1110½ Hay Street, Fayetteville, NC 28305 • preppub@aol.com • (910)-483-6611

EDUCATION

Bachelor of Arts degree in Government, Albion College, Albion, MI; August 2000.
- Member, Epsilon Pi Eta Honor Society; Member, Pi Gamma Mu International Society in Social Science.
- Graduated with a 3.3 GPA.

Associate degree in Criminal Justice, St. Clair County Community College, Port Huron, MI.
- As a Tutor, assisted students having trouble with math and sociology.

COMPUTERS

Very familiar with WordPerfect, PageMaker, MS Word, dBase IV, and Microsoft Excel.
- Offer a proven ability to rapidly master new software and operating systems.

EXPERIENCE

Worked in demanding part-time jobs in order to finance my college education while excelling academically:

SPECIAL ASSISTANT TO THE EXECUTIVE DIRECTOR. Michigan Republican Party's Victory 2000, Lansing, MI (April 1999-present). Was specially recruited for this job which involves overseeing a staff of three while directing fund raising activities and providing support for the campaigns of MI Republicans; play a key role in making decisions regarding which candidates receive contributions.
- Supervise the internship program for college interns.
- Work with Michigan's U.S. Senatorial and Congressional delegation's campaigns to assist them in obtaining any information or assistance they need; also work with MI House of Representative and MI Senate candidates who request help.
- Assist with the Voter Registration Program and massive direct mail efforts.
- Manage expenses for this office.

SPECIAL ASSISTANT. Congressman Daniel Degrow, U.S. House of Representatives, Lansing, MI (Summers, 1998-99). Attended meetings on behalf of the Congressman; spoke on behalf of the Congressman before organizations such as White House Conference on Small Business, Chambers of Commerce, and civic groups.
- Supervised the internship program for college interns.
- Accompanied the Congressman when he traveled in the district; met with constituents.
- Was in charge of the Military Academy nominations for the district.
- Was a link between the Congressman in the District of Columbia and his district.
- Met with constituents on behalf of the Congressman; composed letters to constituents.
- Assisted constituents with obtaining passports and securing help from federal agencies.
- Accompanied the candidate to campaign functions in all 13 counties.
- Organized volunteers and groups throughout the 13 counties; telephoned registered voters; organized rallies; organized and planned highly successful fund raisers while also assisting with fund raising from individuals and Political Action Committees.

OFFICE ASSISTANT. Frederick & Bailey, Attorneys at Law, Lansing, MI (Summer, 1997). Assisted with loan closings, prepared documents for court, assisted with title searches, and provided office support. Responsible for file preparation of all legal documents for child support cases; accompanied attorney to court and communicated with all child support clients while also filing documents at the courthouse.

PERSONAL

Proven ability to excel in stressful and demanding situations. Self-motivated individual.

Date

Exact Name of Person
Title or Position
Name of Company
Address (no., street)
Address (city, state, zip)

History

Dear Exact Name of Person: (or Dear Sir or Madam if answering a blind ad.)

A history major has an extremely versatile degree, and this young professional knows it. She will explore opportunities in banks, public relations firms, consulting companies, and other organizations.

Can you use a highly motivated young professional who offers proven management ability and executive potential?

As you will see from my enclosed resume, I excelled academically in earning a B.A. degree in history while excelling in demanding part-time jobs in banking and sales in order to finance my college education. I began working as a concessionaire in a movie theater when I was 17, and as a youth I learned valuable lessons related to serving customers with a cheerful disposition at all times.

While working in more professional business situations as a college student, I gained valuable insights into internal banking operations and legal/real estate/loan procedures. In one summer job with real estate attorneys, I researched foreclosures, conducted title searches, and analyzed courthouse records. While working for a financial institution I excelled in two different jobs—one as a bank teller and the other as a documents analyst in the internal operations center.

You would find me to be a congenial and poised young person known for "maturity beyond my years." I am a hard worker who understands the importance of working with others as a team in order to maximize profitability and market share in an industry.

I hope you will welcome my call soon to arrange a brief meeting at your convenience to discuss your needs and goals and how I might serve them. Thank you in advance for your time.

Yours sincerely,

Lara Langridge

LARA LANGRIDGE

1110½ Hay Street, Fayetteville, NC 28305   •   preppub@aol.com   •   (910) 483-6611

OBJECTIVE

To contribute to an organization that can use a highly motivated young professional who offers excellent communication skills, a proven ability to serve the public graciously, as well as sales and banking experience which demonstrates my unlimited executive potential.

EDUCATION

Bachelor of Arts degree in History, Macalester College, St. Paul, MN; May 2001.
- Extensively refined my written and oral communication skills in this degree program which stressed the development of top-notch writing, research, analytical, and public speaking ability.
- Excelled academically; was inducted into Phi Alpha Theta History Honor Society and was named to the Dean's List several semesters.

COMPUTER KNOWLEDGE

Banking software: Have operated ASBA computer equipment.
Other software: Am experienced in utilizing MS-DOS, Windows, MS Word, WordPerfect, WordWriter, and MS Works software; offer the ability to rapidly master new software and hardware, and have a personal computer at home.

EXPERIENCE

LAW OFFICE CLERK. Potter & Black, P.A., St. Paul, MN (2000). In a summer job between my junior and senior years of college, gained insight into legal procedures and learned the mechanics of the loan process while assisting real estate attorneys with business transactions.
- Researched foreclosures, conducted title searches, and analyzed courthouse records.
- Wrote letters and was commended for my written communication skills.

BANK TELLER/DOCUMENTS ANALYST. State Employees Credit Union, St. Paul, MN (1996-2000). While excelling academically as a college student, worked part-time at two different locations of this financial institution and also worked at another job on the weekends; learned to manage my time wisely for maximum effectiveness in every activity.
- As a **Bank Teller**, greeted customers, introduced and sold new services, performed data entry and transactions on the computer, consolidated the day's paperwork, and balanced a drawer with more than $10,000 daily in credits and debits.
- As a **Documents Analyst**, worked in a busy operations center where I performed multiple duties including researching bank documents from all branches to solve account problems, retrieving account records, and stocking cancelled checks.

Other experience: *Worked in these jobs in high school during the summers, St. Paul, MN:*
DRY CLEANER CLERK. Took pride in serving customers in a cheerful manner at all times while acting as a counter clerk, operating a cash register, and assisting dissatisfied customers.

SALES REPRESENTATIVE. Was commended for my "natural" sales ability while becoming the highest-volume salesperson during the Christmas holidays and the after-Christmas sales season; developed a new credit policy for the store which is still in use today after becoming skilled in calculating credit accounts and accounting for large amounts of cash.

WAITRESS. For the popular Robie's Seafood Restaurant in St. Paul, learned to perform every job in this 150-person capacity restaurant.

PERSONAL

In high school, was captain of my basketball and tennis teams, and gained valuable confidence and leadership experience—including the ability to motivate others—from athletics. Enjoy mountain biking, hiking, and traveling. Am a keen observer of the stock market.

Date

Exact Name of Person
Title or Position
Name of Company
Address (number and street)
Address (city, state, and zip)

Dear Exact Name of Person: (or Sir or Madam if answering a blind ad.)

With the enclosed resume, I would like to introduce myself and ask you to consider me for a position within your organization where I could contribute to your goals through my education as well as my strategic thinking, problem-solving, and analytical skills.

You will see from my resume that I have recently graduated with a Master of Arts in History, and I authored a highly praised thesis entitled "The Role of the Housewife in the New Georgia 2000 Campaign." Prior to my master's program, I earned an undergraduate degree in History. During graduate school and college, I was active in student activities. I was named Chairperson of the Student Life Committee and was an elected campus leader.

I am skilled in utilizing a variety of tools for conducting research including bibliographies, statistics, automated databases, the internet, and other instruments. I offer excellent communication skills including the ability to skillfully interview others for information and to establish rapport with people at all levels of sophistication.

If you can use an astute thinker, writer, analyst, and communicator who could enhance your strategic efforts, I hope you will contact me to suggest a time when we might meet to discuss your needs and goals and how I might serve them. I can provide outstanding personal and professional references at the appropriate time.

Sincerely,

Ross Meriweather

ROSS MERIWEATHER

1110½ Hay Street, Fayetteville, NC 28305 • preppub@aol.com • (910) 483-6611

OBJECTIVE
To benefit an organization that can use a skilled researcher and analyst with superior thinking, writing, strategic planning, and problem-solving abilities who believes that the solutions to our current and future problems are often discovered through our knowledge of history.

EDUCATION
Received **Master of Arts in History,** Lon Morris College, Jacksonville, TX, December 2000.
- Authored a highly praised thesis entitled *"The Role of the Housewife in the New Georgia 2000 Campaign."*
- Was named Chairperson of the Student Life Committee.

Earned **Bachelor of Arts in History,** Lon Morris College, Jacksonville, TX, 1998.
- Gained a reputation as a campus leader; was elected **Representative** of Houser Hall.
- As an **Orientation Counselor,** derived much satisfaction from acquainting incoming freshmen with all aspects of campus life.
- Appointed to take over as **Co-Head** of Lon Morris College's RHA Entertainment Committee because of my well-known planning, organizational, and management skills.
- Specially selected as **Assistant Director** of the 49er Safewalk, a charitable event.

RESEARCH SKILLS
Skilled in utilizing a variety of tools for conducting research including bibliographies, statistics, automated databases, the Internet, and other instruments.
- Have frequently found that my intense curiosity, thirst for knowledge, and highly intuitive problem-solving ability quickly lead me to the best sources of information.
- Offer excellent communication and interviewing skills along with an ability to quickly establish rapport with knowledgeable officials and obtain needed information through expert interviewing techniques.

EXPERIENCE
FULL-TIME MASTER'S DEGREE STUDENT. Lon Morris College, Jacksonville, TX (1998-2000). While obtaining my Master's degree and completing my thesis, became respected as a leader within the university's residence hall system.
- Completed extensive training in Small Group Teamwork, Small Group Leadership, Innovative Thinking, and other areas sponsored by the Texas Association of Residence Halls and the Southern Association of Residence Halls.
- Earned a reputation as a persuasive communicator and motivator.

ORIENTATION COUNSELOR. Lon Morris College, Jacksonville, TX (1998). While earning my undergraduate degree in History, assisted freshmen in becoming acquainted with college life; also performed as an actor in some plays.
- Refined my public speaking skills while giving presentations to small groups and leading small group discussions.
- Counseled students about life goals, career choices, and personal issues.

CUSTOMER SERVICE REPRESENTATIVE. Blockbuster Video, Jacksonville, TX (1994-98). In this part-time job while in college, was promoted to increasing responsibilities with this fast-growing video chain; was groomed to enter the company's management training program but resigned in order to enter a Master's degree program.

PERSONAL
Extremely analytical yet creative mind. Enjoy finding solutions to stubborn problems.

Date

Exact Name of Person
Title or Position
Name of Company
Address (no., street)
Address (city, state, zip)

Dear Exact Name of Person: (or Dear Sir or Madam if answering a blind ad.)

This young professional is seeking a suitable position in the food service or hospitality industry. She feels that her restaurant industry experience is a valuable addition to her formal degree in Hotel and Restaurant Management.

I would appreciate an opportunity to talk with you soon about how I could contribute to your organization through my education and experience related to the field of restaurant and hotel management.

In 2000 I received an Associate's degree in Hotel and Restaurant Management from Miami University. I have been working since the summer of 1996 as a hostess, waitress, and banquet coordinator. After starting with a family-style restaurant at age 14, I quickly earned a reputation as a mature and responsible young person. I earned the trust of the owner and was soon working all shifts and filling in during the manager's absence.

Very customer-service oriented, I am known for my ability to remain calm and in control even when things are very hectic and busy. I am a team player who motivates others to follow my example of professionalism and dedication to quality service.

I hope you will welcome my call soon to arrange a brief meeting at your convenience to discuss your current and future needs and how I might serve them. Thank you in advance for your time.

Sincerely yours,

Clarissa Wolfe

Alternate last paragraph:
I hope you will call or write me soon to suggest a time convenient for us to meet and discuss your current and future needs and how I might serve them. Thank you in advance for your time.

CLARISSA WOLFE

1110½ Hay Street, Fayetteville, NC 28305 • preppub@aol.com • (910) 483-6611

OBJECTIVE
To contribute through my education and experience related to restaurant and hotel management by offering my motivational and communication skills along with my energy, enthusiasm, and reputation as a dependable and knowledgeable young professional.

EDUCATION
Associate's degree in **Hotel and Restaurant Management,** Miami University, Oxford, OH, 2000.
- Supervised up to seven people while planning, organizing, cooking for, and serving at campus special events, thereby gaining an opportunity to manage details while remaining in control when problems arose.

Studied **Marketing and Small Business Management,** Clinton County Vo-Tech, Oxford, OH.

TRAINING
Completed the following additional programs:
- Sanitation Certification, learned food diseases, bacteria prevention, proper water temperatures, and insect control, Miami University, Oxford, OH.
- Cooking Course, emphasis on preparing, measuring, cooking, and serving food, Clinton County Vo-Tech, Oxford, OH,

SPECIAL KNOWLEDGE
Through training and experience, have gained knowledge of the restaurant business from concept to operation including the following areas:

break-even point analysis	forecasting sales	job descriptions
cleaning/operating supplies	positions and tasks	profit management
preparation and portion control	personnel management	task and job analysis

staffing: recruitment, selection, interviewing, orientation, training
food purchasing: purchasing, storage of different types of food
sanitation: acidity and bacterial growth, food protection, pest control

Use Macintosh and IBM computers with Microsoft Works and MS Word for word processing and spreadsheets.

EXPERIENCE
FOOD SERVICE TEAM MEMBER. McDonald's Hamburgers, Oxford, OH (1998-present). Because of my education and experience in the restaurant business, was able to quickly become familiar with the variety of positions it takes to make a busy fast food restaurant operate smoothly; provided courteous service in all areas.
- Ensured that customers were served rapidly while taking food and drink orders, entering items into the computer, bagging the food, and making change.
- Gained practical kitchen experience cooking meat and assembling sandwiches as well as frying French fries, fish, and chicken nuggets.

HOSTESS and **WAITRESS.** Big Boy East, Oxford, OH (1996-98). Expanded my knowledge of food service by handling functions ranging from greeting customers and seating them, to explaining menu choices, to taking orders, to serving food, to stocking servers' stations, to totaling bills and collecting payments.
- Learned to use the Omron computer system for adding bills.
- Was able to work with the restaurant's bakers while learning to make speciality goods such as strawberry pies, muffins, and cornbread.

PERSONAL
Am a positive and optimistic individual. Offer an energetic, enthusiastic, and outgoing personality. Enjoy contributing to team efforts and seeing customers enjoy services.

Date

Exact Name of Person
Title or Position
Name of Company
Address (no., street)
Address (city, state, zip)

Dear Exact Name of Person: (or Dear Sir or Madam if answering a blind ad.)

With the enclosed resume, I would like to express my strong interest in the position of Program Director for After School Services which you recently advertised.

As you will see from my resume, I offer a track record of involvements which illustrate my true love for children as well as my ability to work effectively with their parents and primary care givers. Although I am excelling in a job as a Sales Representative, I worked for four years previously as a Nanny and Care Giver for professional parents in two different homes. I can provide outstanding references from those families, and they frequently commended me for stimulating the imaginations of their children. I can also provide outstanding references from my current employers but I would appreciate your holding my letter of interest in confidence until after we talk in person.

You will notice from my resume that my computer skills are excellent. I am proficient with software including Microsoft Word and PowerPoint as well as WordPerfect, and I have also used Apple/MacIntosh computers.

It would be my "dream job" to work for an organization that is dedicated to helping and nurturing youth, and I hope you will give me the opportunity to meet you in person and talk with you further about the job. I can assure you that I am a dependable hard worker known for compassion, patience, and understanding, and I also have a "business side" that is practical, down-to-earth, and skilled at using tact and poise in problem solving.

Yours sincerely,

Mary Thompson

MARY THOMPSON

1110½ Hay Street, Fayetteville, NC 28305 • preppub@aol.com • (910) 483-6611

OBJECTIVE

To contribute to an organization that can use a hard-working young professional with excellent communication and computer skills.

EDUCATION

Fourth year student working towards a major in **Human Development and Family Studies with a minor in Communication Studies** from Milligan College, Milligan, TN.
- Inducted into Phi Mu Sorority, Gamma Chi Chapter, 1998-99
- Have completed course work in sign language.

COMPUTERS

Proficient with software including Microsoft Word and PowerPoint; also experienced in using Apple/MacIntosh computers.

EXPERIENCE

SALES REPRESENTATIVE. The Gray Selection, Milligan, TN (1998-present). For the prestigious Gray Selection, I have become involved in a wide range of sales and technical duties.
- Handle extensive responsibility for sales and customer service.
- Design frame and mats for artwork including prints and oils; explain technical details of framing to customers in order to assist customers in making choices among competing styles.
- Manage the store on Sunday on my own; open and close the store.
- Accurately account for money and receipts, and operate the cash register.
- Am known for my poise and tact when dealing with dissatisfied customers and in finding a suitable resolution of their problems.
- Am involved in making inventory buying decisions, and assist in inventory control.

NANNY & PARENT EDUCATOR. Mr. and Mrs. Gary P. Smith, Milligan, TN (1997-98). Reorganized and maintained an orderly household for two working professionals with two young children.
- Cared for the emotional, educational, and physical needs of the children.
- Used my natural creativity and enthusiasm for learning to develop innovative activities which provided educational stimulation.
- Learned how to instruct and work one-on-one with parents.
- Developed a great deal of self-confidence while managing this busy home and acting as the personal assistant to Mr. and Mrs. Smith in personal and financial matters.

NANNY. Dr. and Mrs. Peter Maber, Milligan, TN (1995-98). Cared for children in their own home, and provided stimulating educational opportunities for the children which were greatly appreciated by the parents.

SALES PERSON. Learningsmith, Milligan, TN (1995). Worked during Christmas for a retailer of learning aids and tools.

WAITRESS. Merryville Assisted Living, Milligan, TN (1994-95). At this geriatric facility, waited tables for the facility's residents and became known for my reliability and dependability as well as my cheerful disposition.

PERSONAL

Outstanding personal and professional references upon request. Have a true love for children and a proven ability to relate effectively to their parents and primary care givers. Am known for being compassionate, patient, and understanding.

Date

Exact Name of Person
Exact Title
Exact Name of Company
Address
City, State, Zip

Dear Exact Name of Person: (or Dear Sir or Madam if answering a blind ad):

This slightly older
professional returned to
college to get her degree
after serving in the U.S.
Army briefly and then
working in banking,
telemarketing, and
insurance company
environments. Now she
will try to establish her
career in the human
resources field.

With the enclosed resume, I would like to make you aware of my skills and education related to human resources administration and express my interest in exploring employment opportunities with your organization.

Currently completing my B.A. in Human Resources Management, I have provided human resources support in the medical, financial, as well as the benefits and promotions areas. While serving in the U.S. Army, I gained my earliest exposure to human resources administration as I worked in a Personnel Administration Center supporting 1,200 people. I also became experienced in handling payroll administration for 250 people weekly with a perfect 100% on-time accuracy rate. My experience in human resources and personnel administration while in the U.S. Army was what motivated me to seek my Associate's degree and Bachelor's degree in this area.

In a subsequent position after leaving the military, and while earning my college degree, I supported human resources needs of a medical nature while working with insurance companies and physicians to coordinate physical exams for insured corporate clients. I have refined my communication skills working in customer service positions in a telemarketing firm as well as in the banking industry.

You will notice that I maintained a 3.7 GPA while obtaining an A.A. degree in Human Resources, and I have a 3.6 GPA in my B.A. curriculum. I am seeking a full-time position in a company which can utilize my strengths related to serving customers, assuring the quality of human services provided, and contributing to the company's bottom line.

I can assure you that I am a totally dedicated individual who always makes an effort to excel in all I do, and I have made valuable contributions to every employer for whom I have worked. If my skills and talents interest you, I hope you will contact me to suggest a time when we might meet to discuss your needs.

Sincerely,

Shirley Harell

SHIRLEY HARELL

1110½ Hay Street, Fayetteville, NC 28305 • preppub@aol.com • (910) 483-6611

OBJECTIVE
To offer my background and education related to human resources to an organization that can use a resourceful young professional who offers exceptional time management and communication skills along with a talent for helping others identify and resolve problems.

EDUCATION & TRAINING
Completing **B.A. in Human Resources Management,** Radford University, Radford, VA.
- Am maintaining a 3.6 GPA and have been named to the university's Dean's List in recognition of my "outstanding academic performance."

Earned an **A.A. in Human Resources Management,** Radford University, Radford, VA, 1998; maintained a 3.7 GPA.
- Received training in computer applications, management, and personnel services.

COMPUTERS
Offer proficiency with WordPerfect, MS Word, Excel, and Access.

EXPERIENCE
FULL-TIME STUDENT. Radford University, Radford, VA (1997-present).

MEDICAL RECORDS CLERK. Portamedic Insurance Co., Radford, VA (1998-present). In this part-time job while financing my college degree, provided human resources support of a medical nature while working for a company which conducts physical exams for insured corporate clients, processed requests for medical records from insurance companies.
- Polished already-effective communication skills dealing with agents and physicians while handling sensitive medical records and maintaining their confidentiality.
- Maintained files and payments; prepared correspondence; made follow-up calls to check on file and payment status; coordinated physical exams.
- Maintained a 100% on-time processing rate for weekly status reports required in my capacity as Attending Physician's Statement or APS Clerk.

CUSTOMER SERVICE REPRESENTATIVE. Barnett Bank, Radford, VA (Summer, 1997). Earned teller and customer service responsibilities in the 24-hour-a-day customer service operations center of this banking institution prior to a reorganization caused by a corporate buy-out; I decided to seek another position rather than stay with the acquiring company.
- Opened and closed accounts, IRAs, CDs, and saving bonds.

CUSTOMER SERVICE REPRESENTATIVE. Idleman Telemarketing, Radford, VA (Fall, 1997). While enrolling customers in Blue Cross and Blue Shield health insurance programs, assisted in finding health care providers and advised callers of benefits and options available.

Gained experience in human resources and personnel administration, U.S. Army:
HUMAN RESOURCES COORDINATOR. Germany (1993-96). Gained experience in working with benefits such as travel and personal leave, promotions, and job assessments in a Personnel Administrative Center (PAC) which supported 1,200 people.
- Became skilled in maintaining accurate and timely personnel records and files.

PERSONAL
Operate all standard office equipment including multiline phone systems, fax machines, and copiers. Was entrusted with a Secret security clearance. Can provide excellent references.

Date

Exact Name of Person
Exact Title
Exact Name of Company
Address
City, State, Zip

Interior Design

A big part of what this young person is "selling" on her resume is her experience in various projects while earning her degree. Other than the projects, she has never had any experience in her field. Notice that her Personal section points out that her design portfolio is available on request.

Dear Exact Name of Person (or Dear Sir or Madam if answering a blind ad):

With the enclosed resume, I would like to make you aware of my background as a motivated young professional with exceptional technical, design, and computer skills who offers a track record of accomplishment in visual merchandising as well as in interior design and graphic arts.

As you will see from my enclosed resume, I have a Bachelor of Science degree in Interior Design from Pratt Institute. I studied Modern Nordic Art and Architecture for a semester at the University of Woulu in Finland as the recipient of the H. Michael Weaver Award. While finishing my degree program, I completed several design projects, including the creation of a retail merchandising presentation, plans for a health care office, and a project to renovate a train station for architectural and interior design offices.

Currently a Magazine Coordinator for the country's largest retail bookseller, I oversee all aspects of merchandising for the periodicals department at a 27,000 square foot superstore. With a keen eye for visual impact, I select titles to display "face out" and group similar titles together to increase rack appeal. In an earlier position as a bookseller, I designed creative and effective end cap, cash wrap, window, and tray table displays.

Although I am excelling in my present position and can provide outstanding personal and professional references at the appropriate time, I am interested in exploring career opportunities where I can make full use of my design ability and educational background. I would appreciate your keeping my inquiry in confidence until after we have had the chance to meet.

If you can use a talented young design professional with a strong eye for detail and exceptional communication and organizational skills, I hope you will contact me soon. I assure you in advance that I have an excellent reputation and would quickly become an asset to your organization.

Sincerely,

Janice Carter

JANICE CARTER

1110½ Hay Street, Fayetteville, NC 28305   •   preppub@aol.com   •   (910) 483-6611

OBJECTIVE

To benefit an organization that can use an enthusiastic young professional with exceptional technical and design skills who offers a B.S. in Interior Design along with a strong visual sense which has been proven in challenging design and merchandising environments.

EDUCATION

Bachelor of Science in **Interior Design**, Pratt Institute (a FIDER accredited program), Brooklyn, NY, 2000.
- Studied **Modern Nordic Art and Architecture** for a semester at the University of Woulu in Finland as the recipient of the **H. Michael Weaver Award**, a travel grant for study abroad.
- Awarded the **Architectural Woodwork Institute Scholarship**, 1999.

<u>Projects</u>: Completed several advanced design projects while completing my degree.
- **Retail:** Prepared a booklet and multimedia slide presentation using the computer; refined display techniques used in retail environments, interviewing visual merchandising professionals from Belk department stores and Wrangler jeans while developing this project.
- **Health Care:** Designed a health care information service in the mall where clients could also see a doctor or health care professional; created the internal space, offices, examination rooms, seating area, and lighting.
- **Architectural:** Made substantial contributions on a team project to convert a train station into an office for architects and interior designers; interfaced with other members of the project via teleconferencing between Brooklyn, NY, and Miami, OH.

COMPUTERS

Offer exceptionally strong computer skills which include cross-platform knowledge of both IBM and Macintosh systems. Experienced with modeling and design programs such as AutoCAD R14, Form-Z, and ArchiCAD 4.5, as well as image manipulation and multimedia programs which include Adobe Photoshop 4.0, Illustrator 6.0, and JPEG view slide shows.

EXPERIENCE

With Barnes & Noble, Booksellers, have advanced in the following "track record" of increasing responsibilities for the nation's largest book retailer:
1998-present: **MAGAZINE COORDINATOR.** Brooklyn, NY. Oversee inventory control and merchandising of all magazines and newspapers for this 27,000 square-foot superstore.
- Develop effective marketing strategies for more than 1,600 magazine titles; select magazines with strong visual impact to display "full cover," increasing rack appeal.
- Perform liaison with magazine and newspaper vendors to adjust order quantities according to sales; researched and built relationships with newspaper vendors outside of the area in order to acquire product.
- Designed the initial set-up of the periodicals area for the opening of the store, creating an organizational system to ensure that related titles were merchandised effectively.

INTERN. PBM Graphics, Brooklyn, NY (Summers, 1997 & 1998). Followed the creation of a promotional item for the Denny's restaurant chain through all stages of production while honing my knowledge of printing, layout and design, and film proofing.

AFFILIATIONS

Past member, American Association of Interior Designers Student Chapter. Attended furniture design shows at the Merchandise Mart in Chicago, IL and at Interplan in New York, NY.

PERSONAL

My design portfolio and excellent references are available upon request.

Date

Exact Name of Person
Title or Position
Name of Company
Address (number and street)
Address (city, state, and zip)

Dear Exact Name of Person: (or Sir or Madam if answering a blind ad.)

Although managing a
kitchen has nothing to do
with her professional
objective since earning
her degree in
International Studies, Ms.
McAlister markets the
valuable skills and
abilities she acquired in
that business
management role.

    I would appreciate an opportunity to talk with you soon about how I could contribute to your organization through my versatile experience, education, and the application of my office operations and clerical skills.

    As you will see from my enclosed resume, I attend Spring Hill College where I am pursuing a B.S. in International Studies and already have earned an associate's degree with a concentration in Biology. I am an excellent manager of time who has attended college and worked in often-simultaneous jobs to finance my education. I type at least 40 wpm and am experienced in using Word for word processing applications.

    I have worked in restaurant management as well as in other jobs which have called for strong organizational, supervisory, and managerial skills. My versatile experience includes answering phones and handling general office responsibilities as well as inventory control, merchandising, employee training and supervision, and financial management of small businesses.

    I am an enthusiastic, energetic, and outgoing individual known for my attention to detail as well as my ability to improve bottom-line profitability and the quality of customer service provided.

    I hope you will call or write me soon to suggest a time convenient for us to meet and discuss your current and future needs and how I might serve them. Thank you in advance for your time.

Sincerely,

Katelin McAlister

KATELIN MCALISTER

1110½ Hay Street, Fayetteville, NC 28305 • preppub@aol.com • (910) 483-6611

OBJECTIVE

To offer a well-rounded background in environments where strong customer-service, organizational, supervisory, and managerial abilities are required to a business that can use a detail-oriented young professional with a knack for mathematics.

EDUCATION

Pursuing a **B.S. degree with a concentration in International Studies,** Spring Hill College, Mobile, AL; degree expected in December 2001.
Earned **Associate's degree with a concentration in Biology,** Spring Hill College, 1999.

EXPERIENCE

Am refining my time management as well as my business and supervisory skills while financing my education in these part-time and sometimes simultaneous jobs:
GENERAL MANAGER. SuJin's Kitchen, Mobile, AL (1996-present.) Was credited with increasing overall business income as much as 60% during my work shifts because of my strong service orientation and genuine concern that diners enjoyed their visits.
- Applied my creativity to develop frequent menu changes and promotional ideas which impacted on the level of sales.
- Conducted weekly inventories of food items and supplies and coordinated the process of ordering from three separate retail sources.
- Trained and supervised employees; prepared work schedules.
- Managed business accounting and financial support services while controlling the operating budget.
- Brought about an increase in revenues from large groups by actively marketing the restaurant as a place for business dinners and parties.
- Organized functions for as many as 100 people in a restaurant where one large party could easily equal the average daily income.
- Was relied on for my common-sense approach and ability to cement customer relations which led to increased repeat business.
- Implemented a cost-saving idea which reduced expenses nearly $700 a year.

ASSISTANT MANAGER. Que Pasta, Mobile, AL (1995-96). Had the opportunity to expand my knowledge of small business operations while handling day-to-day activities ranging from supervising a subordinate, to preparing the store for operations, to making food items for sale to customer's orders.

CUSTOMER SERVICE AND TRAINING SPECIALIST. Spaghetti Warehouse, Mobile, AL (Summer, 1995). Provided high quality service in a large-volume restaurant which seated as many as 600 people; was selected to supervise and train new employees.
- Learned to see to every detail while organizing parties for as many as 250 people.

RECEPTIONIST. Another Look, Wittler, AL (Summer, 1994). Gained practical experience in office operations, customer service, and clerical procedures for an exclusive upscale hair salon.
- Gained experience in general office and clerical support activities to include answering telephones and scheduling appointments for four or five stylists and nail technicians.
- Provided support in banking, payroll preparation, and accounting.
- Controlled inventory to include ordering supplies and then pricing new merchandise.

PERSONAL

Have a working knowledge of the French and Thai languages. Received a prestigious biology scholarship. Am a quick learner known for my dedication and ability to adapt.

Date

Exact Name of Person
Title or Position
Name of Company
Address (number and street)
Address (city, state, and zip)

Juris Doctor

Dear Exact Name of Person: (or Sir or Madam if answering a blind ad.)

On this page you will
see an individual who
has earned a law
degree. Compare this
resume to the one on
the next page, which
shows the same
degree but a different
look on the resume.

With the enclosed resume, I would like to make you aware of my interest in exploring employment opportunities with your organization.

As you will see, I have recently earned a Juris Doctor (JD) degree while excelling academically. I was selected by a prominent professor as one of three Webster's Scholars for Property Law, and I won the Property Book Award for achieving the highest grade point in the class. You will see from my resume that I worked part-time as a Research and Administrative Assistant for a faculty member.

Prior to earning my law degree, I worked as Community Director for the March of Dimes and was involved in organizing and managing events while managing volunteers. I have earned a reputation as a caring and dedicated professional.

I hope you will call or write me soon to suggest a time convenient for us to meet and discuss your current and future needs and how I might serve them. Thank you in advance for your time.

Sincerely,

Helen Evers

HELEN EVERS

1110½ Hay Street, Fayetteville, NC 28305 • preppub@aol.com • (910) 483-6611

OBJECTIVE
To benefit an organization that can use an articulate young professional with exceptional communication and organizational skills who offers a strong background in a variety of supervisory, administrative, and clerical roles in legal research and nonprofit environments.

EDUCATION
Completing **Juris Doctor (JD)**, St. Mary's University, San Antonio, TX; degree expected in June of 2001.
- Selected by Professor Pat Herrick as one of three Webster's Scholars for Property Law.
- Was a semifinalist from 30 teams entered in the Client Counseling Competition.
- Received the Property Book Award for the highest grade in the class.

Bachelor of Science, Business Administration, St. Mary's University, San Antonio, TX, 1998.
- Elected Vice President of the Student Alumni Association.
- Recognized as one of the university's Outstanding Seniors; served on the Student/Trustee Liaison Committee.
- President of Alpha Delta Pi Sorority; named to Sorority Women of the Year.

EXPERIENCE
RESEARCH & ADMINISTRATIVE ASSISTANT. Webster's Real Estate Law, Professor Pat Herris, St. Mary's University, San Antonio, TX (1999-present). Perform research, clerical, and administrative duties for the Property Law department of the university.
- Assist with editing and proofreading tasks involved in preparing the latest revision to Webster's Texas Real Estate Law, the standard text on the subject.
- Read and analyze information in the supplement to the current edition, in order to integrate that material appropriately into the main body of the text in the revised edition.
- Research real estate case law to ensure that all citations are listed accurately and correctly illustrate the point of law examined in that section of the text.
- Perform data entry and text editing, and check grammar and spelling, as well as moving blocks of completed text to the appropriate sections of the book.

COMMUNITY DIRECTOR. March of Dimes, San Antonio, TX (1997-1998). Directed events planning; managed recruitment, training, and supervision of volunteers; and handled other administrative tasks for this busy nonprofit organization, the local focus of which is funding the Neo-Natal Intensive Care Unit at Alamo Health Systems.
- Served as Chairperson for the annual March of Dimes Chef's Auction, coordinating with local restaurants to secure their participation; managed 25 volunteers.
- Oversaw all marketing for the event, soliciting donations from corporate sponsors such as Budweiser, Summey Travel, and local medical organizations.
- Organized the March of Dimes Walk-a-thon, assisting in the recruitment, training, and supervision of more than 40 volunteers.

NONPROFIT & COMMUNITY VOLUNTEER. San Antonio, TX (1994-1997). Through my exceptional planning, organizational, and communication skills, made significant contributions working as a volunteer for numerous local charities; this later led to a position in nonprofit management.
- Provided clerical and administrative support as an office volunteer for the San Antonio, TX, CARE Clinic, which offers medical services to the needy.
- Served on fund-raising committees as a volunteer for the Ronald McDonald House.

PERSONAL
Known as a dedicated, self-motivated professional with strong communication and problem-solving skills. Excellent personal and professional references are available upon request.

Date

Exact Name of Person
Title or Position
Name of Company
Address (number and street)
Address (city, state, and zip)

Dear Exact Name of Person: (or Sir or Madam if answering a blind ad.)

With the enclosed resume, I would like to make you aware of my interest in exploring employment opportunities with your organization.

As you will see, I have recently earned a Juris Doctor (JD) degree while excelling academically. I was fortunate to earn my degree in a program which emphasized extensive hands-on experience, and I completed several challenging internships which helped me refine my legal knowledge in practical situations. As an intern with a private law firm, I gained experience in a high-volume real estate practice. As an intern with the District Attorney's office, I gained valuable courtroom experience. As a summer law clerk for attorneys in private practice, I honed my research skills and became proficient with Westlaw and Lexis.

I can provide outstanding personal and professional references, including references from law school professors who would, I am sure, attest to my strong analytical skills and talent for identifying the key issues in complex paperwork.

If you can use a young attorney to complement your fine staff, I hope you will call or write me soon to suggest a time convenient for us to meet and discuss your current and future needs and how I might serve them. Thank you in advance for your time.

Sincerely,

Michael Covert III

MICHAEL COVERT III

1110½ Hay Street, Fayetteville, NC 28305   •   preppub@aol.com   •   (910) 483-6611

EDUCATION

J.D., University of Toledo School of Law, May 2000.

Honors
and
Activities

Dean's List (four semesters)
Volunteer Intern, Allen County D.A.'s Office, Toledo, OH (Spring 1999)
Volunteer Law Clerk, North State Legal Services—indigent work (1998-99)
Orange County Special Olympics, volunteer swimming instructor (Spring 1997)

B.A., Political Science, University of Toledo, May 1997
GPA: 3.490 Rank: 327/1182; top 28%

Honors
and
Activities

Cum Laude; Dean's List (every semester)
Community Big Brother, Toledo Boy's Club (1997-98)
Disc Jockey, college radio station WXYZ (1996)
Intramural golf champion (1995)
Outward Bound Ohio (Summer 1993)

EXPERIENCE

Intern. Office of Janice Doe, Toledo, OH (1999-present). Have gained hands-on experience in a high-volume real estate practice.
* Responsibilities include numerous loan closings, deed preparation, and title searches. In addition, litigation work includes DWI defense, domestic law, and personal injury.

Intern, *Orange County District Attorney's Office*, Toledo, OH (October 1998 to May 1999). Gained extensive negotiating and communication skills in the courtroom. Prosecuted traffic violations and criminal misdemeanors in district court for almost two years.
* Managed very large caseloads in district court.
* Six months experience in juvenile court included several probable cause hearings seeking to try serious offenders as adults.
* Six months experience in superior court included felony and misdemeanor appeal jury trials. Worked closely with victims and witnesses in very serious cases.
* Appointed to courthouse FOCUS group to help improve efficiency within the various departments of courthouse.

Intern, *Orange County District Attorney's Office*, Mylan, OH (Summer 1998).
Took advantage of my third-year practice certification and tried over thirty cases in district court as a law student.
* Interviewed victims and witnesses in preparation for trial.

Summer Law Clerk, *Dobson, Alex, Smith, and Reilly*, Mylan, OH (Summer 1997). Prepared business-related legal memoranda for attorneys.
* Honed research and writing skills.
* Became proficient in WordPerfect, Westlaw, and Lexis.

PERSONAL

Original hometown Toledo, OH. Enjoy golf, fly-fishing, backpacking, and guitar. Founding member and president of a tax-exempt organization whose purpose is to aid orphanages. Proud of my accomplishments as President of both my high school's Key Club and Junior Achievement Club. Ranked #3 out of over 350 students in my high school class.

Date

Exact Name of Person
Title or Position
Name of Company
Address (no., street)
Address (city, state, zip)

Dear Exact Name of Person: (or Dear Sir or Madam if answering a blind ad.)

Can you use a self-starter and fast learner who offers extensive computer knowledge and sharp math skills along with proven abilities related to management and marketing?

While earning my B.S. degree in marketing, I excelled in several "real-world" projects that involved setting up a minor league baseball team, establishing a new franchise "from scratch," and analyzing the financial condition of a major electronics corporation. I am skilled at using several popular software packages.

My mathematical abilities are considered top-notch: I was ranked in the highest percentile of high school students based on my superior math S.A.T. score. I also offer some experience in sales, business management, and customer service through jobs I held prior to earning my college degree.

I am seeking to make a long-term commitment and significant "bottom-line" contribution to a company that can use a versatile and creative young leader with a capacity for hard work.

I hope you will welcome my call soon to arrange a brief meeting at your convenience to discuss your current and future needs and how I might serve them. Thank you in advance for your time.

Sincerely yours,

Clyde Dominey

Alternate last paragraph:
I hope you will call or write me soon to suggest a time convenient for us to meet and discuss your current and future needs and how I might serve them. Thank you in advance for your time.

Although this young professional had very little paid work experience, he did have the good fortune to have marketing projects he could show off on a resume. He is especially interested in finding employment with a sports team in some type of management role, so he made a point of mentioning his marketing project related to starting up a minor league sports team.

CLYDE DOMINEY

1110½ Hay Street, Fayetteville, NC 28305 • preppub@aol.com • (910) 483-6611

OBJECTIVE

I want to contribute to an organization that can use a hard-working young professional who offers a proven ability to creatively apply information with a "bottom-line" orientation.

EXTENSIVE COMPUTER SKILLS

Have used software and programming languages including:

Pascal	SuperCalc 4 spreadsheets	YSTAT	Word
dBase	Word Perfect	UNIX	COBOL

- Excelled in a computer Human Interface course, SIGCHI, Valdosta, GA, 2000.

EDUCATION

Earned **Bachelor of Science (B.S.) degree in Marketing**, Valdosta State University, Valdosta, GA, 2000.

EXPERIENCE

MARKETING TRAINEE. Valdosta State University, Valdosta, GA (1999-00). As a successful candidate for the Bachelor of Science degree, excelled in several "real-world" projects which enhanced my business administration and marketing skills.

- In a project for a **promotion** course, started up a Minor League baseball team for the city of Massey: developed advertising, prepared schedules, prepared consumer literature and discount booklets, and determined logo/team colors.
- In a project for a **retail management** course, established "from scratch" a new Putt-Putt franchise: performed extensive feasibility analysis and prepared in-depth oral/written presentations.
- For a **finance** course, performed extensive in-depth financial analysis, including ratio analysis, of the Apple Computer Company: prepared five-year and 10-year projections.
- For a **marketing** project, collected information to help determine community banking needs and the public's perception of First Interstate Bank.

ACTING STORE MANAGER/MANAGER TRAINEE. Bubba's Breakaway, Massey, GA (Summer, 1998). Was entrusted with occasionally managing this store after learning the internal workings of this fast-food preparation and delivery business serving the area.

Scheduled/directed drivers.	Ordered food/supplies.
Balanced daily receipts.	Answered phones/took orders.
Made bank deposits.	Prepared/delivered food.

SALES CLERK. Boulevard Pawn Shop, Valdosta, GA (Summer, 1997). Acquired excellent customer relations skills and learned valuable inventory control techniques while monitoring a diversified inventory including stereo equipment and firearms.

Other experience: Learned the importance of "attention to detail" as a dishwasher at a seafood restaurant and lifeguard at a country club pool.

MATHEMATICS

Scored a very high 700 on the math portion of Scholastic Aptitude Test (S.A.T.).

KNOWLEDGE & ACADEMIC ABILITY

- Was ranked in the top percentile of high school students in math mastery.
- Was offered an academic scholarship by Valdosta State University.
- Received a Presidential Academic Fitness Award for academic excellence.

PERSONAL

Was elected pledge president in my college fraternity. Enjoy racquetball, golf (12-handicap), skiing, surfing, basketball, softball, and baseball.

Date

Exact Name of Person
Exact Title
Exact Name of Company
Address
City, State, Zip

Mass Communications

Dear Exact Name of Person: (or Dear Sir or Madam if answering a blind ad):

This hard-working young professional has held a variety of part-time jobs in order to finance her education. Now she is eager to find a position in a publishing company or advertising agency where she can refine her creativity and communication skills.

With the enclosed resume, I would like to make you aware of my interest in exploring employment opportunities with your organization. I am completing a Bachelor's degree in Mass Communication with a concentration in Advertising, and I offer a reputation as an articulate and persuasive young professional known for enthusiasm and self-motivation. I have worked nearly full-time throughout college in jobs in the hospitality industry.

During a spring 2000 Practicum I gained experience in selling, preparing, producing, and communicating advertising copy on the air at the university radio station. In addition to gaining on-air time as a DJ, I made cold calls and sold sponsorships to area high schools.

Since the age of fourteen, I have worked in positions that placed me in contact with the public. As a young teenager working in a jewelry store, I was entrusted with the responsibility of selling fine jewelry to discriminating and sophisticated customers, and I proved highly effective in sales and customer service. In later jobs I refined my communication and customer service skills in restaurants and in a "bed-and-breakfast" establishment.

I feel certain that one of my strongest qualities is my ability to deal effectively with people and to inspire confidence and trust in others. I learned how to handle myself with poise in public at an early age. A talented and articulate leader in high school, I was elected to president and vice president positions in clubs and student government.

If you can use a dedicated and mature young professional with high levels of drive, initiative, and energy, I hope you will welcome my call soon when I try to arrange a brief meeting to discuss your goals and how my background might serve your needs. I can provide outstanding references at the appropriate time.

Sincerely,

Beverly Boyce

BEVERLY BOYCE

1110½ Hay Street, Fayetteville, NC 28305　•　preppub@aol.com　•　(910) 483-6611

OBJECTIVE	I want to contribute to an organization that can use a personable, articulate, and detail-oriented young professional with an enthusiastic and energetic personality who offers the proven ability to build strong rapport with customers.
EDUCATION	**College:** Completing a Bachelor's degree in **Mass Communication** (concentration in **Advertising**), University of Virginia, Charlottesville, VA.

- Have completed specialized course work which has included principles of marketing, print media, creative campaign production, design, television production, desktop publishing, photography, speech for radio and television, and radio production.

High School: Graduated from Pine High School, Pine, VA, 1997.

- Was elected to student government leadership roles each year including vice president senior year; served as president of the French Club.
- Elected vice president of "Trojans for Christ."

EXPERIENCE

ADVERTISING SALES REPRESENTATIVE and **RADIO ANNOUNCER.** WCCE 90.1 Radio, University of Virginia, Charlottesville, VA (2000). In a Practicum as a Mass Communication major, acted as a DJ for the university FM radio station playing "light and easy" listening music as well as selling advertising time.

- Raised $600 for the station by making cold calls and selling air time; visited area high schools and obtained sponsorships for top students.
- Processed paperwork after selling ads and then created the advertising copy.
- Performed production work as well as doing live on-the-air ads.

Polished my "people skills" as well as communication, organizational, and time management abilities in restaurant industry positions while attending college:
HOSTESS. On the Border Mexican Restaurant, Charlottesville, VA (1999-present). Contribute to the smooth operation and quality of service in this new and popular restaurant.

COOK and **WAITRESS.** Mexican Restaurant, Pine, VA (1997-99). Gained a wide range of knowledge in all aspects of small business operations while handling everything from waiting on and serving customers, to cooking, to hiring and training staff.

HOSTESS, COOK, and **WAITRESS.** Waverly's Bed and Breakfast, Pine, VA (1996-97). Worked approximately 20 hours a week while attending school and contributed in several functional areas: cleaned, provided customer service, and cooked.

LIFEGUARD. Pine City Pool, Pine, VA (1995-96). Gave private swimming lessons to infants, children, and adults; supervised open swimming for club members and their guests; arranged swim meets and parties.

Other experience: SALES & CUSTOMER SERVICE CLERK. The Jewelry Inn, Pine, VA. From the age of 14, worked in this family business and became skilled in tailoring my sales pitch to the customer while selling fine jewelry; was credited with increasing the percentage of daily sales through my ability to analyze the customer and provide what they wanted.

COMPUTERS　　Familiar with Windows, DOS, PageMaker, Word, and WordPerfect.

PERSONAL　　Feel that one of my greatest strengths is the ability to communicate ideas and concepts.

Date

Exact Name of Person
Title or Position
Name of Company
Address (number and street)
Address (city, state, and ZIP)

Master of Education in Counseling

While earning her degree, this caring professional completed internships which helped her refine her skills and knowledge related to counseling.

Dear Exact Name of Person: (or Sir or Madam if answering a blind ad.)

I would appreciate an opportunity to talk with you soon about how I could contribute to your organization through my wide variety of experience in working with diverse client populations while applying my counseling skills, enthusiasm, and ability to work effectively with people.

With a master's degree in Counseling and bachelor's degree in Psychology, I offer a strong educational background which I have utilized in positions which called for the ability to be a caring and concerned listener who could make effective professional judgments. You will see from my enclosed resume that I have completed internships in counseling which have given me exposure to children as young as three who have experienced physical and/or sexual abuse. I have also worked with adults receiving marriage counseling along with middle school students involved in violence intervention programs.

Known for my ability to provide effective leadership and keep group and individual sessions on target, I have consistently been able to provide high quality care to populations of mentally or physically handicapped children, adults in a group home setting, and children participating in a variety of sports activities.

I am a self-confident individual with strong counseling skills as well as a firm grasp of program planning, case management, as well as the administrative support required to keep programs operating and productive.

I hope you will welcome my call soon to arrange a brief meeting to discuss your current and future needs and how I might serve them. Thank you in advance for your time.

Sincerely,

Sophia Yuan-Chin

Alternate last paragraph:
I hope you will call or write me soon to suggest a time convenient for us to meet and discuss your current and future needs and how I might serve them. Thank you in advance for your time.

SOPHIA YUAN-CHIN

1110 ½ Hay Street, Fayetteville, NC 28305 • preppub@aol.com • (910-483-6611

OBJECTIVE   To obtain a permanent position in the mental health field that utilizes my educational background, organizational and program management skills, and planning abilities.

EDUCATION   **Master of Education in Counseling**, University of Saint Francis, Joliet, IL, 2000.
* Graduated *magna cum laude.*
Bachelor of Arts in Psychology, University of Saint Francis, Joliet, IL, 1998.

EXPERIENCE   **INDIVIDUAL AND FAMILY COUNSELING INTERN.** The Center for Individual and Family Therapy, Joliet, IL (1998-2000). Provided age and situationally appropriate counseling for individuals in a variety of age groups ranging from young children to middle-age adults, acted as a co-leader for therapy groups for sexually abused girls, and provided marital therapy.
* Helped develop the curriculum for two counseling groups—the four-year-olds and the nine to 12-year-old group of sexually abused females—including reorganizing guidelines in such a way that future leaders would have a foundation for additional groups.
* Provided a buffer between sexually and/or physically abused children and their parents during supervised visitations scheduled after gaining the children's trust.
* Led groups so that each member was given an opportunity for individual growth.
* Staffed the front desk on rotation for intake and referrals.

COUNSELING INTERN. Joliet School District, Joliet, IL (1998). Assisted the counseling staff at Morton Middle School in the implementation of in-school counseling under the sponsorship of "Second Step—Joliet Committee for Children," a violence intervention program.
* Participated in support activities including facilitation of violence intervention classes, attendance at parent conferences, and individual or group meetings with students.
* Experienced first hand the positive effects of an early intervention initiative which taught the students alternatives and solutions to potentially dangerous situations.

CAMP COUNSELOR. Joliet Parks and Recreation, Joliet, IL (summer 1998). For the city's special programs summer camp, provided support for physically and mentally handicapped children in overnight as well as day-camp settings.
* Supervised a wide range of areas including assistance with general hygiene, dressing, and meals as well as evening and overnight activities.
* Planned and conducted outdoor group activities for as many as 11 children of varying abilities and temperaments.

FACILITY ASSISTANT. Reilly International, Kent, IL (Summer, 1997). As assistant to the facility manager, provided support to mentally disabled home residents as well as supervising five staff members in an intense work environment.
* Challenged residents to take the maximum responsibility for decisions such as daily life skills, money management, and social interaction.

Highlights of other experience: Enjoyed working with young people and encouraging them to set and maintain high personal goals and standards.
* Coached high school long-distance runners with an emphasis on personal improvement and team involvement (spring 1996) as well as teaching a variety of sports to elementary and middle school youth for the YMCA (1996).

PERSONAL   Can provide outstanding personal and professional references.

Date

Exact Name of Person
Title or Position
Name of Company
Address (number and street)
Address (city, state, and zip)

Mathematics

Dear Exact Name of Person: (or Dear Sir or Madam if answering a blind ad.)

Although the job on his resume as Carpenter's Helper has nothing to do with his mathematics degree, prospective employers take a positive view of a young man who has worked hard to earn his degree. Even jobs outside the mathematics field can help an individual gain excellent work habits.

I would appreciate an opportunity to talk with you soon about how I could contribute to your organization through my strong interest in the field of geotechnical engineering, quality control and inspection, and materials testing as well as through my experience, education, and communication skills.

You will see by my enclosed resume that, while earning my B.S. in Mathematics, I gained practical experience in summer and part-time positions which included Concrete Technician and Engineering Technician.

I offer well-developed communication skills partially as a result of my eight years of service in the U.S. Army where I was heavily involved in training and supervision of teams of up to nine well-trained people. I also refined my ability to communicate effectively during a period where I tutored students in mathematics at a college learning center where most of my students needed assistance in precalculus or calculus.

My computer skills include familiarity with Windows and UNIX operating systems with some experience in programming in Pascal. I enjoy technical challenges and learning new theories and mechanics.

I hope you will welcome my call soon to arrange a brief meeting at your convenience to discuss your current and future needs and how I might serve them. Thank you in advance for your time.

Sincerely yours,

David Callahan

Alternate last paragraph:
I hope you will call or write me soon to suggest a time convenient for us to meet and discuss your current and future needs and how I might serve them. Thank you in advance for your time.

DAVID CALLAHAN

1110½ Hay Street, Fayetteville, NC 28305 · preppub@aol.com · (910) 483-6611

OBJECTIVE

To offer my analytical and mathematical abilities to an organization that can use a technically oriented young professional with a reputation as a team player known for outstanding communication, problem-solving, and planning abilities.

EDUCATION

Bachelor of Science degree in Mathematics, Virginia Tech, Blacksburg, VA, 2000.
- Was inducted into Pi Mu Epsilon National Mathematics Honor Society as a math major with a 3.5 GPA, spring semester 1999.
- Earned departmental honors in mathematics in recognition of my high GPA and completion of a semester of directed study with a presentation made to department faculty.
- Became a member of the Mathematical Association of America (MAA), 1998.

TECHNICAL KNOWLEDGE

Familiar with the Windows and UNIX operating systems and use computer software such as Lotus 1-2-3, dBase, MS Word and WordPerfect; have experience with programming in Pascal.

LANGUAGE

Fluently speak, read, and write Spanish
- Have traveled extensively throughout Central and South America.

EXPERIENCE

Gained practical experience and refined my time management skills while juggling the demands of attending college full time and working to help finance my education:

CARPENTER'S HELPER. Allton Construction, Blacksburg, VA (1998-2000). Earned a reputation as a dependable and trustworthy employee while learning commercial carpentry working on ceilings and dry walls; was rehired in 2000 based on my performance during the summer of 1999.

QUALITY ASSURANCE CLERK. Roadway Package System, Hartwood, VA (Summer, 1998). Polished customer service skills while involved in activities including redirecting packages which had been improperly routed, processing damaged parcels, maintaining various types of records and documentation, and responding to customer complaints and problems.
- Was cited as the driving force behind providing satisfactory quality assurance operations for the first time since the terminal was built.

MATHEMATICS TUTOR. Germanna Community College, Blacksburg, VA (Summer and Fall 1998). Applied my well-developed communication skills and mathematical abilities while helping students experiencing difficulties in subjects such as precalculus and calculus.
- Became adept at explaining technical subject matter concisely and clearly.
- Refined customer service skills while assisting in resource center operations.

ENGINEERING TECHNICIAN. Geowave Materials Testing, Inc., Blacksburg, VA (Summer, 1997). Further enhanced my knowledge of concrete testing and learned soil testing techniques while preparing reports prior to collecting samples.

MILITARY EXPERIENCE: Served my country in the U.S. Army for eight years and was promoted ahead of my peers to management; supervised teams of up to nine people.

PERSONAL

Working knowledge of German. Enjoy reading scientific/technical books on subjects such as quantum mechanics. Like technical challenges and learning new theories .

Exact Name of Person
Exact Title
Exact Name of Company
Address
City, State, Zip

Mechanical Engineering

Dear Exact Name of Person (or Dear Sir or Madam if answering a blind ad):

If you look at his
resume, you will see that
Mr. Friedenthal has
experienced a wide
variety of work
situations! This can
influence prospective
employers positively,
because a widely
experienced employee
will often be a more
insightful problem solver
on the job.

With the enclosed resume, I would like to introduce you to an educated, meticulous professional with excellent communication and organizational skills as well as a background in medical, surgical, and logistics environments which require attention to detail.

I am currently excelling in a rigorous Mechanical Engineering degree program while working part-time to finance my education. My academic excellence has earned me a position on the Dean's List for the last two semesters, and I will receive my Associate's degree in 2001. I have already completed a number of courses in Computer Aided Drafting and the operation of related software, including: Technical Drafting 1 and II, AutoCAD 1 and II, CAD/CAM (using AutoCAD R14 and R15), and Drafting Design I using AutoCAD. I have also taken a course on Pro-Engineer, which is a design and production program used to automate the mechanical development of a product from conceptual design through production.

As you will see from the enclosed resume, I have previously worked as a Surgical Technologist, providing operating room support and assistance in surgical procedures from appendectomies to open heart surgery. I gained experience in the use of new instruments, equipment, and procedures as well as in integrating new technologies with the existing equipment and procedures already in use. Prior to my medical career, I served my country in the U.S. Air Force as an Air Cargo Loading Supervisor and Air Evacuation Medical Specialist, positions which required constant attention to detail.

If you can use a self-motivated, meticulous computer-aided drafting professional with excellent communication and organizational skills and a growing knowledge of CAD and related software, I look forward to hearing from you soon to suggest a time when we might meet. I can provide outstanding personal and professional references at the appropriate time and would quickly become a worthy addition to your company.

Sincerely,

Jack Friedenthal

JACK FRIEDENTHAL

1110½ Hay Street, Fayetteville, NC 28305 • preppub@aol.com • (910) 483-6611

OBJECTIVE	To benefit an organization that can use an educated, meticulous computer-aided drafting professional with excellent communication and organizational skills who offers a background in medical, surgical, and logistics environments requiring careful attention to detail.

EDUCATION

Bachelor's Degree in Mechanical Engineering, Bentley College, Waltham, MA, 2001.
- Made the Dean's list for the last two semesters.

Have completed the following courses directly related to Computer-Aided Drafting:

Technical Drafting I	Technical Drafting II
AutoCAD	CAD/CAM
Drafting Design I (using AutoCAD R13 and R14)	

Graduated from the **Surgical Technology Program,** Bentley College, Waltham, MA, 1993.

EXPERIENCE

COLLEGE STUDENT. Bentley College, Waltham, MA (1998-present). Currently excelling in a rigorous degree program while working part-time to finance my education.
- Completed numerous courses in Computer-Aided Drafting and related software.

CASHIER and ACTING GENERAL MANAGER. Etna Snack Mart, Waltham, MA (1998-present). Perform a variety of customer service, cashier, stocking, and shelving duties while completing my college degree.
- Have become the trusted "right arm" to the general manager, and handle a variety of management, customer service, accounting, and other activities.
- Act as General Manager of three stations in the absence of the owner.

SURGICAL TECHNICIAN. Bentley Medical Center, Waltham, MA (1993-1998). Served as a member of the surgical team in this busy hospital environment.
- Assisted the surgeon in the performance of surgical procedures.
- Prepared operating room for surgeries, ensuring that all necessary supplies and equipment were available; broke down surgical cases after procedures were completed.
- Restocked surgeries and prepared case carts for the next day's surgical cases.
- Cleaned, disinfected, and performed sterilization procedures on surgical instruments and equipment.

Highlights of earlier experience: proudly served my country in the Air Force.
AIRCRAFT CARGO SUPERVISOR. Charleston AFB, Charleston, SC (1990-1992). Exercised careful planning and attention to detail in calculating the weights and balances of aircraft cargo and/or passengers to be placed on the aircraft; these calculations were used by the flight crew to prepare the aircraft for flight.
- Supervised a ground loading crew of eight employees, loading and unloading aircraft according to established procedures.
- Oversaw the configuration and set-up of aircraft for Emergency Medical Evacuation.

AIR EVACUATION MEDICAL SPECIALIST and **MEDICAL SPECIALIST.** Charleston AFB, Charleston, SC and Homestead AFB, FL (1986-1990). Provided medical care to patients both in-flight and in hospital environments.

PERSONAL

Outstanding personal and professional references are available upon request.

Medical Billing Certification

Here is an example of a
resume in which the
previous work
experience has nothing
in common with the
degree program.

Dear Sir or Madam:

With the enclosed resume, I would like to make you aware of my background as an enthusiastic young professional with an education in Medical Billing who offers proven skills related to medical office administration, records management, and medical billing which have been tested in busy hospital environments.

Recently, I have been excelling as a Night Auditor for several different hotels while pursuing my diploma in Medical Billing. Using Microsoft Excel, I generated revenue and expense reports as well as reconciling daily receipts to ensure that all funds are accounted for. I have been recognized by these employers as an enthusiastic, reliable worker who adheres to a high work standard while providing exceptional customer service.

Earlier, I served with distinction as a Medical Corpsman in the U.S. Navy. While assisting nursing professionals and physicians in busy hospital environments, I performed a number of medical and administrative functions, including patient screening, updating and maintenance of patient medical records, phlebotomy, and patient billing. I completed in-patient registration of new clients, screening the patient and creating a file containing their medical history and major complaint. While serving as Medical Receptionist in the Medical Clinic, it was also my responsibility to obtain patient insurance information, file insurance claims, perform patient education, and provide administrative and clerical support to the office.

As you will see from my enclosed resume, I have recently completed a diploma program in Medical Billing from an accredited correspondence school, which included course work in Medical Terminology, Medical Claims Procedures, and CPT/ICD-9 coding. I have also received a diploma in Medical Science and graduated from the U.S. Navy's three-month Medical Corpsman School, completing courses in a variety of medical disciplines. I feel that my strong combination of education and practical experience would make me a valuable addition to any medical office.

Highly regarded by my previous employers, I can provide outstanding letters of recommendation at the appropriate time. I assure you in advance that I have an excellent reputation and would quickly become an asset to your organization.

Sincerely,

Gerald Faich

GERALD FAICH

1110½ Hay Street, Fayetteville, NC 28305 • preppub@aol.com • (910) 483-6611

OBJECTIVE

To benefit an organization that can use an enthusiastic, reliable young professional with strong communication and organizational skills who offers an education in medical billing and experience in medical office administration, patient screening, billing, and auditing.

EDUCATION

Completed **Certification in Medical Billing** through an accredited correspondence course, 2000. Courses included:

Medical Terminology	Anatomy and Physiology
Procedural Coding	Diagnostic Coding
Medical Claims Procedures	CPT/ICD-9 Coding

Earned diploma from a Screener's course in Medical Science, Great Lakes, IL, 1999.
Graduated from the U.S. Navy Medical Corpsman School, a three-month program which included courses in:

Venipuncture and Phlebotomy	Medical Records Management
Patient Screening and Assessment	Medical Office Administration

COMPUTERS

Familiar with popular computer systems and software including Windows , Microsoft Word, and Microsoft Excel. Have quickly mastered new software, including a variety of proprietary systems specific to the military and to the medical profession.

EXPERIENCE

NIGHT AUDITOR. Various locations throughout Fargo, IL (1998-present). Have served with distinction, working simultaneously as Night Auditor and "Manager on Duty" for several different hotels while completing my education in Medical Billing.

- Generated daily revenue and expense reports in Microsoft Excel and reconciled daily receipts to ensure that all funds were accounted for; handled large volumes of cash.
- Supervised the night shift hotel staff while performing customer service, bookkeeping, and guest check-in.
- Personally credited with increasing total revenue at one hotel by seven percent.
- Recognized by my employers as an enthusiastic, reliable worker who adheres to a high work standard and excels at customer service; can provide letters of recommendation.

NURSING ASSISTANT. U.S. Navy, Great Lakes, IL (1996-1998). After completing extensive military training in various medical disciplines, served as a Hospital Corpsman; assisted nurses and physicians, providing patient care in busy hospital environments.

- Performed patient screening and initial assessment for more than 100 patients per week; utilized extensive knowledge of medical terminology and abbreviations.
- Completed patient registration, verifying insurance information and utilizing the DEERS military dependent eligibility system; gained valuable experience in medical billing.
- Updated and maintained medical records for more than 1,000 patients, documenting all medical visits, treatments, and changes to patients' medical history.
- Served as a Medical Receptionist at the Medical Clinic; answered phones, scheduled appointments, screened patients, and pulled, updated, maintained, and filed charts.
- Operated a computer, utilizing a variety of proprietary software specific to military medical environments to prepare reports, patient histories, and other documents.
- Conducted patient education related to subjects such as side effects of prescribed medication and proper home care procedures for patients being released.

PERSONAL

Enthusiastic individual with a results-oriented attitude. Outstanding references.

Nanny and Governess School

This recent graduate of Nanny and Governess School will seek a situation with a high-profile family with multiple children who need a well-groomed and well-educated nanny to help raise and educate their affluent children. Here is an example of a resume which will probably be sent to families by way of the placement service at the school where she graduated.

Dear Sir or Madam:

With the enclosed resume, I would like to make you aware of my background as a nanny and governess as well as my desire to put my experience to work for a high-profile family. I am single and can travel as extensively as the family requires.

With a reputation as an outgoing and intelligent young person, I can provide outstanding personal and professional references. I have served in situations in which children had recently lost their mother due to illness or a tragic accident, and I am experienced in helping children cope with grief and loss.

My interest in becoming a nanny grew out of my early child care work experiences. I learned that children tend to bond naturally to me, and I discovered my ability to nurture them while helping them gain independence and self confidence. I am known for my high moral standards, and I would be attracted to a situation in which a family subscribed to strong moral and ethical values.

Highly regarded by my previous employers, I can provide outstanding letters of recommendation at the appropriate time. I assure you in advance that I have an excellent reputation and would quickly become an asset to your family.

Sincerely,

Tanya Rutledge

TANYA RUTLEDGE

1110½ Hay Street, Fayetteville, NC 28305 • preppub@aol.com • (910) 483-6611

OBJECTIVE   To actively participate in supplying children with a stable and loving environment while seeing that children in my care have fun while enjoying intellectually stimulating activities.

EDUCATION   Graduated from the **English Nanny & Governess School, Inc.**, Storm Lake, IA, 2000.
- Completed three months in-house and a six-month internship in the Child Growth and Development course of study.
- Specialized course work included nutrition, health, hygiene, welfare, and safety as well as courses emphasizing cultural enrichment; language, literature, music, art, and creative play.
- Earned *certifications* in Infant-through-adult CPR, AAA Defensive Driving, and Red Cross Standard First Aid.
- Completed a Field Practicum during which I provided in-home care for four children for the Smith family – a four month old, an 18 month old, a four year old, and a six year old.

Working toward a **B.S. in Child Psychology** in my spare time, Buena Vista University, Storm Lake, IA, 2000; completed specialized course work in English and psychology.

EXPERIENCE   **CERTIFIED PROFESSIONAL NANNY (CPN).** Courtney and Winston Smith, Storm Lake, IA (2000-2001). Cared for seven-year-old Parker and six-year-old Dillon with duties including preparing meals, providing transportation to and from various activities, and providing companionship and care for indoor and outdoor activities.
- Supervised two young boys and helped them with their homework; supervised activities while their friends were in the home to play; also volunteered in their classrooms.

DATA ENTRY CLERK. Independence Network, Winston, IA (1999). Performed data entry as well as general office duties such as filing, faxing, copying, and answering phones.

CHILD CARE PROVIDER. Toddle Tots Day Care Center, Storm Lake, IA (1997-98). Handled a wide range of daily child care from changing diapers, to preparing lunches, to feeding baby food and bottles, to toilet training, to art activities, to singing and rhyming reading, to outdoor activities.

CHILD CARE PROVIDER. Beth and Jim Brutner, Storm Lake, IA (1996-97). Took care of three children – Mark who is now 10, Shane who is seven, and Elisa who is three.
- Handled daily care including changing diapers, feeding, toilet training, meal preparation, and play and learning activities.
- Performed light housekeeping such as laundry and dishes.
- Provided supervision for play groups.

CHURCH NURSERY WORKER. Our Lady of Good Council Church, Storm Lake, IA (1993-96). Cared for children during Sunday morning worship services.

INTERESTS   Through my wide-ranging interests and hobbies, can communicate and relate to others in many areas: photography, art, pottery and ceramics, plays and musicals, reading, hiking and climbing, horseback riding, camping, traveling, and baseball.

PERSONAL   Experienced with children of all ages, am energetic, honest, and compassionate with a good sense of humor. Am a self-starter who is willing to try new things.

Date

Exact Name of Person
Exact Title
Exact Name of Company
Address
City, State, Zip

Natural Sciences

Dear Exact Name of Person (or Dear Sir or Madam if answering a blind ad):

A career in nursing is
ahead of this young
professional, and she is
using her resume to
show off her medical
skills, office skills,
certifications, license,
honors, education, and
experience. The cover
letter gives her a chance
to add the "warmth" and
"personality" that can
sometimes be lacking in
a resume.

With the enclosed resume, I would like to make you aware of my strong educational background in science and medicine, my highly developed analytical and problem-solving skills, and my extensive laboratory experience.

As you will see, I am currently completing a Bachelor of Science degree in Natural Sciences with a concentration in Biology from Wright State University. In addition to the rigorous course load of my degree program and my teaching responsibilities, I have taken on courses from the biotechnology program, which have provided me with the opportunity to develop cutting edge knowledge and learn to operate state-of-the-art laboratory equipment. While learning the fundamentals of DNA manipulation, I have used micropipettes, centrifuges, thermocyclers, and gel electrophorens apparatuses. I have studied techniques of DNA cloning, restriction digestion, transformation, plasmid isolation, bacterial culturing, and gel electrophorese. During a one-year project, I assisted on work involving the cloning of microbial resistant genes from the clinical isolation of *Klebsiella pneumoniae*.

If you can use an educated professional with highly-developed analytical and technical skills who offers a strong background in laboratory testing, I look forward to hearing from you soon to suggest a time when we might meet to discuss your needs. I can assure you in advance that I have an excellent reputation and would rapidly become a valuable addition to your organization.

Sincerely,

Elka Westervelt

ELKA WESTERVELT

1110½ Hay Street, Fayetteville, NC 28305 • preppub@aol.com • (910) 483-6611

OBJECTIVE To benefit an organization that can use an articulate and intelligent young professional with exceptional technical and analytical skills who offers a strong educational background in scientific and medical testing in laboratory environments.

EDUCATION Completing a **Bachelor of Science degree in Natural Sciences**, with a concentration in Biology, Wright State University, Dayton, OH. Will receive degree in May, 2001.
Have studied a wide range of difficult courses related to science and medicine, including:

Cellular and Molecular Biology	Techniques in Microbiology	Genetics
Radiation Biology	Comparative Anatomy	Chemistry I
Integrated Zoology	Calculus w/Analytic Geometry	Chemistry II
General Physics I, II, & III	Anatomy & Physiology I & II	Botany
Ecology and Evolution	Elementary Statistics	Spanish I & II
Animal Development	Intro To Computer Science	
Vertebrate Physiology	Special Problems (lab assignments)	

Completed 52 hours of **field experience teaching science** to local high school students.

TECHNICAL SKILLS Excelled in a number of additional courses from the biotechnology program, developing skills in the following areas:

- Fundamentals of DNA manipulation using state-of-the-art equipment such as micropipettes, centrifuges, thermocyclers, and gel electrophorens apparati.
- Techniques of DNA cloning, restriction digestion, transformation, plasmid isolation, bacterial culturing, and gel electrophorens.
- Spent a year on work involving the cloning of microbial resistant genes from clinical isolation of *Klebsiella pneumoniae.*

EXPERIENCE **TELEMARKETER.** Big Starr Telemarketing, Dayton, OH (Summers 1998, 1999, 2000). During summer break, demonstrated my exceptional verbal communication and listening skills while excelling in this stressful telephone direct sales environment.

- Quickly developed a rapport with customers, uncovered their objections, and used product knowledge and persuasion to close the sale.
- Provided direct marketing sales and support, presenting customers with the benefits and advantages of various products offered by the company.

CUSTODIAN. North High School, Dayton, OH (1997). In a part-time job while in college, performed general maintenance, cleaning, and landscaping services in order to beautify and prepare the school's interior, exterior, and grounds for the fall enrollment.

SEWING MACHINE OPERATOR. D& D Jeans, Dayton, OH (1996-1997). Worked in this commission-based position in a busy clothing production plant.

COOK and **CASHIER.** Burger King, Dayton, OH (1994-1996). Honed my skills in teamwork and time management while cooking and providing customer service for this local branch of the large national fast food chain.

- Was frequently called upon to accept the additional responsibility of training new employees due to my patience and exceptional communication skills.
- Provided customer service, taking food orders and operating a cash register.

PERSONAL Excellent personal and professional references are available upon request.

Nursing

The resume shows off internships which have helped her gain valuable knowledge.

Dear Sir or Madam:

I would appreciate an opportunity to talk with you soon about how I could contribute to your organization through my formal education as a Registered Nurse as well as through my outstanding personal qualities.

As you will see from my resume, I completed several clinical rotations while earning my nursing degree; these gave me hands-on experience in medical-surgical nursing, newborn and maternal care nursing, and psychiatric nursing. In every situation, I was commended for my excellent communication skills and ability to deal professionally with doctors, nurses, patients, administrators, and other personnel.

I was extremely active as a student was involved in the Nursing Students Association and was an elected delegate to the National Student Nurses Association Conference in New York. I have always been regarded as an outgoing individual with an ability to relate well to people on all levels.

You would find me in person to be a congenial individual who always strives to do my best in all situations. I am a mature individual who raised two children before embarking on my lifelong dream of becoming a nurse. I can provide outstanding personal and professional references.

I hope you will call or write me soon to suggest a time convenient for us to meet and discuss your current and future needs and how I might serve them. Thank you in advance for your time.

Sincerely,

Ragina Raftery

RAGINA RAFTERY

1110½ Hay Street, Fayetteville, NC 28305 • preppub@aol.com • (910) 483-6611

OBJECTIVE   To contribute to an organization that can use a Registered Nurse with excellent judgment and decision-making skills who offers a strong desire to make a significant contribution to medical, surgical, and patient care activities.

EDUCATION   **Associate of Applied Science degree in Nursing,** Averett College, Danville, VA, 2000. Completed Rape Crisis Intervention Volunteer Training, January 1999.

RN LICENSE   Valid until February 13, 2002.

CERTIFICATIONS   Certified Nursing Assistant I and II; CPR Certified.

MEDICAL SKILLS   • Trained in patient assessment, medication administration, catheterizations, sterile dressing changes, charting, and patient education.
• Skilled in using IV pumps, CPM (continuous passive motion) machine, and AccuChek.

OFFICE SKILLS   • Computer knowledgeable.
• Skilled in using office machines including faxes, copiers, printers, and typewriters.

EXPERIENCE   *1998-2000--While earning my nursing degree, have excelled in the following clinical rotations:*
Medical-Surgical Nursing Clinical Rotation: Danville Medical Center, Danville, VA. Provided total patient care while administering medications, assisting with activities of daily living including body mechanics, nutrition, and safety.
• Took vital signs; made dressing changes.
• Learned tracheotomy suctioning techniques.
• Applied sterile dressings and handled tube feedings.

Maternal and Newborn Nursing: Danville Medical Center, Danville, VA. Attended mothers through labor and delivery of infants.
• Became proficient in relaxation techniques during labor.
• Became a breast-feeding specialist.
• Completed one rotation in Neonatal ICU.
• Cared for critically ill newborns as well as healthy newborns.

Psychiatric Nursing: Danville Hospital, Danville, VA. Was commended for my compassion-ate attitude and my excellent communication skills while working in the adult unit.

1996-98: While earning my nursing degree, also worked part-time for LOMAC, Danville, VA: As **TREASURER**, was proudly associated with this fine organization and played a key role in the daily business operation of the day program for autistic adults; LOMAC is a nonprofit organization funded by the county, and it has evolved into the County Mental Health Day Program of today!
• Worked closely with the Board of Directors and was accountable to the board.
• Was responsible for more than $70,000 per year in cash and disbursements.

HONORS   • Member, Nursing Students Association, Averett College.
• Delegate, National Student Nurses Association Conference in New York.

Date

Exact Name of Person
Exact Title
Exact Name of Company
Address
City, State, Zip

Nursing

The Objective of the resume is a blend of all-purpose and specific. He mentions his specialized knowledge of the automotive industry as well as his sales and management skills which are transferable to any field.

Dear Exact Name of Person (or Dear Sir or Madam if answering a blind ad):

With the enclosed resume, I would like to acquaint you with my exceptional organizational and communication skills as well as my experience in Phlebotomy and as a Certified Nursing Assistant I & II.

A Certified Nursing Assistant, I have earned a certification in Phlebotomy from the American Society of Phlebotomy Technicians as well as a certification in Medical Terminology. Currently pursuing an Associate's degree in Nursing in the evenings at Carthage University, I expect to complete the requirements for the Licensed Practical Nurse program by June of 2000 and the Registered Nurse requirements in June of 2001.

In my most recent position, I worked a four-month internship in Phlebotomy at several area hospitals. Earlier in a four-month Certified Nursing Assistant Internship, I maintained tracheostomies and catheters, inserted and cleaned feeding tubes, and assisted nurses in providing patient care.

While pursuing my nursing degree and working in the above positions, I simultaneously oversee the operation of J & D 24-hour Towing, a successful small business. I interview and hire all new employees, handle accounts payable and receivable, and process weekly payroll. In an earlier position with Quick Stop, I served as Assistant Manager in this convenience store chain. I feel that my versatile experience, supervisory skills, and education would make me a valuable addition to your organization.

If you can use a highly motivated professional with strong organizational and communication skills, I hope you will contact me to suggest a time when we might meet. I can assure you that I have an excellent reputation and would quickly become an asset to your organization.

Sincerely,

Young Sikh Sondheimer

YOUNG SIKH SONDHEIMER

1110½ Hay Street, Fayetteville, NC 28305   • preppub@aol.com   • (910) 483-6611

OBJECTIVE
To contribute to an organization that can use a dedicated and hard-working medical professional with exceptional communication and organizational skills as well as certifications in Phlebotomy and as a Certified Nursing Assistant I & II.

EDUCATION
Completing **Associate's** degree in **Nursing** program at Carthage College, Kenosha, WA.
- Will complete the Licensed Practical Nurse requirements in June, 2000, and the Registered Nurse requirements in June, 2001.

Completed the Phlebotomy, Certified Nursing Assistant I & II, and Medical Terminology courses, Carthage College, Kenosha, WA, 1999.

CERTIFICATION
Certified in Phlebotomy, American Society of Phlebotomy Technicians, certificate XYZ123, 1999.
Certified Medical Assistant I & II, certificate #0922929, 1999.
Earned a certification in Medical Terminology, certificate #0923931, 1999.

EXPERIENCE
COLLEGE STUDENT and **SMALL BUSINESS OWNER.** J & D 24-hour Towing, Kenosha, WA (1996-present). Assumed ownership of his business after the death of my father; oversee all operational aspects of this successful towing company while simultaneously pursuing my Associate's degree in Nursing.
- Interview and hire all new employees; process weekly payroll and manage accounts payable/accounts receivable.
- Update and maintain all licenses and permits.

Completed the following internships while pursuing my Associate's degree in Nursing and simultaneously running a small business:
PHLEBOTOMY INTERNSHIP. Veterans Administration Hospital, Kenosha, WA; Good Hope Hospital, Kenosha, WA; and Harnett Manor, Lillith, WA (1999). Completed this internship program while earning my certification in phlebotomy.
- Prepared patients for phlebotomy, sterilizing the venipuncture site, and tying off the vein before drawing blood for laboratory testing and diagnosis.
- Retrieved records from the computer to determine what tests are to be performed.
- Maintained strict adherence to safety regulations and guidelines related to the handling and disposal of all blood products and related biohazards.

INTERNSHIP, CERTIFIED NURSING ASSISTANT I & II. Veterans Administration Hospital, Kenosha, WA; Good Hope Hospital, Kenosha, WA; and Harnett Manor, Lillith, WA, 1998. Performed the duties of a CNA while completing a four-month internship; assisted nurses in providing patient care while pursuing my nursing degree.
- Performed tracheostomies and administered catheters; cleaned and maintained catheters and tracheostomy tubes; turned stroke and heart patients every two hours.

ASSISTANT MANAGER. Quick Stop, Kenosha, WA (1993-1996). Managed this busy location of the regional convenience store chain; oversaw all facets of operation, including human resources, inventory control and purchasing, loss prevention, and accounting.
- Supervised five employees; interviewed, hired, and trained all new personnel.
- Balanced cash registers and safe, tracking all discrepancies and recording overages, shortages, and sales figures on daily transaction logs.

PERSONAL
Excellent personal and professional references are available upon request.

Date

Exact Name of Person
Exact Title
Exact Name of Company
Address
City, State, Zip

Dear Exact Name of Person (or Dear Sir or Madam if answering a blind ad):

This young Registered
Nurse has many clinical
rotations and much
leadership experience
to show off on his
resume.

With the enclosed resume, I would like to make you aware of my desire to explore employment as a Registered Nurse.

As you will see, I will shortly graduate with an Associate's degree in Nursing and am seeking employment in the San Diego area, where my extended family is from. While earning my degree, I excelled in numerous clinical rotations and internships. I have worked in med-surg, ortho/neuro, labor and delivery, long-term care, psychiatric, and substance abuse environments.

I have taken the time to work actively in student organizations, and I have held numerous elected offices in student nursing associations. I can provide outstanding personal and professional references.

If you can use an educated professional with highly developed analytical and technical skills, I hope you will contact me to suggest a time when we might meet to discuss your present and future needs. I can assure you in advance that I have an excellent reputation and would rapidly become a valuable addition to your organization.

Sincerely,

Andrew Reese

ANDREW REESE

1110½ Hay Street, Fayetteville, NC 28305 • preppub@aol.com • (910) 483-6611

OBJECTIVE   I want to contribute to an organization that can use a skilled young nursing professional who offers proven management and leadership skills.

CERTIFICATIONS   Certified Nurse Aide II.
CPR Certification.

LICENSES   Will take the NCLEX-RN in June 2001.

EDUCATION   **Associate Degree in Nursing (ADN) degree,** Drexel University, Philadelphia, PA; will graduate May 2001. **Current GPA 3.89.**
- Named to President's List; inducted into Phi Theta Kappa Honor Society.
- Will pursue Bachelor of Science in Nursing in my spare time after receiving RN license.
Graduated from Chambers Senior High School, Philadelphia, PA, 1995.
Extensive management and leadership training as a U.S. Army professional, 1995-98.

EXPERIENCE   **NURSING INTERN & NURSING STUDENT.** Drexel University, Philadelphia, PA (1998-present). Have excelled academically, in clinical rotations, and in leadership positions with the Pennsylvania Association of Nursing Students (PANS) and the Drexel Association of Nursing Students (ANS).
Clinical Rotations: Have received the highest-possible evaluations of my performance in these clinical rotations:
- **Med/Surg:** Rainey Memorial Hospital, Fall 1999 and Fall 2000. Refined skills in patient care and administered oral medications; provided advanced care in Fall 2000.
- **Ortho/Neuro:** Philadelphia Medical Center, Spring 1999. Administered parenteral and IV medications; expanded my assessment skills with adult patients.
- **Labor & Delivery/Newborn:** Philadelphia Medical Center, Summer 1999. Administered IVs; refined my assessment skills related to newborns and mothers.
- **Long-Term Care:** Carrol Nursing Home, Fall 1998. Administered medications and feedings via gastrostomy tubes; gained skills in long-term care geriatric nursing.
- **Psychiatric:** Hope Hospital, Fall 1998. Gained insights into psychiatric care.
- **Substance Abuse:** Blunt Avenue Clinic, Spring 1998. Learned about substance abuse nursing practices.

Leadership in Professional Organizations: Have been elected Breakthrough to Nursing Director in both the state (PANS) and the Drexel nursing associations.
- Awarded the PANS Nursing Scholarship at PANS Annual Convention, Oct 1999.
- For the Drexel Association of Nursing Students, supervised recruiting activities; achieved a 95% retention rate of second-year students while aggressively recruiting new first-year student members.
- For the Philadelphia Association of Nursing Students, am supervising membership recruitment and retention for all 78 nursing schools in Pennsylvania.
- Represented the state nursing association at the Pennsylvania State Legislature; have played a key role in planning the 2001 mid-year conference.

MEDEVAC OPERATIONS MANAGER. U.S. Army, Ft. Sill, OK (1995-98). For a medevac company at a large U.S. military base, was promoted to manage an average of seven people and up to 40 personnel while assuring the availability of 15 helicopters and other medevac assets; maintained and organized inspectable aircraft maintenance records; received "Commendable" ratings in five inspections.

PERSONAL   Can provide outstanding references. Proven leadership and management skills.

Date

Exact Name of Person
Exact Title
Exact Name of Company
Address
City, State, Zip

Dear Exact Name of Person (or Dear Sir or Madam if answering a blind ad):

Here is another resume
of a technical
professional who has
clinical rotations to show
off.

With the enclosed resume, I would like to make you aware of my background as an articulate young professional with exceptional communication, organization, and patient care skills who offers an educational background and clinical rotation experience in various occupational therapy environments.

As you will see from my enclosed resume, I am currently excelling both academically and in clinical rotations while completing my Bachelor of Science degree in Occupational Therapy. Currently maintaining a **3.89 GPA**, I will graduate in May and test for certification as an Occupational Therapist Registered in September of 2000. I previously earned an Associate of Applied Science degree in Accounting and completed two years college course work in Biology before entering the Occupational Therapy program.

I have excelled in clinical rotations at Charles Mental Health Center and at Northeastern Regional Rehabilitation Center, where I demonstrated my creativity, problem-solving ability, and therapeutic skills. In addition to preparing a multimedia in-service presentation for the Occupational Therapy department using Microsoft PowerPoint, I also designed and created a new adaptive tool for patients with hemiparesis. Currently, I am beginning a Pediatric Outpatient rotation.

If you can use a dedicated, accomplished young professional with a strong desire to make a contribution in the field of Occupational Therapy, I look forward to hearing from you soon. I assure you in advance that I have an excellent reputation and would quickly become an asset to your organization.

Sincerely,

Deborah Lucas

DEBORAH LUCAS

1110½ Hay Street, Fayetteville, NC 28305　•　preppub@aol.com　•　(910) 483-6611

OBJECTIVE　To offer my education and experience in Occupational Therapy to an organization that could benefit from the services of a creative and dedicated professional with exceptional communication, problem-solving, and patient care skills which have been tested in a variety of clinical environments.

EDUCATION　**Bachelor of Science in Occupational Therapy**, Hastings College, Hastings, NE; currently maintaining a **3.89 GPA**, will graduate May, 2000.
- Named to the **President's Honor List** three times, for achieving a perfect **4.0 GPA** for the semester, and the **Dean's List**, for a **3.5 GPA** or better.
- Received the prestigious Thomas Foundation scholarship, a $16,000 award in recognition of my extensive hours of volunteer work.
- Completed two years of college-level course work towards a Bachelor of Science in Biology at Hastings College before entering the Occupational Therapy program, 1997-1999.

Associate of Applied Science degree in Accounting, Hastings Community College, Hastings, NE, 1996.

CERTIFICATIONS　Will test for Occupational Therapist Registered through the National Board for Certification in Occupational Therapy, September 18, 2000.

AFFILIATIONS　Member, American Student Occupational Therapy Association, 1997-present.
Treasurer, Phi Beta Lambda, 1997-1999.

EXPERIENCE　**OCCUPATIONAL THERAPY INTERN** and **STUDENT.** Hastings College, Hastings, NE (1999-present). Have excelled academically, in clinical rotations, and in leadership positions with the American Student Occupational Therapy Association.
Clinical Rotations: Have received the highest-possible evaluations of my performance and been praised for my creativity and problem-solving while completing these clinical rotations:
Pediatric Outpatient: Caring Hands, Hastings, NE (Mar 1999-present). Apply my growing knowledge and exceptional care skills while providing occupational therapy to children.
Rehabilitation: Northeastern Regional Rehabilitation Center, Hastings, NE (Jan-Mar 1999). Demonstrated creativity and problem-solving while further honing my patient care skills during this clinical rotation at a major regional rehabilitation center; performed patient assessment and evaluation in order to establish a plan of care.
Mental Health: Charles Mental Health Center, Hastings, NE (May-Aug 1998). Gained valuable experience in helping clients with schizophrenia and bipolar disorder to develop problem-solving ability as well as social and communication skills; held a money management workshop and conducted weekly money management group meetings to help patients achieve a greater sense of personal responsibility.

THERAPY ASSISTANT. Titus Rehabilitation Hospital, Hastings, NE (1994-1996). Performed more than 240 hours of volunteer work, assisting with patient activities under the supervision of an Occupational Therapist.

ACCOUNTING CLERK and **DATA ENTRY CLERK.** Kearns Guidance & Navigation Corporation, Charles, NE (1992-1994). Started with this major defense contractor as a Data Entry Clerk and quickly advanced to a position of increased responsibility.

PERSONAL　Excellent personal and professional references are available upon request.

Date

Exact Name of Person
Title or Position
Name of Company
Address (number and street)
Address (city, state, and zip)

Dear Exact Name of Person: (or Sir or Madam if answering a blind ad.)

With the enclosed resume, I would like to initiate the process of being considered for employment within your organization. I am in the process of permanently relocating to your area where both my wife and I have family. We will be permanently settling in the area around May 15, 2001, after my college graduation on May 7.

As you will see from my resume, I have recently earned my Associate of Applied Science in Paralegal Technology in an ABA-approved program in Kentucky. With a 4.0 GPA, I am graduating as the #1 student in my class. While excelling academically, I was selected as Honorary Legal Research Assistant at my college because of my academic standing and personal reputation. In that capacity I tutor students and assist faculty in projects that involve legal writing and research. I also have worked 15 hours a week in a paid job as an Assistant Manager while earning my degree.

Prior to enrolling in my current degree program, I excelled as a Legal Specialist in the U.S. Army, and I received 15 medals, awards, and certificates in recognition of my outstanding skills and exceptional performance. As a Legal Specialist I worked with numerous attorneys and was entrusted with the responsibility for supervising legal work performed at numerous organizations.

You will also see from my resume that I have worked as a Paralegal for the past five months in an internship with one of the city's most respected law firms. I have gained exposure to real estate, corporate law, civil litigation, personal injury, and criminal defense.

You would find me in person to be a congenial individual, and I can assure you that my legal research and legal writing skills are top-notch. If you can use a hard worker who could become a valuable part of your organization, I hope you will call to suggest a time when I can make myself available for a personal interview at your convenience. Thank you in advance for your time.

Sincerely,

Harry Hooper

HARRY HOOPER

1110½ Hay Street, Fayetteville, NC 28305 • preppub@aol.com • (910) 483-6611

OBJECTIVE   To become a contributing member of a law firm that can use a versatile paralegal who offers experience with real estate law, corporate law, civil litigation, personal injury, and criminal defense along with outstanding analytical, research, and communication skills.

EDUCATION   **Associate of Applied Science in Paralegal Technology** (an ABA-Approved Program), Georgetown College, Georgetown, KY; graduation date is May 7, 2001.
- With a 4.0 GPA, I will graduate *summa cum laude* and am ranked #1 in my class.
- Named to Phi Theta Kappa Society, which requires a GPA above 3.5.
- Consistently named to President's and Dean's Lists; Active member, Paralegal Club.
- Selected as Honorary Legal Research Assistant; coursework included:

Legal Research	Partnership/Corporate Law	Civil Litigation
Tort Law	Criminal Procedures	Family Law
Case Analysis/Reasoning	Contract Law and the UCC	Investigations

Other legal training: While serving in the U.S. Army as a **Legal Specialist,** completed extensive legal training in addition to the Army's nine-week **Legal Specialist Training Program.**

EXPERIENCE   **PARALEGAL.** Morris and Blake, P.A., Georgetown, KY (January 2001-May 2001). Was successful in being selected for this Paralegal Internship with one of the city's most respected law firms; excelled in this part-time job while retaining my #1 position in my graduating class; can provide outstanding references from this firm.
- Have assisted Attorney Morris with his real estate and corporate law practice.
- Assisted Attorney Blake in civil litigation, personal injury, and criminal defense.
- Was commended by both attorneys for significantly reducing their research time through my excellent analytical skills and research ability.
- Learned how to title search and how to prepare loan closing packages.

LEGAL RESEARCH ASSISTANT. Georgetown College, Georgetown, KY (1999-present). Was selected for this honorary role at my college because of my personal reputation and GPA; tutored students in legal research methodology.
- Assisted faculty members with projects which required excellent legal writing skills.

LEGAL SPECIALIST. U.S. Army, Ft. Hood, TX (1996-99). Provided legal services for a 500-soldier organization while working under the supervision of numerous military attorneys.
- Supervised two employees while managing legal work performed in three organizations.
- Prepared Article 15's, Separation Packets, Powers of Attorney; and Charge Sheets.
- Coordinated Article 32 hearings, 15-6 investigations, and line-of-duty investigations.
- Prepared correspondence for the signature of military executives.
- **Honors and awards:** Received 15 medals, ribbons, and Certificates of Achievement which included the Army Commendation Medal, Army Achievement Medal, National Defense Service Medal, Humanitarian Service Medal, and others.

Other experience: ASSISTANT MANAGER. Video Wares, Dallas, TX (1997-May 1998). Worked part-time 15 hours a week while earning my degree; supervised two employees.

COMPUTERS   Highly computer literate. Familiar with Westlaw, Michie's, Premise, Microsoft Word, WordPerfect, Enable, and Harvard Graphics. Excellent references on request.

PERSONAL   Excellent references. Relocating to Rhode Island where my wife and I have family.

Date

Exact Name of Person
Exact Title
Exact Name of Company
Address
City, State, Zip

Dear Exact Name of Person (or Dear Sir or Madam if answering a blind ad):

With the enclosed resume, I would like to make you aware of my interest in obtaining a position in a health services field where I could utilize the knowledge and skills which I am developing as I pursue an Associate's degree from the Physical Therapy Assistant's program at Palomar College.

As you will see, I have been pursuing my degree part-time while excelling in various positions with the California Department of Transportation. While completing my general studies requirements I have maintained a 3.85 GPA and was elected to the National Honor Society. I was accepted into the Physical Therapy Assistant's program beginning with the fall semester of 2000. I hold current certifications in Community CPR and First Aid, and I have already completed a number of courses related to the health sciences.

In prior experience with the California Department of Transportation I have shown myself to be an articulate communicator and persuasive leader as well as a dedicated and reliable team player who applies imagination and ingenuity to problem-solving. Currently an Auditor, I demonstrate my strong attention to detail while over-seeing accountability for a $32 million road construction project. Earlier I exhibited exceptional leadership and communication skills while managing and training a three-man survey crew.

I am highly regarded by my present employer and can provide outstanding references and letters of recommendation at the appropriate time. However, I am interested in exploring opportunities in the health services field.

If you can use a motivated and compassionate young professional whose growing knowledge of physical therapy and exceptional communication and organizational skills could benefit your organization, I would appreciate the opportunity to speak with you about your needs and how I could serve them. I assure you in advance that I have an excellent reputation and could quickly become an asset to your organization.

Sincerely,

Nigel Kramer

NIGEL KRAMER

1110½ Hay Street, Fayetteville, NC 28305   •   preppub@aol.com   •   (910) 483-6611

OBJECTIVE

To benefit an organization that can use an accomplished young professional with a strong desire to make a contribution to the health care field.

EDUCATION

Pursuing **Physical Therapy Assistant Associate's Degree**, Palomar College, San Marcos, CA.
- Named to the National Honor Society, am maintaining 3.85 GPA.

Courses related to the medical field which I have completed or am completing include:

Anatomy & Physiology I	Basic Chemistry I & II
Health Sciences Physics	General Psychology
Developmental Psychology	First Aid & CPR
Anatomy & Physiology II	General Microbiology

Previously completed nearly four years of college-level course work towards a Bachelor of Science in Business Administration, Pacific Union College, Angwin, CA.

CERTIFICATIONS

Hold current certifications in First Aid and Community CPR (adult, child, and infant).

AFFILIATIONS

Member, National Honor Society, 2000.

COMPUTERS

Familiar with many popular computer operating systems and software programs, including Windows and Microsoft Word, Excel, Access, and PowerPoint.

EXPERIENCE

STUDENT. Palomar College, San Marcos, CA (1999-present). Demonstrate exceptional time management skills, excelling in my college studies while working full-time for the California Department of Transportation.
- Currently maintaining a 3.85 GPA in the Physical Therapy Assistant program.

RESIDENT ASSISTANT. Palomar College, San Marcos, CA (1998-present). In a part-time job, provide guidance and supervision for dormitory activities for up to 20 male students.
- Was recognized as **Resident Assistant of the Year for 2000** on the basis of my leadership, counseling ability, and resourceful problem-solving style.

With the California Department of Transportation, have advanced in the following "track record" of increasing responsibilities:
1998-present: **AUDITOR.** San Marcos, CA. Promoted to this job from a position as Transportation Technician II; excelled in this difficult position requiring careful attention to detail while simultaneously pursuing my college education.
- Audit all records and reports submitted to the DOT in relation to the $32 million I-95 construction project.
- Verify accuracy of all documentation, ensuring that all records and reports are in compliance with applicable California standards and specifications.
- Monitored compensation made to the contractor on behalf of the state to guarantee that all monthly payment amounts were accurate.
- As a semi-independent auditor, excelled at performing liaison between contractors and CDOT officials, providing a fair and impartial assessment of the facts.

1996-1998: **TRANSPORTATION TECHNICIAN II.** San Marcos, CA. Oversaw the work of a survey crew, organizing and planning survey work to be done on various road construction.

PERSONAL

Excellent references on request.

Date

Exact Name of Person
Exact Title
Exact Name of Company
Address
City, State, Zip

Dear Exact Name of Person: (or Dear Sir or Madam if answering a blind ad):

With the enclosed resume, I would like to make you aware of my education as a Physician Assistant as well as my extensive experience in surgical environments as a Certified Surgical Technologist. I am interested in exploring employment with you as a Surgical Physician Assistant.

As you will see from my resume, I completed my Associate of Science and earned a diploma as a Surgical Technologist, and I have worked as a Surgical Technologist at Malibu Regional Hospital. I am highly skilled in operating room procedures and am known for my dedication to providing the highest quality patient care. I am also skilled in interacting with staff and physicians and am known for my ability to establish and maintain effective working relationships with people at all levels.

While excelling in my full-time job, I have also excelled academically while completing the Physician Assistant Program at Pepperdine University. You will see from my resume that I have completed rotations in orthopedics, family practice, pediatrics, internal medicine, surgery, and obstetrics and gynecology. In 2001, I will be involved in rotations in vascular surgery, dermatology, urology, psychiatry, emergency medicine, and public health.

If you can use a dedicated young Physician Assistant who is highly experienced in surgical and medical environments, I hope you will contact me to suggest a time when we might meet in person to discuss your needs. I can provide outstanding references at the appropriate time.

Sincerely,

Su H. Chung

SU H. CHUNG

1110½ Hay Street, Fayetteville, NC 28305   •   preppub@aol.com   •   (910) 483-6611

OBJECTIVE   To benefit an organization that can use a skilled young Physician Assistant dedicated to the highest standards of patient care who offers a background as a Certified Surgical Technologist along with extensive experience in surgical and medical environments.

EDUCATION   Completing **Physician Assistant Program,** Pepperdine University, Malibu, CA; degree to be awarded May 2001; have excelled academically; named to **President's List** and **Dean's List**; inducted into **Tri Beta Biological Honor Society.**
Completed **Associate of Science (A.S.) degree** and a **Diploma as a Surgical Technologist**, Malibu Technical College, Malibu, CA, 1996.
• Elected President, Surgical Technology Club.
One year of college in general studies, Pacific Union College, Angwin, CA, 1992-94.

CERTIFICATIONS   Certified in Advanced Cardiac Life Support (ACLS).
& AFFILIATIONS   AAPA: American Academy of Physician Assistants.
CAPA: California Academy of Physician Assistants.

EXPERIENCE   **CERTIFIED SURGICAL TECHNOLOGIST.** Malibu Regional Hospital, Malibu, CA (1996-present). Am known for my dedication to providing the highest quality patient care in the process of performing surgical assisting and surgical first-assisting.

PHYSICIAN ASSISTANT ROTATIONS: While completing Physician's Assistant School, have excelled in the following rotations:
Orthopedics: Alabaster Hospital, Malibu, CA (5/10-6/99). Performed assessment and treatment of trauma patients; handled reducing, casting, splinting of fractures; performed hardware removal, X-ray interpretation, surgical first assisting, inpatient care, suturing, and handled operative orders and notes.
Family Practice: Heritage Family Practice, Malibu, CA (6/99-7/99). Was involved in inpatient rounds and care; took dictations; performed assessment, diagnosis, and treatment of a wide variety of conditions; performed routine gynecological exams.
Pediatrics: Malibu Public Health, Malibu, CA (7/99). Handled well baby exams. Performed Denver II assessments along with assessment, diagnosis, and treatment of childhood illnesses. Provided school and sports physicals.
Family Practice: Langolier Medical Center, Langolier, CA (8/99). Handled the diagnosis and treatment of a wide variety of conditions while also performing office procedures such as toe nail removal, steroid injections, sebaceous cyst incisions, and gynecological exams.
Internal Medicine: Alabaster Hospital, Malibu, CA (8/99-10/99). Was involved in the daily management and care of inpatients and ICU patients. Handled procedures including thoracentesis, abdominocentesis, joint aspiration, and lumber puncture. Monitored ventilator patients and stress testing.
Surgery: Village Surgical Associates, Malibu, CA (10/99-11/99). Was involved in surgical first assisting, suturing, performing daily rounds, and providing patient care.
Obstetrics and Gynecology: Alabaster Hospital, Malibu, CA (11/99-12/99). Handled routine OB-GYN assessment exams, vaginal/C-section deliveries, surgical first assisting, and suturing.
Rotations scheduled for 2001:

Vascular Surgery	**Urology**	**Emergency Medicine**
Dermatology	**Psychiatry**	**Public Health**

PERSONAL   Excellent personal and professional references are available upon request.

Date

Exact Name of Person
Title or Position
Name of Company
Address (no., street)
Address (city, state, zip)

Dear Exact Name of Person: (or Dear Sir or Madam if answering a blind ad.)

Mr. Troy has made a career change by pursuing his degree in Police Administration. He will use this versatile all-purpose letter to approach various police departments and municipalities in order to determine his options.

I would appreciate an opportunity to talk with you soon about how I could contribute to your organization through my degree in Police Administration.

A recent graduate from Strayer University, Washington, DC, with a B.S. degree in Police Administration, I completed specialized course work which included law enforcement, criminal law, community-based corrections, and the legal aspects of the criminal justice system. Other classes in sociology, social problems, abnormal psychology, statistics, and computer science gave me a well-rounded base of knowledge. The degree program also gave me an opportunity to participate in two internships where I observed members of the District of Columbia Police Department on duty and gained insight into the day-to-day operations of a metropolitan police department.

I hope you will welcome my call soon to arrange a brief meeting at your convenience to discuss your current and future needs and how I might serve them. Thank you in advance for your time.

Sincerely yours,

Paul Edward Troy

Alternate last paragraph:
I hope you will call or write me soon to suggest a time convenient for us to meet and discuss your current and future needs and how I might serve them. Thank you in advance for your time.

PAUL EDWARD TROY

1110½ Hay Street, Fayetteville, NC 28305 • preppub@aol.com • (910) 483-6611

OBJECTIVE
To offer my education in the field of police administration to an organization that can use a mature young professional who offers strong computer, sales, and communication abilities.

EDUCATION
B.S. degree in Police Administration, Strayer College, Washington, DC, 2000.
- Completed specialized course work including the following:

principles of sociology	crime and delinquency	law enforcement
contemporary social problems	the court system	criminal law
civil rights and the constitution	abnormal psychology	juvenile justice
legal aspects of the justice system		community corrections

Attended University of Missouri-Rolla, Rolla, MO.

POLICE INTERNSHIPS
Completed two 40-hour Police Administration Internships with the District of Columbia Police Department, Washington, DC, summer and fall, 1999.
- Was exposed to the day-to-day functions of the department; shadowed police officers and dispatchers as well as detectives investigating homicides.

EXPERIENCE
Refined my time management skills while gaining practical work experience and building a reputation as a detail-oriented and hard-working young professional in these jobs while also attending college full time:
MATERIAL HANDLER. Nyles Warehouse, Inc., Washington, DC (2000). In a part-time job while financing my college education, gained experience in operating material-handling equipment including forklifts and power jacks as well as in activities including loading trucks, preparing items for cold storage, separating items into categories, and cleaning a warehouse.

ADMINISTRATIVE ASSISTANT. American Division Association, Inc., Washington, DC (Summers, 1998 and 1999). Provided this professional association of 50,000 active global members with secretarial support which included answering phone calls and giving information about activities.
- Increased my familiarity with using Word for word processing various documents for the association.
- Processed information from members and kept address files current.
- Learned to operate copy machines and produced approximately 280 eight-to-ten page monthly bulletins for the association.
- Was very proud and pleasantly surprised at receiving the President's Award given at a national convention in honor of my many hours of service and dedication.

ADMINISTRATIVE ASSISTANT. Environmental Protection Agency, Washington, DC (summer 1996). Learned to work independently while applying my analytical skills in investigating environmental issues.

COMPUTERS
Offer experience in using MS Word for word processing on IBM compatible PCs.

LANGUAGE
Speak and read Spanish fluently; have a fair grasp of written Spanish.

PERSONAL
Enthusiastic, energetic, and creative. Truly like people and enjoy meeting and getting to know and help others. Offer strong problem-solving skills and a drive to succeed.

Date

Exact Name of Person
Exact Title
Exact Name of Company
Address
City, State, Zip

Dear Exact Name of Person (or Dear Sir or Madam if answering a blind ad):

The background of this
professional will no
doubt be an advantage
to him as he attempts to
launch a career in the
public sector.

With the enclosed resume, I would like to introduce you to an enthusiastic, articulate, and mature young professional with exceptional organizational, communication, and computer operations skills as well as a versatile background and a newly minted degree in Political Science.

Most recently, I have been assisting the Director for European Studies at the University of Miami's Regional Studies Center. I have refined my communication skills while coordinating with major universities on their Regional Studies programs. With strong computer skills I have used the Internet extensively in addition to other media to secure material for use in training.

In previous positions as a Peer Counselor and German Tutor for the University of Miami, I utilized my communication skills while counseling students on issues from personal to academic tutoring students having difficulty with the German foreign language program.

As you will see from my resume, I have one semester left to complete the program requirements for a Bachelor of Science in Political Science with a minor in German from the University of Miami, and will receive my diploma in December; I am currently maintaining a 3.7 GPA. I already hold an Associate of Arts in General Studies from the University of Montana, and I received a certification as an English-German translator and a Spanish-German correspondent from a translator's school in Germany.

If you can use an enthusiastic, articulate, and educated young professional with exceptional communication, organizational, and computer operation skills, I hope you will contact me to suggest a time when we might meet to discuss your needs. I can assure you that I am highly regarded by all who have worked with me and could quickly become a valuable asset to your organization.

Sincerely,

Robert Gollance

ROBERT GOLLANCE

1110½ Hay Street, Fayetteville, NC 28305　　•　　preppub@aol.com　　•　　(910) 483-6611

OBJECTIVE　　To benefit an organization that can use an enthusiastic and articulate young professional with exceptional organizational, communication, and computer operations skills in addition to strong foreign language skills and a newly minted degree in Political Science.

EDUCATION　　Maintained a 3.7 GPA in the **Bachelor of Science program in Political Science** with a minor in German, University of Miami, Coral Gables, FL; to be awarded December, 2000. **Associate of Arts degree in General Studies,** University of Montana, 1998. Certified as an **English-German translator and Spanish-German correspondent,** Translator's School, Germany, 1997.

COMPUTERS　　Proficient in Windows and Word, Excel, Access, PowerPoint, Outlook, and WordPerfect.

AFFILIATIONS　　Member, University of Montana University College Alumni Association.
Vice President, University of Miami Political Science Club.
Member, Phi Sigma Iota—International Foreign Language Honor Society.

EXPERIENCE　　**RESEARCH ASSISTANT AND INTERN.** University of Miami, Miami, FL (Summer, 2000). Served an internship in this prestigious center, assisting the Director for European Studies at the Regional Studies Center.
- Contacted major universities to obtain information on their Regional Studies programs.
- Conducted research via books, magazines, the Internet, and other media to secure material that could be used for the next training cycle.
- Performed clerical and secretarial tasks, such as typing, filing, and photocopying.

PEER COUNSELOR. Counseling Center, University of Miami, Coral Gables, FL (Summer, 1999). In a largely Christian counseling center, provided a secular and nonjudgmental viewpoint appreciated by many students.
- Counseled students on a wide range of issues, from personal to academic; referred students to advanced counseling when necessary.
- Managed the counseling office independently when the Staff Psychologist was not in.
- Provided students with the opportunity to discuss problems in a confidential environment.
- Further honed my communication skills, learning to listen actively and interpret body language.

GERMAN TUTOR. University of Miami, Coral Gables, FL (Summer, 1998). Assisted students taking German language courses in improving their grammar, pronunciation, and comprehension of the German language and culture.
- Provided coaching and supplementary instruction for students having difficulty with course work in German.
- Increased my communication skills by gaining an outsider's view of my native language while preparing teaching aids and lessons for the classes.

Other experience: **SALES ASSOCIATE.** Optical Shop, Montana (1997-1998). Assisted customers in the selection of eyeglasses and frames; operated a lensometer; transposed prescriptions; repaired, adjusted eyeglasses; accounting and customer service.

PERSONAL　　Excellent personal and professional references are available upon request.

Date

Exact Name of Person
Exact Title
Exact Name of Company
Address
City, State, Zip

Psychology with Counseling Concentration

A cover letter gives you an opportunity to tell the employer things that are more difficult to communicate in a resume. For example, the cover letter provides an opportunity to communicate that Ms. Menke is relocating to Brownsville.

Dear Exact Name of Person: (or Dear Sir or Madam if answering a blind ad)::

With the enclosed resume, I would like to make you aware of my background as an educated, articulate young professional who offers exceptional communication and organizational skills as well as experience in dealing with diverse populations in customer service and public speaking environments.

I am in the process of relocating to the Brownsville area due to my husband's transfer from GTE. I will be permanently established in the area by June 1, 2001, and I would appreciate the chance to speak with you concerning career opportunities within your organization.

As you will see from my resume, I have recently completed a Bachelor of Arts in Psychology with a concentration in Counseling from Emory University, where I graduated **magna cum laude** with a **3.7 cumulative GPA**. Throughout my collegiate career, I have excelled academically while managing a family and a home. Earlier I graduated **cum laude** with an Associate of Arts with a concentration in Education at Darton College, maintaining a **3.5 GPA**. I also completed a number of travel industry management and training courses through my employers, and am highly computer literate.

Although my previous experience has been as a Branch Manager and Travel Agent for various companies in the travel industry, I feel that the exceptional communication skills, strong "people" focus, and public speaking ability which I have honed in this field will serve me well in counseling environments.

I hope you will welcome my call soon when I try to arrange a brief meeting to discuss your goals and how my background might serve your needs. I can provide outstanding references at the appropriate time.

Sincerely,

Norma Menke

NORMA MENKE

1110½ Hay Street, Fayetteville, NC 28305 • preppub@aol.com • (910) 483-6611

OBJECTIVE

To benefit an organization that can use a human services professional with exceptional communication, organizational, and customer service skills who offers an education in psychology and counseling as well as experience in dealing with diverse populations.

EDUCATION

Bachelor of Arts in **Psychology** with a concentration in Counseling, Emory University, Atlanta, GA, 2000.
- Graduated **magna cum laude**, maintaining a **3.7 cumulative GPA**.
- Completed research projects examining the long-term effect of uniform school dress codes on achievement scores and the effects of culture on teenage pregnancy; received "A's" on both projects.

Courses related to counseling and psychology included:

Abnormal Psychology	Principles of Sociology I & II	General Psychology
Cognitive Psychology	Theories of Personality	Theories of Learning
Physiological Psychology	Social Psychology	Learning & Memory
Psychology of Aging	Child Psychopathology	Psychological Statistics
Psychological Testing & Measurement		Psychology of Adjustment
Introduction to Clinical Psychology & Counseling		History in Psychology
Comprehensive Applications in Behavioral Science		Research Methods

Associate of Arts with a concentration in Education, Darton College, Albany, GA, 1998.
- Graduated **cum laude**, with a **3.5 cumulative GPA**.

COMPUTERS

Familiar with many of the most popular computer operating systems and software, including: Windows and Microsoft Word, PowerPoint, Works, and Publisher.
Also familiar with United Airlines Apollo and American Airlines SABRE reservation systems and other software specific to the travel industry.

EXPERIENCE

COLLEGE STUDENT. Emory University, Atlanta, GA (1998-present). Honed my time management skills attending college full-time while managing a home and family.

BRANCH MANAGER. Sato Travel, Atlanta, GA (1996-1998). Oversaw all operational aspects of this local travel agency; interviewed, hired, and trained a travel agent while assisting customers with the planning and scheduling of hotel, airline, rental car, and cruise ship reservations and travel itineraries.
- Completed a company-sponsored management training program; coordinated and negotiated with vendors, and set up new customer accounts.
- Created and implemented innovative and effective marketing strategies and promotions which resulted in quadrupling the office's sales within a one-year period.
- Conducted public speaking engagements at monthly "newcomers" and Chamber of Commerce meetings, presenting Sato's products and services to local consumers.
- Wrote travel articles for the local newspaper on a regular basis.

Highlights of earlier experience: Excelled in earlier positions as a **TRAVEL AGENT**, assisting customers with travel itineraries and reservations; provided exceptional customer service while dealing in a tactful and diplomatic manner with customers who were often upset due to problems with travel arrangements.

PERSONAL

Excellent personal and professional references are available upon request.

Date

Exact Name of Person
Title or Position
Name of Company
Address (number and street)
Address (city, state, and ZIP)

Dear Exact Name of Person: (or Dear Sir or Madam if answering a blind as.)

Can you use a creative and intelligent young professional who offers well-developed verbal and written communication skills along with personal qualities of adaptability, dependability, and dedication to excellence?

As you will see from my enclosed resume, I received my Bachelor of Arts degree from Marymount University. My college years were an opportunity for gaining an education and growing in self-motivation, self-awareness, and a sense of responsibility as a citizen of the community. Through practical experience in summer jobs, I learned to work with others on a team and adapt to a wide range of situations where physical strength and common sense was important in order to do a good job.

I have always been able to deal with people in settings which have ranged from adolescents attending a summer camp, to customers in retail stores, to general laborers, to professors and instructors in academic environments.

Known for my sensitivity and artistic talents, I have a lot to offer any organization that values hard work, determination, honesty, and concern for others.

I hope you will welcome my call soon to arrange a brief meeting at your convenience to discuss your current and future needs and how I might serve them. Thank you in advance for your time.

Sincerely yours.

Alexander La Salla

Alternate last paragraph:
I hope you will call or write me soon to suggest a time convenient for us to meet and discuss your current and future needs and how I might serve them. Thank you in advance for your time.

ALEXANDER LA SALLA

1110½ Hay Street, Fayetteville, NC 28305   •   preppub@aol.com   •   (910) 483-6611

OBJECTIVE

To apply my creativity along with my outstanding verbal and written communication skills to an organization that can use an intelligent and caring young professional who possesses a strong desire to contribute to an organization that values initiative and dedication.

EDUCATION

Earned a **Bachelor of Arts (B.A.) degree in Religious Studies,** with a minor in Music, Marymount University, Arlington, VA, 2000.
- Elected President of the Religious Association.
- Refined my written and oral communication skills in this degree program which required the preparation of numerous written papers and reports that involved extensive research and the application of strong analytical skills.

EXPERIENCE

Earned a reputation for dependability, reliability, and integrity in summer and part-time jobs including the following, which called for adaptability and strong communication skills:

CASHIER and **CUSTOMER SERVICE SPECIALIST.** Hamm Sporting Goods, Arlington, VA (2000). Learned how to operate a cash register while refining my customer service and sales skills in this busy retail location.

ASSISTANT. Borough Motor Company, Arlington, VA (1999). Gained experience in basic mechanics while assisting the car rental staff by answering phones, running errands, and washing cars.

FIELD INSPECTOR. Protect Advisory Service, Arlington, VA (1998). As a "cotton scout," inspected fields for certain insects and checked the growth rate of the cotton crops.

GENERAL LABORER. Greenway Landscaping, Arlington, VA (1997). Learned my capacity for physical labor while assisting in planting and lawn care for residential and commercial customers.

CAMP COUNSELOR. The Arlington YMCA, Camp Gull, Arlington, VA (summers 1993-96). As a counselor for four consecutive summers, learned patience while spending 24 hours a day with groups of up to 15 twelve year olds and set an example for them in character, values, and morality.
- Became adept at providing good listening skills while counseling the campers and being sensitive to the needs of other counselors.
- Singled out for the camp's administrative staff, became the youngest member in my last year at the camp; was the golf instructor and ran the entire program.

COMPUTERS

Proficient with Microsoft Excel, Lotus 1-2-3, MS Word, and WordPerfect software.

VOLUNTEER INVOLVEMENT

Have contributed time in a homeless shelter as a member of a team preparing and serving meals as well as providing a safe place for disadvantaged people.

HONORS & AWARDS

Was recognized for my strong leadership qualities at a young age; have earned numerous awards and honors in academics and athletics and for community service.

PERSONAL

A well-rounded, creative, and artistic individual, enjoy writing poetry, drawing, painting, playing guitar, and listening to and composing music. Very physically fit, am an avid golfer.

Date

Exact Name of Person
Exact Title
Exact Name of Company
Address
City, State, Zip

Dear Exact Name of Person (or Dear Sir or Madam if answering a blind ad):

This young professional is oriented toward teaching, and that is why he is accentuating the student teaching internship.

With the enclosed resume, I would like to make you aware of my background, degree, and leadership abilities as well as of my strong interest in education.

As you will see, I have recently graduated from Castleton State College in Castleton, VT, where I earned my B.S. in History with teacher certification in Social Studies. I was named to the National Dean's List and inducted into Kappa Delta Pi, a national honor society for education majors. While maintaining a GPA of 3.4, I completed my student teaching at E.E. Cummings High School in April with a 400-hour block of practical classroom experience. I had previously completed 40-hour practicums at three area high schools.

My work experience includes distinguished service in the U.S. Air Force where I advanced in rank well ahead of my peers and earned a reputation as a dynamic and exceptional performer at all stages of my military career. I gained the bulk of my experience in the fields of logistics and supply operations management where I was consistently described as an enthusiastic and results-oriented professional who could be counted on to find ways to increase productivity and efficiency while eliminating waste and excess. I have controlled multimillion-dollar inventories, prepared budgets, trained and supervised personnel, and built new operations from the ground up.

The recipient of two Meritorious Service and three Air Force Commendation Medals, I was often singled out as an exceptional leader and manager who demonstrated expertise in every measurable area of performance. I have always enjoyed the opportunity to mentor and guide others and feel that I am highly effective in accomplishing this goal. If you can use a mature professional with an enthusiastic and energetic style, I hope you will contact me to suggest a time when we might meet to discuss your needs. I can assure you in advance that I could rapidly become an asset to your organization.

Sincerely,

Martin Caverley

MARTIN CAVERLEY

1110½ Hay Street, Fayetteville, NC 28305 • preppub@aol.com • (910) 483-6611

OBJECTIVE

To contribute through my education as well as my outstanding communication and interpersonal skills for the benefit of a school system which can use a mature professional with a reputation for obtaining results and increasing productivity.

EDUCATION

Bachelor of Science in **History with Teacher Certification in Social Studies,** Castleton State College, Castleton, VT, 2000. Named to the **National Dean's List** in 1999-2000, and inducted into **Kappa Delta Pi**, a national honor society for education majors, in 1999; current GPA 3.4.
- Completed a concentrated 400-hour block as a Student Teacher at E.E. Cummings High School, Castleton, VT, 2000.
- Completed three 40 hour semesters of field experience at area high schools in 1998-1999.

Associate of Arts in **Management**, Community College of the Air Force, 1996.

COMPUTERS

Proficient with many of the most popular computer operating systems and software including Windows, Microsoft Word, Excel, and PowerPoint; E-mail; and the Internet.

EXPERIENCE

STUDENT TEACHER. E.E. Cummings High School, Castleton, VT (2000). Assisted the teacher with homeroom and taught one class of World History and two classes of Politics, Economics, and Law to as many as 27 ninth through 12th grade students; assembled course materials, prepared lesson plans, issued assignments, and administered quizzes.

Advanced in rank ahead of my peers and held managerial roles in the U.S. Air Force:
CHIEF OF SUPPLY AND LOGISTICS SUPPORT. Ft. Campbell, KY (1996-1977). As a key member of the Group Commander's staff, was described as a "dynamic" and "superior performer" and credited with developing and implementing improvements to policies and procedures for one of the Air Force's largest fighter groups, consisting of 51 aircraft, an operations section, and a maintenance department.
- Managed and wrote the Operating Instructions for a $26 million aviation petroleum, oils, and lubricants (POL) program.

LOGISTICS OPERATIONS MANAGER. Pope AFB, NC (1995-96). Recognized for single-handedly improving numerous key programs through a combination of initiative, enthusiasm, and the application of expert knowledge of aviation logistics support actions.
- Converted an aviation POL program from a manual to an automated system.

SUPPLY AND MAINTENANCE SUPPORT MANAGER. Korea (1994-95). Supervised eight employees, establishing and controlling procedures which allowed 285 organizations with 2,400 vehicles and 58 aircraft to respond within 15 minutes to requests for flight services.
- Provided the leadership which allowed the unit to achieve fully operational status above 90% and pre-packaged spare parts kits requests to be filled 95% of the time.

SPECIAL INVENTORY MANAGER. Beale AFB, CA (1992-94). Supervised a staff of 22 personnel and controlled a $14 million inventory of high-priority and readiness spare parts kits.
- Handpicked to build an operation in the United Kingdom from the ground up, managed a $4 million supply account and served as resource advisor for a $320,000 budget.

PERSONAL

Honored with two prestigious Meritorious Service and three Air Force Commendation Medals in recognition of "distinguished service" and exceptional accomplishments.

Exact Name of Person
Title or Position
Name of Company
Address (number and street)
Address (city, state, and ZIP)

Social Work

Dear Exact Name of Person: (or Dear Sir or Madam if answering a blind ad.)

Graduating magna cum laude is an accomplishment, and this young graduate emphasizes the fact.

I would appreciate an opportunity to talk with you soon about how I could contribute to your organization through my education and high level of interest in the human services field by applying my knowledge related to social work and counseling.

As you will see from my enclosed resume, I graduated *magna cum laude* from Baker University in Baldwin City, KS, with a Bachelor of Social Work degree. My areas of concentration included 15 credit hours in Family and Children's Services and an additional 21 hours of Psychology which included Adolescent, Child, and Developmental Psychology.

During an internship at Franklin Memorial Hospital in Baldwin City, I earned the respect of medical professionals in a hospital setting where the social work aspect of patient care was of secondary importance. During this period I gained experience in areas such as interviewing patients and their family members, assessing their needs, and networking through the community order to make referrals to outside agencies.

I have developed a reputation as an empathetic and caring professional with excellent listening and analytical skills. Very patient and nonjudgmental, I respect the need for confidentiality in client care. An excellent manager of time, I am familiar with proper and accepted procedures for collecting data, identifying and assessing needs, and keeping complete and accurate records.

I hope you will welcome my call soon to arrange a brief meeting at your convenience to discuss your current and future needs and how I might serve them. Thank you in advance for your time.

Sincerely yours.

Patricia Lane Wise

Alternate last paragraph:
I hope you will call or write me soon to suggest a time convenient for us to meet and discuss your current and future needs and how I might serve them. Thank you in advance for your time.

PATRICIA LANE WISE

1110½ Hay Street, Fayetteville, NC 28305 • preppub@aol.com • (910) 483-6611

OBJECTIVE   To contribute through my education and interest in the field of social work and counseling to an organization that can benefit from my personal qualities and reputation as an empathetic and caring professional who excels at listening, interviewing, and counseling.

EDUCATION   **Bachelor of Social Work (B.S.W.) degree**, Baker University, Baldwin City, KS, 2000.
- Graduated *magna cum laude* with a 3.68 GPA from one of only three accredited schools of social work in the state.
- Was elected to membership in **Phi Kappa Phi Honor Society** in recognition of my placement in the top 5% of my class.
- Earned recognition from the **Golden Key National Honor Society** for my academic accomplishments.
- Completed 15 semester hours of work with a concentration in Family and Children's Services.
- Excelled in 21 hours of studies in Psychology which included courses in Adolescent Psychology, Child Psychology, and Developmental Psychology.

EXPERIENCE   **SOCIAL WORK INTERN.** Franklin Memorial Hospital, Baldwin City, KS (1999-2000). Gained practical experience in a hospital setting by conducting interviews with patients and their families, arranging for home health care, coordinating plans for hospice care, and arranging for patients to be placed in nursing homes or rest homes.
- Became familiar with local resources and referred clients and their families to support agencies and services within the community.
- Completed paperwork and proper documentation of all interviews and actions.
- Learned the importance of following procedures for identifying and assessing needs, collecting data, interviewing, and keeping complete and accurate records.

SALES ASSOCIATE. Brody's Department Store, Baldwin City, KS (1998). Learned valuable time management skills while assisting with customer purchases, returns, or layaway of clothing and accessories along with helping with stocking.

PHYSICAL THERAPY CLINIC VOLUNTEER. Regional Rehabilitation Center, Baldwin City, KS (1997). Contributed more than 100 hours of time working with pediatric physical therapy patients; assisted the physical therapy staff members in moving the children, playing with them and giving them individual attention, and observing their condition.
- Gained awareness of how different each patient is and how fragile the emotional state of a child can be when forced to spend long periods of their life hospitalized.

WAITRESS. Huggmugger's Grill, Baldwin City, KS (1996). Earned a reputation as a friendly, helpful, and cheerful individual who could be counted on to remain calm and professional.

CUSTOMER SERVICE SPECIALIST. Belk Department Store, Grason, KS (1993-95). Learned to be adaptable and quickly master new tasks: took care of such day-to-day activities as accounting for petty cash/register money, wrapping gifts, typing, taking credit applications, processing gift certificates, and handling returned checks/layaways/complaints.

PERSONAL   Skilled at interviewing—concisely paraphrase, clarify, and summarize what others have said. Am patient and non-judgmental with respect for the importance of confidentiality.

Date

Exact Name of Person
Exact Title
Exact Name of Company
Address
City, State, Zip

Sociology

Dear Exact Name of Person (or Dear Sir or Madam if answering a blind ad):

A versatile job hunt is what Ms. Pratt has in mind. She is primarily oriented toward social services environments, nonprofit organizations, and teaching.

With the enclosed resume, I would like to offer my services to a company that can make use of a confident and highly motivated professional with strong organizational and communication skills and a firm commitment to making a difference in the lives of others.

As you will see, I have recently completed my Bachelor of Arts in Sociology. While pursuing my degree, I worked as a student teacher and attended extracurricular seminars in order to further prepare myself to work in this field. Being a mother of two and a military spouse, I feel that my personal experience as well as my education and background make me uniquely qualified to serve the needs of our community.

In previous positions, I have shown myself to be a versatile and results-oriented team player who also works well with little or no supervision. For example, I quickly learned the spreadsheet program used by First Union to access and modify account information and I also compiled and published the bank's monthly newsletter.

If you can use an enthusiastic and knowledgeable counselor or teacher, I hope you will contact me to suggest a time when we might meet to discuss your present and future needs, and how I might meet them. I can assure you in advance that I could rapidly become an asset to your organization.

Sincerely,

Edith Pratt

EDITH PRATT

1110½ Hay Street, Fayetteville, NC 28305   •   preppub@aol.com   •   (910) 483-6611

OBJECTIVE To benefit an organization that can use a confident and highly motivated individual with strong organizational and communication skills along with a firm commitment to making a difference in the lives of others.

EDUCATION **Bachelor of Arts in Sociology,** Albion College, Albion, MI, 2000.
Attended numerous seminars to supplement my degree program, including modules on good parenting, the difficult child, homework skills, and abuse issues.

COMPUTERS Proficient with numerous popular software programs including Word.

EXPERIENCE **COLLEGE STUDENT.** Albion College, Albion, MI (1997-2000). Completed my Bachelor of Arts degree in Sociology.

KINDERGARTEN STUDENT TEACHER. Roosevelt Elementary School, Albion, MI (2000). Was a Student Teacher Assistant while completing my Bachelor's degree.
- Planned and executed various activities, such as reading to the students, arts and crafts, and music.
- Supported the regular classroom teacher in the implementation of lesson plans.
- Developed excellent rapport with the children under my care; assisted those having difficulty with reading, spelling, and math.

ADMINISTRATIVE ASSISTANT, LOAN DEPARTMENT. First Union Bank, Albion, MI (1997-1999). In a part-time job, prepared consumer loan paperwork and entered it into a database; compiled and published the bank's monthly newsletter.
- Entered consumer loan information into a computer; utilized the software to retrieve and modify existing files.
- Utilized computers to check account balances and payment status of existing loans.
- Prepared financial documents and maintained the filing system.

POSTAL WORKER/MAIL HANDLER. U.S. Post Office, Jacksonille, FL (1996). Excelled in this physically strenuous and mentally stressful environment, performing a variety of different tasks; as an Equipment Operator, operated mail processing machines, binding machines, automated labeling equipment, embossing and addressing machines, bundle belt, return-to-sender machines, as well as machines for casing, stacking, lifting, and loading.

MICROFILMING TECHNICIAN. State Board of Health, Jacksonville, FL (Summer, 1995). Transferred official documents from hard copy to microfilm; prepared/sealed documents to be microfilmed; produced microfilm of birth certificates, marriage certificates, and adoption papers; once the documents were transferred to microfilm, packed original paper copies for long-term storage.

Other experience: **TUTOR** and **SUPERVISOR.** Albion Urban League, Albion, MT. Excelled in summer jobs for two summers. In the first summer, worked as a Tutor for young children; in the second summer, supervised 25 young tutors aged 16-20 in tutoring children aged K-5 in reading and writing.

PERSONAL Excellent personal and professional references on request.

Date

Exact Name of Person
Exact Title
Exact Name of Company
Address
City, State, Zip

Dear Exact Name of Person (or Dear Sir or Madam if answering a blind ad):

With the enclosed resume, I would like to offer my services to a company that can make use of a caring and compassionate professional with a Master's degree in Special Education Counseling.

As you will see, prior to earning my master's degree, I worked as a Child Service Coordinator, Maternal Outreach Worker, and Special Education Counselor. I have refined my knowledge and base of skills in three separate internships while earning my master's degree.

If you can use an enthusiastic and knowledgeable counselor, I hope you will contact me to suggest a time when we might meet to discuss your present and future needs, and how I might meet them. I can assure you in advance that I could rapidly become an asset to your organization.

Sincerely,

Evelyn Hannah

EVELYN HANNAH

1110½ Hay Street, Fayetteville, NC 28305 • preppub@aol.com • (910) 483-6611

OBJECTIVE
I want to contribute to an organization that can use an experienced young professional with a proven ability to rapidly master new tasks and knowledge.

EDUCATION
Pursuing **Master's degree in Special Education Counseling,** Albertson College, Caldwell, ID; degree expected 2001.
Earned **Bachelor of Science degree in Applied Science,** Caldwell Junior College, Caldwell, ID, 1999.
Completed **Associate in Applied Science degree in Human Services Technology,** Caldwell Junior College, Caldwell, ID, 1996.
Human Services Internships:
- Department of Social Services, Caldwell, ID; 100 hours; administrative and office work.
- Field Counselor, Caldwell Junior College, Caldwell, ID; 75 hours; internship emphasized planning, organizing, and counseling skills
- Drug and Alcohol Abuse Counselor, Field Placement; 66 hours.
- Practicum and Observation, Caldwell Vocational Institute; 30 hours.

EXPERIENCE
MASTER'S DEGREE STUDENT. Albertson College, Caldwell, ID (1999-present). Am completing my Master's degree in Special Education Counseling.

SPECIAL EDUCATION COUNSELOR. Walker School, Caldwell, ID (1997-99). As a Support Mother for pregnant teenagers, assisted young women with goal setting and encouraged them to stay in school while interacting with other agencies and sources of support for these young women.
- Planned workshops and monthly support group meetings.
- Maintained accurate records on clients; made home visits and established cordial relationships with the families and significant others in the women's lives.
- Decided that I wished to continue my education in special education at the Master's degree level.

MATERNAL OUTREACH WORKER. Girls Group Home, Caldwell, ID (1994-97). Counseled pregnant women and assisted them with goal setting.
- Taught parenting classes and was involved in community outreach.
- Provided support to families of pregnant teenagers.
- Facilitated the use of external resources provided by other agencies and community service organizations.
- Made appropriate referrals to agencies.
- Provided follow-up and served as client advocate.

CHILD SERVICE COORDINATOR. Caring Kids Service, Caldwell, ID (1990-94). Worked with 22 high-risk children experiencing developmental delay; also counseled families.
- Assessed parent child interaction.
- Performed service planning and worked as part of a team to accomplish multifaceted goals on behalf of the children.
- Acted as a lay person of a local consortium which determines eligibility for the infant toddler program in coordination with six agencies and parents.

PERSONAL
Can provide strong personal and professional references.

Date

Exact Name of Person
Exact Title
Exact Name of Company
Address
City, State, Zip

Dear Exact Name of Person (or Dear Sir or Madam if answering a blind ad):

With the enclosed resume, I would like to express my interest in exploring employment opportunities with your company and make you aware of my strong communication and management skills as well as my experience related to public relations, customer service, and sales/marketing.

While earning my B.A. degree from Austin College, I worked nearly full-time throughout college in jobs which gave me an opportunity to refine my communication and management skills. In my current position as a Customer Service Representative with a national company, I am excelling in sales and marketing. In a key measured area of my job performance, I have maintained a 30% rate on membership retention, nearly 20% higher than the company's weekly goal. The company has offered me a promotion into management upon my college graduation in May, but I have decided to seek employment elsewhere.

During public relations and media relations internships with an international industrial corporation and a major medical center, I was involved in public relations activities which allowed me to express my creativity in writing and producing effective public service announcements. Within a Fortune 500 company environment, I edited a weekly newsletter and performed editing, layout, and design of a monthly publication for which I selected articles, photographs, and other material. For both the medical center and the industrial corporation, I compiled an extensive list of local and regional contacts in print, radio, and television media for use in public relations campaigns. I excel in planning and organizing special events.

If you can use an accomplished young professional whose exceptional communication, public relations, and sales skills have been proven in a variety of challenging environments, I hope you will contact me to suggest a time when we might meet to discuss your needs. I offer unusually strong communication skills and management abilities which complement my naturally dynamic and outgoing personality, and I am confident that I could become valuable to a company that can use a dynamic hard worker known for personal initiative and reliability.

Sincerely,

Whitman Muscarell

WHITMAN MUSCARELL

1110½ Hay Street, Fayetteville, NC 28305 • preppub@aol.com • (910) 483-6611

OBJECTIVE

To benefit an organization that can use an enthusiastic young professional with exceptional communication and motivational skills who offers a background in public relations, project development, customer service, and telemarketing.

EDUCATION

Bachelor of Arts in Speech/Theater with a concentration in Telecommunications, Austin College, Sherman, TX, degree to be awarded May, 2001.
- Have worked nearly full-time throughout college in order to finance my education; my normal schedule consisted of classes from 9 am-3 pm and work from 3 pm-11 pm.

COMPUTERS

Familiar with many popular computer systems and software, including Microsoft Word, Excel, and Access; Windows, and spreadsheets.

EXPERIENCE

Worked approximately 30 hours weekly in these jobs while earning my college degree:
CUSTOMER SERVICE REPRESENTATIVE. MARK International, Sherman, TX (1998-present). In a part-time job for this major telemarketing company with call centers in Sherman, Kansas City, and Minneapolis, have excelled in customer service and direct sales/marketing.
- Although I have been offered a promotion into management after college graduation, I have decided to pursue other opportunities.
- Receive a large volume of in-bound sales calls, answering questions and taking customer orders; have become known for my good manners and gracious style.
- Sell club memberships, extended warranties, and other offers to customers.
- Complete detailed documentation when additional research and follow-up is required.
- Aggressively ensure retention of club membership; maintain a minimum 30% rate on membership saves, nearly 20% better than weekly goals set by the company.

PUBLIC RELATIONS COORDINATOR. Michelin Tire Company, Sherman, TX (2000). As an **intern** with this company, performed public relations, editing, and project development activities at a local manufacturing facility of the Michelin Tire Company.
- Planned, developed, and created a public service announcement for Michelin.
- Edited and compiled written and graphic material for the weekly newsletter.
- Performed editing, layout, and design for the company's monthly publication.

MEDIA RELATIONS COORDINATOR. Valley Medical Center, Sherman, TX (1998). As an **intern** with a major medical center, handled project development, events coordination, public relations, and administrative duties.
- Developed concepts for, wrote, and produced several public service announcements.
- Created a list of local, and regional contacts from print, radio, and television media.
- Wrote and developed press releases and other publicity; compiled media lists.

PUBLIC RELATIONS ASSISTANT. Austin College, Sherman, TX (1998). Developed press releases for the students, faculty, and staff of this large state university

Other sales and marketing experience while attending college:
- Performed direct phone sales of food products for a major food company.
- Sold debt consolidation/mortgage loan products for a financial institution.

PERSONAL

Aggressive, goal-oriented individual with an outgoing personality. Excellent references.

Date

Exact Name of Person
Exact Title
Exact Name of Company
Address
City, State, Zip

Dear Exact Name of Person (or Dear Sir or Madam if answering a blind ad):

With the enclosed resume, I would like to express my interest in exploring employment opportunities with your company and make you aware of my background in sports administration.

After earning my B.S. degree in Communications, I worked as a Sports Producer and Director and then applied my communications skills as a Public Affairs Officer in the U.S. Army.

While earning my master's degree in Sports Administration, I had many opportunities to refine my computer operations skills with virtually all the software programs used to create documents and communicate with the public. I am skilled at utilizing the latest versions of Adobe PageMaker, Macintosh Quark XPRESS, and Microsoft Publisher, and I am experienced with Corel.

If you can use an experienced professional whose exceptional communication, public relations, and sales skills have been proven in a variety of challenging environments, I hope you will contact me to suggest a time when we might meet to discuss your needs and how I might serve them. I can provide outstanding personal and professional references at the appropriate time.

Sincerely,

Kenneth Lesser

KENNETH LESSER

1110½ Hay Street, Fayetteville, NC 28305 • preppub@aol.com • (910) 483-6611

EDUCATION

Master's degree in Sports Administration, Alfred University, Alfred, NY, 2000.
- Selected from 300 applicants for one of 25 positions in this "premier" program.
- Excelled in more than 170 "practicum" hours in three areas of emphasis: the Sports Information Director's office, sports and NCAA compliance, and ticket office procedures.
- Completed a 40-hour program in desktop publishing using Macintosh Quark XPRESS.

B.S. degree in Communications, Ball State University, Muncie, IN, 1990.
- Named Distinguished Military Graduate based on management and leadership.

TRAINING

Excelled in various executive training programs for junior military officers.

EXPERIENCE

MARKETING/SALES/SPORTS PROGRAMMING DIRECTOR. Ramon's Inc., Alfred, NY (1999-present). In an internship, develop and manage key promotions and timely advertisements while selling advertising options to businesses in an entertainment atmosphere.
- Direct nightly sports programming utilizing satellite, video tape, cable and NTN Communications systems, stressing interesting and popular programming.

EVENT INFORMATION COORDINATOR. Independence Arena Company, Alfred, NY (1998-99). In an internship, coordinated the staffing and training of employees in addition to preparing and presenting Arena event information and schedules.
- Processed sales and cash receipts for season tickets, mini-plans, groups, playoffs, and batch orders, ensuring that discounts, prices, and payments were accurate.

SALES REPRESENTATIVE. Ticketron, New York, NY (1996-98). Generated, renewed, and maintained accounts for season tickets, partial plans and group outings for the sporting events held in New York City. Contacted key decision makers regarding executive suites.

PUBLIC AFFAIRS OFFICER. Ft. Bragg, NC, and Saudi Arabia (1992-96). As an Army officer, gained extensive media, community, and public relations experience as the "voice" and "face" of the famed Special Forces Command during the war in the Middle East and also during the overthrow of Panamanian dictator Manuel Noriega.
- Coordinated three ABC "Home Show" broadcasts; earned award for best "special" Home Show of all time.
- Provided Time/Life books with most of the material needed for a book on "The New Soldier."

SPORTS PRODUCER AND DIRECTOR. Athens Video Works, Alfred, NY (1990-92). Supervised 10 people as the producer and director of sports coverage with an emphasis on football and basketball: managed pre-production coordination, set-up, production quality, and post-production editing.

SKILLS & AFFILIATIONS

Experienced in using various telecommunications equipment.
Hold membership in the National Press Photographer's Association.
Member of 10-person committee bringing minor league baseball to Alfred, NY.

PERSONAL

Secret security clearance. Am an expert parachutist who has earned jump "wings" from three countries. Volunteer with the Special Olympics.

Date

Exact Name of Person
Exact Title
Exact Name of Company
Address
City, State, Zip

Trust Management

Dear Exact Name of Person (or Dear Sir or Madam if answering a blind ad):

This young professional is seeking his first job in trust management in the financial services arena. He will probably approach banks and other financial institutions including mortgage bankers, credit unions, and savings and loan associations.

With the enclosed resume, I would like to express my interest in exploring employment opportunities with your company.

While earning my B.B.A. degree, I excelled academically and received a prestigious scholarship. The program I attended has one of the strongest concentrations in Trust Management in the country, and I have become knowledgeable of financial planning and trust instruments.

You will see from my resume that I have worked since I was a youth. I began working as a farm worker at the age of 11 or 12, and I quickly advanced into management roles which made me responsible for migrant workers. I have earned a reputation as a prudent decision maker who excels in thinking strategically while maintaining strict attention to detail in all matters.

If you can use a young professional with strong communication and analytical skills, I hope you will contact me to suggest a time when we might meet to discuss your needs and how I might serve them.

Sincerely,

Liam McDonald

LIAM McDONALD

1110½ Hay Street, Fayetteville, NC 28305 • preppub@aol.com • 910) 483-6611

OBJECTIVE

I want to contribute to a financial institution that can use a dedicated young professional who seeks a career in personal trust management with an emphasis in estate planning and investments.

EDUCATION

Completing **Bachelor of Business Administration (BBA) in Trust Management** with a Minor in Financial Planning and a Trust certificate from Beloit College, Beloit, WI, May 2000.
* Excelled academically with a 3.55 GPA in my major.

Scholarships:
* Received the Mason Williams Scholarship valued at approximately $13,000 because of my outstanding academic record in high school.
* Received the President's Scholarship valued at $600.00.

Extracurricular Activities:
* Member of the Trust Club.
* Member of the Society for the Advancement of Management.
* Participant in the Stock Market Game.

Courses:
* Courses have included Estate and Gift Tax, Qualified Retirement Plans, Estate Planning, Management Trust Departments, Trust Law, and Investments.

EXPERIENCE

ENTREPRENEUR. McDonald Produce Farms, Carson, WI (1998-present). As the son of a successful entrepreneur in the agricultural business, worked on a farm throughout my childhood and learned the business.
* Established "from scratch" a business which I operated for profit during the summer months during high school and college; made a profit of $15,000 annually while only working a few months a year.
* Developed a niche business which concentrated on chemical applications to improve the production of produce, and which made volume sales to retailers.
* Personally approached retailers; handled all sales and marketing for the business.
* Refined my time management and strategic planning skills.

FARM EMPLOYEE. McDonald Farms, Carson, WI (1992-present). Since childhood, have been actively involved in my father's business, and have gained valuable management skills while assisting him in the management of a multifaceted family farm which includes 2,500 head of swine and 130 cattle.
* Handled veterinary work in addition to being trained in management skills.

COMPUTERS

Proficient in using computers including Lotus 1-2-3, Word, Access, and Excel.

PERSONAL

Single and willing to relocate or travel to meet the needs of my employer. Outstanding personal and professional references upon request. Enjoy hunting, snow skiing, fishing, and spending time with family and friends.

Date

Exact Name of Person
Exact Title
Exact Name of Company
Address
City, State, Zip

Dear Exact Name of Person (or Dear Sir or Madam if answering a blind ad):

With the enclosed resume, I would like to make you aware of a dedicated, experienced veterinary technician with exceptional communication and organizational skills and a background in internal medicine, emergency care, and pharmacy environments.

I am currently completing an internship at an animal hospital, performing the same duties that I had as a Veterinary Intern at Centre Veterinary Clinic in Danville, KY. In that position, I assisted the veterinarian in all phases of treatment, taking vital signs, drawing blood, administering medications, and performing other duties as needed.

I have also worked in an emergency care environment as a Veterinary Technician and I learned to deal with stressful situations while caring for with sick or injured pets, interacting with distressed pet owners and assisting with emergency procedures.

I have earned an Associate of Applied Science in Veterinary Technology from Centre College, and I am a Registered Veterinary Technician with the state of Kentucky. I feel that my education and experience in a variety of clinical environments will be an asset to your organization.

If you can use a compassionate veterinary technician with strong organizational and communication skills and a background in internal medicine, emergency care, and pharmacy environments, I hope you will contact me to suggest a time when we might meet to discuss your needs. I can assure you in advance that I would quickly become a valuable addition to your organization.

Sincerely,

Shannon Henry

SHANNON HENRY

1110½ Hay Street, Fayetteville, NC 28305 • preppub@aol.com • (910) 483-6611

OBJECTIVE   To benefit an organization that can use a dedicated and experienced veterinary technician with exceptional organizational and communication skills, a strong attention to detail, and a background in internal medicine, emergency care, and pharmacy environments.

EDUCATION   **Associate of Applied Science degree in Veterinary Technology,** Centre College, Danville, KY, 2000.
Graduated from Metzer High School, Danville, KY.

CERTIFICATIONS   Kentucky Registered Veterinary Technician #957.
Kentucky Board Certified Veterinary Technician #2004.

EXPERIENCE   **VETERINARY INTERN.** Centre Animal Hospital, Danville, KY (1999-present). Perform a wide variety of functions in this extremely busy veterinary clinic.
- Work in the pharmacy, dispensing medications and typing labels.
- Handle duties similar to those I performed at Centre Veterinary Specialists.

VETERINARY INTERN. Centre Veterinary Specialists, Danville, KY (1998). Provided a number of services in support of the veterinarians in this practice which focuses on internal medicine and serves as an emergency care facility at nights and on weekends.
- Performed patient assessments, taking vital signs, and communicating pertinent information to the veterinarian in an accurate and timely manner.
- Assisted veterinarians in all phases of treatment.
- Made triage determinations, both physically and over the telephone.
- Operated radiography equipment, taking views and developing X-ray film.
- Drew blood and executed complete blood counts, including differentials; placed IV catheters.
- Administered medication including chemotherapy.
- Restrained animals appropriately to avoid injury to the patient or the care team.
- Interacted with and educated pet owners on issues related to surgical aftercare, diet and exercise, and other areas.

VETERINARY INTERN. Centre Animal Hospital, Danville, KY (1996-1997). Rapidly performed patient assessments and assisted the veterinarian under stressful conditions in this busy animal emergency care facility.
- Assisted the veterinarian in emergency surgeries and other emergency procedures.
- Safely restrained and calmed injured animals so they could be treated without causing them further harm.
- Interacted with pet owners who were upset, calming them and quickly obtaining information vital to the appropriate treatment of the patient's emergency condition.

Other experience:
SALES ASSOCIATE. Yours Truly Cards & Gifts, Danville, KY (1995-1996). Assisted customers in the selection and purchase of merchandise; responsible for cash handling and balancing cash receipts.

PERSONAL   Excellent personal and professional references are available upon request.

ABOUT THE EDITOR

Anne McKinney holds an MBA from the Harvard Business School and a BA in English from the University of North Carolina at Chapel Hill. A noted public speaker, writer, and teacher, she is the senior editor for PREP's business and career imprint, which bears her name. Early titles in the Anne McKinney Career Series (now called the Real-Resumes Series) published by PREP include: *Resumes and Cover Letters That Have Worked, Resumes and Cover Letters That Have Worked for Military Professionals, Government Job Applications and Federal Resumes, Cover Letters That Blow Doors Open,* and *Letters for Special Situations.* Her career titles and how-to resume-and-cover-letter books are based on the expertise she has acquired in 20 years of working with job hunters. Her valuable career insights have appeared in publications of the "Wall Street Journal" and other prominent newspapers and magazines.

Judeo-Christian Ethics Series

BIBLE STORIES FROM THE OLD TESTAMENT

Katherine Whaley

Familiar and not-so-familiar Bible stories told by an engaging storyteller in a style guaranteed to delight and inform. Includes stories about Abraham, Cain and Abel, Jacob and David, Moses and the Exodus, Judges, Saul, David, and Solomon. (272 pages)

"Whaley tells these tales in such a way that they will appeal to the young adult as well as the senior citizen."
–*Independent Publisher*

Trade paperback 1-885288-12-3—$18.00

BACK IN TIME

Patty Sleem

Published in large print hardcover by Simon & Schuster's Thorndike Press as a Thorndike Christian Mystery in November 1998.
(306 pages)

"An engrossing look at the discrimination faced by female ministers." – *Library Journal*

Trade paperback 1-885288-03-4—$16.00

A GENTLE BREEZE FROM GOSSAMER WINGS

Gordon Beld

Pol Pot was the Khmer Rouge leader whose reign of terror caused the deaths of up to 2 million Cambodians in the mid-1970s. He masterminded an extreme, Maoist-inspired revolution in which those Cambodians died in mass executions, and from starvation and disease. This book of historical fiction shows the life of one refugee from this reign of genocide.
(320 pages)

"I'm pleased to recommend *A Gentle Breeze From Gossamer Wings*. Every Christian in America should read it. It's a story you won't want to miss – and it could change your life."
— Robert H. Schuller, Pastor, Crystal Cathedral

Trade paperback 1-885288-07-7—$18.00

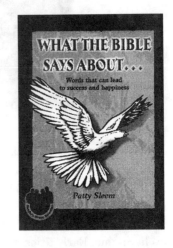

WHAT THE BIBLE SAYS ABOUT… Words that can lead to success and happiness

Patty Sleem

A daily inspirational guide as well as a valuable reference when you want to see what the Bible says about Life and Living, Toil and Working, Problems and Suffering, Anger and Arguing, Self-Reliance and Peace of Mind, Justice and Wrong-Doing, Discipline and Self-Control, Wealth and Power, Knowledge and Wisdom, Pride and Honor, Gifts and Giving, Husbands and Wives, Friends and Neighbors, Children, Sinning and Repenting, Judgment and Mercy, Faith and Religion, and Love.
(192 pages)

Hardcover 1-885288-02-6—$20.00

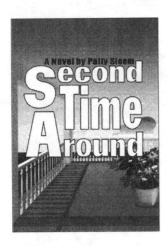

SECOND TIME AROUND

Patty Sleem

"Sleem explores the ugliness of suicide and murder, obsession and abuse, as well as Christian faith and values. An emotional and suspenseful read reflecting modern issues and concerns." – *Southern Book Trade*
(336 pages)

Foreign rights sold in Chinese.
Hardcover 1-885288-00-X—$25.00
Trade paperback 1-885288-05-0—$17.00

RESUMES AND COVER LETTERS THAT HAVE WORKED

Anne McKinney, Editor

More than 100 resumes and cover letters written by the world's oldest resume-writing company. Resumes shown helped real people not only change jobs but also transfer their skills and experience to other industries and fields. An indispensable tool in an era of downsizing when research shows that most of us have not one but three distinctly different careers in our working lifetime. (272 pages)
"Distinguished by its highly readable samples...essential for library collections."
– *Library Journal*
Trade paperback 1-885288-04-2—$25.00

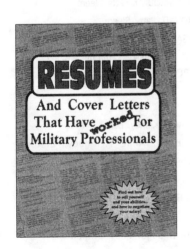

RESUMES AND COVER LETTERS THAT HAVE WORKED FOR MILITARY PROFESSIONALS

Anne McKinney, Editor

Military professionals from all branches of the service gain valuable experience while serving their country, but they need resumes and cover letters that translate their skills and background into "civilian language." This is a book showing more than 100 resumes and cover letters written by a resume-writing service in business for nearly 20 years which specializes in "military translation." (256 pages)
"A guide that significantly translates veterans' experience into viable repertoires of achievement." – *Booklist*
Trade paperback 1-885288-06-9—$25.00

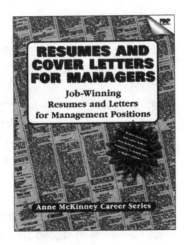

RESUMES AND COVER LETTERS FOR MANAGERS

Anne McKinney, Editor

Destined to become the bible for managers who want to make sure their resumes and cover letters open the maximum number of doors while helping them maximize in the salary negotiation process. From office manager to CEO, managers trying to relocate to or from these and other industries and fields will find helpful examples: Banking, Agriculture, School Systems, Human Resources, Restaurants, Manufacturing, Hospitality Industry, Automotive, Retail, Telecommunications, Police Force, Dentistry, Social Work, Academic Affairs, Non-Profit Organizations, Childcare, Sales, Sports, Municipalities, Rest Homes, Medicine and Healthcare, Business Operations, Landscaping, Customer Service, MIS, Quality Control, Teaching, the Arts, and Self-Employed. (288 pages)
Trade paperback 1-885288-10-7—$25.00

GOVERNMENT JOB APPLICATIONS AND FEDERAL RESUMES:
Federal Resumes, KSAs, Forms 171 and 612, and Postal Applications

Anne McKinney, Editor

Getting a government job can lead to job security and peace of mind. The problem is that getting a government job requires extensive and complex paperwork. Now, for the first time, this book reveals the secrets and shortcuts of professional writers in preparing job-winning government applications such as these:
The Standard Form 171 (SF 171) – several complete samples
The Optional Form 612 (OF 612) – several complete samples
KSAs – samples of KSAs tailored to jobs ranging from the GS-5 to GS-12
Ranking Factors – how-to samples
Postal Applications
Wage Grade paperwork
Federal Resumes – see the different formats required by various government agencies. (272 pages)
Trade paperback 1-885288-11-5—$25.00

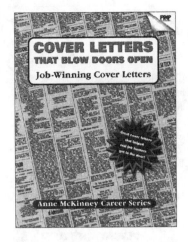

COVER LETTERS THAT
BLOW DOORS OPEN
Anne McKinney, Editor
Although a resume is important, the cover letter is the first impression. This book is a compilation of great cover letters that helped real people get in the door for job interviews against stiff competition. Included are letters that show how to approach employers when you're moving to a new area, how to write a cover letter when you're changing fields or industries, and how to arouse the employer's interest in dialing your number first from a stack of resumes. (272 pages) Trade paperback 1-885288-13-1—$25.00

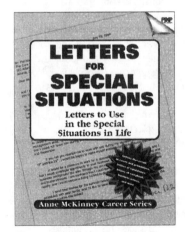

LETTERS FOR SPECIAL SITUATIONS
Anne McKinney, Editor
Sometimes it is necessary to write a special letter for a special situation in life. You will find great letters to use as models for business and personal reasons including: letters asking for a raise, letters of

resignation, letters of reference, letters notifying a vendor of a breach of contract, letter to a Congressman, letters of complaint, letters requesting reinstatement to an academic program, follow-up letters after an interview, letters requesting bill consolidation, letters of reprimand to marginal employees, letters requesting financial assistance or a grant, letters to professionals disputing their charges, collections letters, thank-you letters, and letters to accompany resumes in job-hunting. (256 pages)
Trade paperback 1-885288-09-3—$25.00

PREP Publishing Order Form

You may purchase any of our titles from your favorite bookseller! Or send a check or money order or your credit card number for the total amount*, plus $3.20 postage and handling, to PREP, Box 66, Fayetteville, NC 28302. If you have a question about any of our titles, feel free to e-mail us at preppub@aol.com and visit our website at http://www.prep-pub.com

Name: _____

Phone #: _____

Address: _____

_____

E-mail address: _____

Payment Type: ☐ Check/Money Order ☐ Visa ☐ MasterCard

Credit Card Number: _____ Expiration Date: _____

Check items you are ordering:

☐ $25.00—RESUMES AND COVER LETTERS THAT HAVE WORKED.

☐ $25.00—RESUMES AND COVER LETTERS THAT HAVE WORKED FOR MILITARY PROFESSIONALS.

☐ $25.00—RESUMES AND COVER LETTERS FOR MANAGERS.

☐ $25.00—GOVERNMENT JOB APPLICATIONS AND FEDERAL RESUMES: Federal Resumes, KSAs, Forms 171 and 612, and Postal Applications.

☐ $25.00—COVER LETTERS THAT BLOW DOORS OPEN.

☐ $25.00—LETTERS FOR SPECIAL SITUATIONS.

☐ $16.00—BACK IN TIME. Patty Sleem

☐ $17.00—(trade paperback) SECOND TIME AROUND. Patty Sleem

☐ $25.00—(hardcover) SECOND TIME AROUND. Patty Sleem

☐ $18.00—A GENTLE BREEZE FROM GOSSAMER WINGS. Gordon Beld

☐ $18.00—BIBLE STORIES FROM THE OLD TESTAMENT. Katherine Whaley

☐ $20.00—WHAT THE BIBLE SAYS ABOUT... *Words that can lead to success and happiness.* Patty Sleem

New titles!

☐ $16.95—REAL-RESUMES FOR SALES. Anne McKinney, Editor

☐ $16.95—REAL-RESUMES FOR TEACHERS. Anne McKinney, Editor

☐ $16.95—REAL-RESUMES FOR CAREER CHANGERS. Anne McKinney, Editor

☐ $16.95—REAL-RESUMES FOR STUDENTS. Anne McKinney, Editor

☐ $16.95—REAL ESSAYS FOR COLLEGE AND GRAD SCHOOL. Anne McKinney, Editor

☐ $10.95—KIJABE...An African Historical Saga. Pally Dhillon

_____ **TOTAL ORDERED (add $3.20 for postage and handling)**

Volume discounts on large orders. (910) 483-6611 for more information.

Would you like to explore the possibility of having PREP's writing team create a resume for you similar to the ones in this book?

For a brief free consultation, call 910-483-6611 or send $4.00 to receive our Job Change Packet to PREP, Department STU, Box 66, Fayetteville, NC 28302.

QUESTIONS OR COMMENTS? E-MAIL US AT PREPPUB@AOL.COM